DYING TO LIVE

DYING TO LIVE

Susan Blackmore is Senior Lecturer in Psychology at the University of the West of England. She has been researching in parapsychology for twenty years and her current research interests include the effects of meditation, the origins of belief in the paranormal and astrology. She is author of *Beyond the Body*, hailed as 'the definitive text on out-of-body experiences', and *The Adventures of a Parapsychologist*, an autobiography describing her endless search for evidence of the paranormal. She is a frequent contributor to television and radio and writes for several magazines and national newspapers. She lives in Bristol with her two children.

DYING TO LIVE

NEAR-DEATH EXPERIENCES

SUSAN BLACKMORE

 Prometheus Books

59 John Glenn Drive
Buffalo, New York 14228-2197

Published 1993 by Prometheus Books

Originally published 1993 by
Grafton, An Imprint of HarperCollins *Publishers,* London

97 96 95 94   5 4 3 2

Library of Congress Cataloging-in-Publication Data

Blackmore, Susan, J., 1951–
    Dying to live : near-death experiences / Susan Blackmore.
        p.   cm.
    Includes bibliographical references.
    ISBN 0-87975-870-8
    1. Near-death experiences. I. Title.
BF1045.N4B53   1993
133.9′01′3—dc20   93-24749
                                                                  CIP

Printed in the United States of America on acid-free paper.

To my children, Emily and Jolyon, who are both in this book.

Contents

Acknowledgements

I would like to thank the many people who have helped me in the writing of this book. In some way everyone who has ever helped me to think or who has criticized my ideas in any way at all ought to be thanked, for the basic ideas behind my book involve a whole way of looking at life and death that has developed throughout my own life and goes on developing all the time. Among these many are John Crook, who has taught me much about Buddhism and meditation, Ken Ring, whose diametrically opposed views are a constant source of dialogue and interest, and my parents who also disagree with almost everything I believe in but help me in their arguments as well as through their loving support. In particular, my mother read early drafts of the book and encouraged me to make it more readable.

I would also like to thank all the people who have come close to death and have told me their stories. This includes many who have written to me, as well as the survivors of cardiac arrest who kindly consented to discuss their experiences with me. Also Dr Vann Jones, consultant cardiologist at Bristol Royal Infirmary, who referred his patients to me, and the Bristol and Weston District Medical Research Committee, who helped pay for the expenses incurred in interviewing patients. Finally, thanks also to Glenn Roberts who passed on to me his entire collection of papers on the near-death experience and to friends at the Universities of Bristol and Bath where I did much of the research that went into this book.

Preface

What is it going to be like when I die? Will I be lonely and frightened, in pain and in anger? Will the grim reaper thrust me into darkness and terror against my will?

There are very few of us who have not thought about our own deaths, or pushed the thought steadfastly away. As young children we begin to think about dying. As we gain a strong sense of self and who we are the thought of death becomes more and more threatening. It is inconceivable that Mummy will ever be dead, let alone me.

It is no wonder that we like to deny death. Whole religions are based on that denial. Turn to religion and you may be assured of eternal life. You cannot die, you have a soul, a spirit, an everlasting inner being that will not succumb to the ravages of worms and putrefaction.

Of course, this comforting thought conflicts with science. Science tells us that death is the end and, as so often, finds itself opposing religion. Interestingly, the greatest conflict of all has been about our origins, not our end. Darwin's *The Origin of Species*, first published in 1859, caused a controversy which is still not dead after a century and a half (44). He proposed that the simple process of natural selection could account for the evolution and diversity of living things.

The idea is, I believe, the simplest and most beautiful in all of science. Indeed, it is so simple and obvious that it is sometimes hard to remember how important it is to understanding ourselves. It is just this. You need a system for reproducing things that is not exact copying – it produces variation. And you need an environment in which there is not room for all the things that are made. Obviously some things survive and some do not. And the ones that survive pass on copies more similar to themselves than to the dead ones. That's all. Out of that simple principle comes the whole of evolutionary theory and our understanding of our own origins.

The problem with evolution is, and has always been, that it leaves little room either for a grand purpose to life or for an individual soul.

The environment moulds the progress of evolution and it in turn is part of that evolutionary process. In fact, the whole planet can be seen as an interdependent living system, as it is in the Gaia hypothesis (122). We are each just tiny parts of that living, evolving whole. As parts of the whole we are indispensable; as individuals each of us is eminently dispensable.

There is no future heaven towards which evolution progresses. And no ultimate purpose. It just goes along. Yet our minds have evolved to crave purposefulness and cling to the idea of a self because that will more efficiently keep alive the body and perpetuate its genes. In other words, our evolution makes it very hard for us to accept the idea of evolution and our own individual pointlessness.

It is perhaps not surprising that in the United States there are still powerful lobbies for equal time to be given to the theory of 'creation' in teaching biology in schools. The idea that God created us all for a special purpose is a lot more palatable than the idea that we just got here through the whims of 'Chance and Necessity', as the French biologist Jacques Monod (132) put it, even though it has no evidence to support it and provides no help in understanding the nature of the living world. And people will fight, and even die, for the ideas they like best.

Death is an idea they do not like. The self is an idea they do like; an everlasting self they like even better.

It is over a hundred and thirty years since science seriously tackled the nature of human origins. Is it ready to tackle the nature of human death? I think so. The past twenty years have seen great strides forward. The discovery and study of near-death experiences has taught us about the experience of nearly dying. Progress in medical science has increased our understanding of what happens when the brain begins to fail. Psychology is delving ever more deeply into the nature of that precious self. This book is an attempt to explore what psychology, biology and medicine have to say about death and dying. Are you ready to find out what it's going to be like when you die?

Susan Blackmore
Bristol, 1992

Coming Close to Death

In 1989 I received a letter from a seventy-year-old widow. She had never met me but had read about my work in a newspaper and wanted to tell me of her own experience. This is what she wrote:

About twenty-nine years ago I lived in a small town in Leicestershire. I had very bad legs and backache. The local doctor said all women my age had backache . . .

Two years later I collapsed [and] after a lot of tests and X-rays it was found I had a spinal tumour.

I was taken to Derby and . . . while I was being operated on I saw some very odd lights flashing and heard a loud keening noise. Then I was in the operating theatre above everyone else but just high enough to see over everyone's shoulders. I was surprised to see everyone dressed in green and wearing short wellingtons. I remember how everything shone. I looked down and wondered what they were all looking at and what was under the cover on the long table. I saw a square of flesh, and I thought, 'I wonder who it is and what they are doing.' I then realized it was me. I heard someone say, 'He looks very tired, but he's going to Portugal on a fishing holiday after this.'

Some months later during a checkup I asked if the man who had operated on me had gone to Portugal on holiday after I had been operated on. I was told 'Yes'.

One day the pain was so intense, I could hear myself talking, what about I don't know. Suddenly, amidst all this pain (I was still in the dark), I saw a light, very faint and in the distance. It got nearer to me, and everything was so quiet, it was warm, I was warm, and all the pain began to go. When I finally stood out of the dark and into this light, it was the most beautiful thing I have ever seen, soft, warm, translucent. I was finally there, and I felt as if someone had put their arms around me. I was safe, no more pain, nothing, just this lovely lovely caring sensation . . .

Then my husband was again visiting me with my children. I was only vaguely aware of them, I drifted off, I could again see this light, I couldn't wait to go back down that tunnel.

My husband bent over me, patted me on the cheek and said, 'I've been thinking things over, don't you worry about what's going to happen to me and the kids after you've gone. I won't marry anyone who won't be good to us'! I drifted off down this passage to the peace and calm, and as I stood there surrounded by all this loveliness I saw my two children's lovely faces looking at me. I thought, 'Please, God, don't let my children grow up without a mother,' and everything gradually faded away. I was back and I never went there again.

This story touched me, as do so many accounts of near-death experiences. Mrs Freeman (as I shall call her) seemed to have gone somewhere she recognized – that wonderful feeling of 'going home' at last. Experiences like this affect people deeply; in this case Mrs Freeman wanted to write and tell me about it nearly thirty years later. Does this answer our question: what is it going to be like when I die?

I think it fair to conclude that if we come close to death, or if people we love are going to die, this is how it might be – a reassuring thought. Facing illness and the possibility of death is not so difficult if you know it is likely to involve feeling warm, safe and loved, but can we conclude anything *more* than that from the near-death experience?

Conclusions can run wild and in diametrically opposed directions. The most common response of experiencers and commentators alike is 'Why have I been afraid of death all my life? There is nothing to be afraid of in this!'(164). Indeed, most NDErs go further, claiming that now they know there is life after death.

Others wax lyrical about the meaning of the near-death experience. The President of the International Association for Near-Death Studies, recently described it as a powerful paranormal experience that frees experiencers from an awareness of the five senses and moves them quickly to that level of consciousness in which telepathic communication is a norm. Not content only with telepathic communication she went on to suggest that NDErs find themselves in a space/time dimension of different vibrations and higher frequencies than those of the everyday world (58).

At the other extreme are those who dismiss the visions as meaningless hallucinations. Californian psychologist Ron Siegel shows how the descriptions given by dying persons are virtually identical to descriptions given by persons experiencing drug-induced hallucinations (216). He concludes that NDEs are nothing more than hallucinations, based on stored images in the brain.

Similarly, after a thorough review of the literature, two British psychiatrists concluded that no one reporting an NDE can properly be considered to have died, that all the separate elements can occur in non-life-threatening situations and that typical NDEs can be chemically induced (191).

Are any of these views correct? Can we, by research or by any other method, find out? By reviewing what has been learned about NDEs I hope this book will bring us some answers.

LIFE AFTER DEATH OR A DYING BRAIN?

The fundamental choice to make is between two alternative points of view.

The first choice could be termed the 'Afterlife Hypothesis'. This suggests that the NDE is a glimpse into life after death. There are many versions of this hypothesis but most often they claim that the tunnel is some kind of passageway to the next life, the bright light is the light of heaven or the world beyond, and the people one meets in that world are the real surviving personalities of people who have died before and with whom one will spend an eternity after death. The traveller is believed to be the person's soul or spirit, freed from its earthly ties. Paranormal events are only to be expected because the soul is travelling in a non-material world beyond the limitations of space and time.

The second choice could be termed the 'Dying Brain Hypothesis'. All the phenomena of the NDE are believed to be products of the dying brain; hallucinations, imaginings and mental constructions that will ultimately stop when the brain's activity stops. If this hypothesis is true then NDEs tell us nothing about life after death.

Which (if either) is correct?

The afterlife view is far more popular. Surveys show that over half the population believes in some kind of life after death (15, 92, 224, 226). In fact, the latest Gallup poll in the United States found that 70 per cent believe in life after death, a figure that has not changed much since the Second World War (70) and the common reaction of NDErs is to think they have been given personal proof that they will live after they die (68, 79). But popularity is not proof; neither is a compelling personal experience.

An NDE can change a person's life for ever but it is not necessarily evidence for life after death. To explore what it can tell us about ourselves we can look at the arguments used to bolster the two hypotheses.

The Afterlife Hypothesis

Four main kinds of argument for the reality of an afterlife are often used:

1. The 'consistency argument' is that NDEs are similar around the world and throughout history. The only possible explanation for this, so the argument runs, is that NDEs are just what they appear to be – the soul's journey out of the body,

through a tunnel to another world that awaits us after death. Consistency, it is argued, amounts to evidence for an afterlife.

2. The 'reality argument' is that NDEs feel so real that they must be what they appear to be, a real journey to the next world. Anyone who has had an NDE knows it is real because they have been there. Those who haven't cannot know what it is like. In this argument, feelings of reality amount to evidence.

3. The 'paranormal argument' is that NDEs involve paranormal events which cannot be explained by science. These are therefore evidence that the NDE involves another dimension, another world, or the existence of a non-material spirit or soul. No purely materialist hypothesis can explain the paranormal so paranormality amounts to evidence.

4. The 'transformation argument' is that people are changed by their NDEs, sometimes dramatically for the better – becoming more spiritual and less materialistic. This proves, so the argument goes, that they have had a spiritual experience involving another world. For this reason only could their transformation have come about and it is these aftereffects that amount to the evidence.

These arguments have a strong appeal and, in various forms, appear again and again, as much in conversations over dinner or a drink as in the popular and scientific literature. But they are not necessarily either logical or correct.

The Dying Brain Hypothesis

Just two main arguments are most often used for the dying brain hypothesis. Interestingly, the first one is the same as for the afterlife hypothesis but for quite different reasons.

1. The 'consistency argument' is that NDEs are similar around the world and throughout history. The reason, this argument

goes, is that everyone has a similar brain, hormones and nervous system and that is why they have similar experiences when those systems fail.

2. The 'just like hallucinations' argument maintains that all the features of the NDE can occur under other conditions, not near death, and therefore can be explained in terms of hallucinations or normal imagery.

I shall tackle each one of these arguments in the course of this book to find out just how compelling they are. We shall find that the answers lead us far beyond either of these two simplistic hypotheses.

Let us begin at the beginning, with the 'consistency argument' (in both its forms). We have to find out firstly whether it is really true that NDEs are consistent and, if so, whether this provides evidence for either view.

So are NDEs universal and are they always the same?

The pioneer of the idea, indeed the pioneer of the whole NDE movement, was Raymond Moody, an American doctor and philosopher who began collecting accounts of NDEs as part of his clinical practice. It was in 1975 that his ground-breaking book *Life After Life* was published (133). It was a simple book but dramatic in its impact. It was no more than a compilation of accounts from people who had come close to death and lived to tell the tale. Many had had cardiac arrests and been resuscitated, though some had had their close encounters through other, less medically demanding means. All of them, however, described similar experiences and this similarity became part of the idea's selling power, with phrases such as 'startlingly similar in detail' on the book's cover. It was also this similarity that enabled Moody to produce his now famous composite account (133, pp. 21–3). Since no book on NDEs would be complete without it I make no apologies to those who have read it before (though I would point out that it could equally be a 'she'):

A man is dying and, as he reaches the point of greatest physical distress, he hears himself pronounced dead by his doctor. He begins to hear an uncomfortable noise, a loud ringing or buzzing, and at the same time feels himself moving very rapidly through a long dark tunnel. After this, he suddenly finds himself outside of his own physical body, but still in the immediate physical environment, and he sees his own body from a distance, as though he is a spectator. He watches the resuscitation attempt from this unusual vantage point and is in a state of emotional upheaval.

After a while, he collects himself and becomes more accustomed to his odd condition. He notices that he still has a 'body', but one of a very different nature and with very different powers from the physical body he has left behind. Soon other things begin to happen. Others come to meet and to help him. He glimpses the spirits of relatives and friends who have already died, and a loving, warm spirit of a kind he has never encountered before – a being of light – appears before him. This being asks him a question, non-verbally, to make him evaluate his life and helps him along by showing him a panoramic, instantaneous playback of the major events of his life. At some point he finds himself approaching some sort of barrier or border, apparently representing the limit between earthly life and the next life. Yet, he finds that he must go back to the earth, that the time for his death has not yet come. At this point he resists, for by now he is taken up with his experiences in the afterlife and does not want to return. He is overwhelmed by intense feelings of joy, love and peace. Despite his attitude, though, he somehow reunites with his physical body and lives.

Later he tries to tell others but he has trouble doing so. In the first place, he can find no human words adequate to describe these unearthly episodes. He also finds that others scoff, so he stops telling other people. Still, the experience affects his life profoundly, especially his views about death and its relationship to life.

Of course, not all the accounts in Moody's book fitted this formula precisely. Some were much shorter and included fewer elements. Others seemed to dwell on some parts of the experience to the exclusion of others. Nevertheless, the pattern was clear and the similarity obvious.

At the time there was something of an outcry from other doctors and from psychologists and physiologists. This was all too fanciful, they said; after all, the experiences were just hallucinations. Some critics claimed they could not be proved or they were invented or exaggerated. Others said they were just products of Western peoples' expectations. This last argument is important. Moody was claiming far more than the simple fact that a lot of Americans being resuscitated from cardiac arrests had had similar experiences. He was claiming, or at least strongly implying, that the experience he outlined so graphically was common to all human beings; that this is what happens when we die and it is relevant to every one of us.

If this is really true we should expect NDEs to be substantially the same the world over. There are at least three ways of looking at this: the historical, the cross-cultural and the developmental. Have people always reported these experiences throughout the ages or are they just a twentieth-century phenomenon? Do they occur in other cultures or are they a product of Western education, religion or medicine? And are they the same in children who have had less chance to take on religious and cultural expectations?

We can answer these questions with a (necessarily brief) excursion into distant times and places.

TRAVELS FROM DISTANT TIMES

The most famous historical case is probably that from Plato, who considered death to be central in the work of philosophy. Indeed, in the *Phaedo* Socrates proclaims that true philosophers make death and dying their profession. Plato's famous story of a return from death is recounted in the *Republic*.

Er was a Greek soldier who was left for dead on a funeral pyre. Before he was burned he awoke to describe what he had experienced on a journey out of his body. Along with other spirits he travelled to a place where the souls are judged, with openings or passageways to heaven or to punishment. Other souls were stopped and judged for what they had done in this life but Er was sent back to earth to tell others about the life beyond. He awoke back in his body, not knowing how he had returned.

In Tibetan Buddhist literature there are also the *das-lok* or 'returned from the dead' writings. There are hundreds of accounts of people who have come back to life before being cremated or buried. Usually the dead person meets with deceased relatives and friends or famous people of old, and is asked to take messages back to the living. Thereafter the person is often transformed into a wandering prophet or teacher, warning people to avoid evil and cultivate goodness (141).

If it were not for the obvious similarities to Moody's accounts these stories might plausibly be taken as the kind of useful myth that is propagated in many cultures. Its function might be to ensure belief in life after death and eventual judgement for everybody's wrongdoings and hence to enforce good behaviour.

The same might easily be said of another such myth, this time intended to enforce the ritual of burning a fire for four days after a person's death. But again there is a similarity to modern NDEs. The myth comes from a culture centuries and thousands of miles away from ancient Greece or Tibet: the North American Indians of the early nineteenth century. Mr Henry Rowe Schoolcraft was travelling in the Mississippi valley, collecting tales from the Indians he met, aware that, with the encroachment of the white man, these oral traditions might soon become altered or lost. The following tale was told by the Chippewas.

A warrior chief, so the story goes, took a small party and met his enemies on the open plain. Though his warriors were brave and ultimately triumphed, he was killed and his body left on the battlefield. In the usual way it was propped up against a tree, with all the chief's equipment to hand and his headdress in place.

The odd thing was that while his body was being prepared he felt everything that was happening. Yet he could not make his warriors understand, however much he shouted and yelled. Eventually they left and he struggled with great anguish to follow them. His rage only increased as they travelled the long journey back to his village where the men were greeted with joy at their victory and with questions about his own fate. In answer to these, the men described how he had perished.

'It is not true', replied the indignant chief, with a loud voice, 'that I was killed and left upon the field. I am here! I live! I move! See me! Touch me! I shall again raise my lance in battle and sound my drum in the feast.' But nobody seemed conscious of his presence, and they mistook his loud voice for the whispering winds (208 p. 406).

Next he went to his wife who was mourning at his death. He asked for food but she only heard a buzzing in her ears. Exasperated, he struck her on the forehead but she only complained of a slight headache. Then he remembered that he had heard that sometimes the spirit is permitted to leave the body and wander about. It took him four long days to return to the battlefield and find his body and then there was a fire in his path. He thought he would never get back, until he leapt right through the flame and awoke, hungry and exhausted. Somehow he walked the long way back to the village for the second time, to the utter amazement of all his people to whom he explained that they must light a fire for four nights after death to save the departed soul from having to do this task itself.

Although its value in enforcing burial rituals is clear, this story is similar to modern NDEs in describing the out-of-body travels and the frustrating inability to affect the physical world. And it comes, long ago, from a culture that can have had little contact with outsiders.

This impotence of the travelling soul to make itself heard appears in another ancient legend, this time from Lithuanian folklore. A man who expressed too much curiosity about life after death got his just deserts when he fell into a coma and awoke without pain. He left his bed to sit near the stove only to see his wife enter and start screaming, 'He is dead, he is dead!' He tried to calm her, and failed, finally seeing his own body lying on the bed. But still he did not realize what had happened. It was only when he accompanied his family to the cemetery for the funeral and kissed his own body along with them, that he grasped the truth. At this moment he re-entered his body, sat up, left the grave, and returned home with his family (96).

Is it odd that this Lithuanian traveller was so stupid as not to realize what was going on? Not at all. And here is something worth thinking about. Imagine you are nearly dead. There must be something seriously wrong or you would not be in this state. You are hardly likely to be at your best and brightest. You may also be very fearful of death, not wanting to lose everything you have always worked for, identified with, or taken as the meaning of your life. Now, suddenly, everything is topsy-turvy, you are drifting above the scene, unable to affect anything, terrified of losing everything and everyone you hold dear. I do not think it at all surprising that you would be confused.

This brings to mind a comment by Stephen Levine in his book *Who Dies?*, a book about preparing for death in life. 'Occasionally,' he writes, 'I hear people say, "Oh, don't worry, when the time comes I'll do the proper meditations." Good luck! Because when it comes time, the energies you have now may very well not be present' (117 p. 28). Just like the Chippewa chief or the Lithuanian inquirer, you may be too confused, too afraid or in too much pain to have any clear understanding of what is going on.

Is it this that provides the motivation for the manuals on dying? In our culture we are not much used to the idea of using life to prepare for death but many other cultures have developed special training techniques for learning how to die. They teach people what to expect of death and the skills needed to prepare for it so that confusion will not overtake them when the time comes.

The earliest of these is the *Egyptian Book of the Dead* but the most famous is probably the *Tibetan Book of the Dead* or *Bardo Thodol* (57, 7). This was intended to be studied by Tibetan

Buddhists during life and read to them on their deathbed to help guide them through the experiences of dying, either to choose an auspicious next life or to escape from the wheel of death and rebirth altogether. Among the experiences described are loud roaring noises, bright lights and personifications of emotions, attachments and desires in the form of Tibetan deities.

The well-known *Bardo Thodol* is only part of extensive teachings on death in the Tibetan tradition. A central teaching of the Buddha is that of impermanence; everything, including oneself, is impermanent, transitory and ever-changing. Death is the supreme teacher of impermanence and there are meditations on death, inspirational stories about the deaths of great lamas and methods of training the mind for the transference of consciousness at death (141).

The difference between these teachings and the folk-tales we have been considering – and it is a very big difference – is that in Buddhism these experiences are not meant to be taken literally as a topology of the next life, or as a description of actual places to be visited by a real soul departing from the body. Rather, they are products of the mind or expressions of form out of emptiness. To understand this means more than just seeing them, in a Western psychological way, as mental images or hallucinations. The notion of mental emptiness is not merely the opposite of mental fullness. I shall return to this in due course when we look at the transformations that NDErs undergo and what this tells us about the nature of mind.

For now, let us pursue the similarities with modern NDEs a little further and compare the *Tibetan Book of the Dead* with the other major manuals of dying, the medieval ones. There were many such guides, written to help the Christian seeker to die well and also to behave better in this life.

The *Book of the Craft of Dying* begins by explaining that, for those not skilled in dying, death 'seemeth wonderfully hard and perilous, and also right fearful and horrible'. Therefore the book is for teaching and comforting 'them that be in point of death ... for doubtless it is and may be profitable generally, to all true Christian men, to learn and have craft and knowledge to die well' (36). It then includes a commendation of death and a list of the devil's temptations of the dying, including loss of faith, despair triumphing over hope, impatience, complacence or spiritual pride and an occupation with outward or temporal things. There are questions to be asked of the dying while they can still understand, instructions to those who are going to die and, finally, prayers to be said over the dying.

I stated earlier that in our culture we are not much used to the idea of learning how to die, but there are signs that this is changing. Today, there are probably more books on death than ever before, including translations of the ancient texts, books from the hospice movement, the study of death and dying, the 'New Age' and from modern spiritual teachings.

How do you learn to die willingly? When the trappings of the various religious traditions are stripped away there seems to be one underlying route – and that is to learn to live willingly. What prevents us from living life as it is? Our own desires, our clinging to what we think of as good and bad, acceptable and unacceptable, a terrible calamity or great good fortune. For most people, their own death or that of their children or their lovers is a terrible disaster to be feared and avoided at all cost. But really this is only an extension of the fear that we will look old and ugly, that the phone will (or won't) ring, or the bill be too high, that the party won't go well, and so on. Learning to welcome any of this as it comes, without the resistance made of judgement, is learning to live, and this in turn will mean learning to die.

This is, perhaps, the simplest way – simple but difficult. It is also a way that comes hard to us because of our biological nature. To stay alive as animals we have to strive to get food and to get on better than other people. From that striving come greed, ownership and fear of loss. The biggest loss of all is, of course, the loss of ourselves because by the time we face death most of us have built up a huge superstructure called 'me' that is impossible to dissolve. Some of the teachings aimed at preparing us for death are about ways to let go of that self. The self, they teach, is illusory. Let it go in life and truth will reveal itself in both life and death.

Although the medieval teachings on death were teachings to prepare for a Christian afterlife, they also contained teaching on this more general point. *Tower of all Towers* explains 'Against his will he dieth that hath not learned to die. Learn to die and thou shalt con [learn] to live, for there shall none con to live that hath not learned to die; and he shall be cleped a wretch that cannot live and dare not die' (36 p. 127).

There are many other medieval writings on death and, as to be expected from within this Christian tradition, many have to do with the judgement or reward and punishment for deeds committed in life. Many also deal with death as a kind of journey; a journey from an enfeebled or dying body to a glorious body in another world.

The many forms this journey took in medieval times is described in detail in the work of Harvard lecturer on the study of religion, Carol Zaleski, in her book *Otherworld Journeys* (239). What is striking about these accounts is how horrible they are compared to most modern ones.

In the seventh-century *Vision of Barontus*, for example, the traveller is struck down by a fever after divine office and is found writhing on the floor pointing at his throat before he chokes into unconsciousness. While the monks around him chant and spread holy water about the place, he is grappling with two loathsome demons who have him by the throat and drag him towards hell. At three in the morning the monks begin to pray for his recovery and it is apparently at this moment that the archangel Raphael starts fighting with the demons for his soul. By Vespers the monks see the signs of death and start praying instead for his soul. Meanwhile the archangel is taking Barontus on a journey to appear before the tribunal of the eternal judge. Finally, at cock crow, Barontus revives, sits up and praises God, much to the astonishment of his companions.

These stories can be as nasty as one can imagine and human imagination can be nasty indeed; sinners are tossed between fire and ice, devoured by dragons, roasted forever on devils' barbecues, or pinned to the ground with red hot nails. Then there is the test bridge, which appears in many different forms but usually consists of a narrow bridge over some kind of fiery or fetid river or deep dark pit to a beautiful land beyond. For the just and good the narrow path is easily walked but for the wicked it can become as sharp as a sword, or slippery and dark, and after thousands of years trying to cross they eventually fall screaming into the boiling depths.

Although superficially quite unlike modern NDEs this tale does include the idea of judgement. Indeed, this is a recurring theme in the medieval accounts. But whereas in modern accounts the judgement is usually a self-judgement or judgement by a loving being or warm light, in these older tales it is by divine power and the punishment is meted out by the most horrific creatures that the imagination can conjure. Even so, Zaleski concludes that 'Whatever its guise, the review of deeds is essentially an encounter with oneself' (239 p. 27).

Zaleski sums up the similarities and differences she found between modern and medieval accounts of people who died and were revived again. In both, the first step is a kind of dualistic parting of body and soul, with the separated spirit looking down on its former dwelling place with indifference or contempt, hovering and able to watch the scene with detachment. Then begins the journey proper, signalled by the arrival of guides or by symbols of travel such as paths, valleys or tunnels. The guide interprets the scenes of the journey and emphasizes the need for spiritual instruction in this life and the next. The pivotal episode is the self-confrontation in which the visionaries meet their own thoughts, words and deeds, learn the weight of their souls or review their life and bring judgement on themselves.

Both modern and ancient stories, though this is only rarely and briefly found in the older accounts, can include a mystical experience, in which thinking and feeling fuse, unmediated awareness floods in, and the journey is suspended. An instant later the play resumes and the traveller feels compelled to return, sometimes against his will, to life, returning transformed from an 'ordinary guy' into a prophet or visionary (239 p. 188).

These few examples from distant times suggest that most of the features of the Moody-type experience have a long history.

The emphasis varies, the experiences can be vastly different in detail, but still the similarities come through clearly. This in turn suggests the possibility that not only have NDEs been similar throughout the ages but that this is why so many traditional beliefs are also so similar (191).

What, then, of the present time? If NDEs are universal, as some have claimed, then they should not be confined to the West but should cross cultural as well as historical barriers.

ACROSS CULTURES TODAY

The answer, for the moment, is that we do not have enough evidence to be sure. There is certainly a similarity in the beliefs most people hold about themselves. A key assumption in most of these travellers' tales is that a human being is something more than a body; a soul or spirit or some other entity, which can separate at death or even before death and travel about on its own.

This way of looking at ourselves is compelling. In our Western philosophical tradition it was formalized in the seventeenth century by René Descartes in what has come to be known as Cartesian Dualism. Descartes distinguished two fundamentally different kinds of things, *physical* or *extended* substance and *thinking* substance. For him, mind and brain were made of quite separate kinds of stuff.

Western philosophers and scientists have long argued cogently and powerfully against this dualist view and the few who still defend it, such as neurophysiologist Sir John Eccles, philosopher Sir Karl Popper (173) or psychologist John Beloff (10), are in a tiny minority amongst academics. However, most other people seem to agree with Descartes. The dualist temptation is so great. Just as we do not like to imagine that we will one day die, so we do not like to think of ourselves as just an ever-changing and perishable body, controlled by an information-processing brain. Our experience seems to suggest that we have some aspect of ourselves that stays the same throughout our life, that is, if you like, 'the real me'. If you believe this, it is not such a big step (though neither is it a logical one) to believing that this 'something' can leave the body and travel outside it.

It is not surprising, then, to find that most other non-Western cultures share at least this much. Dean Sheils (212) compared the beliefs of over sixty different cultures by consulting ethnographic accounts in the 'Human Relations Area Files'. He found only three that claimed no belief in anything like this. Of fifty-four cultures for which some information was reported, twenty-five (or nearly half) claimed that most people could travel out of their bodies in this way and another twenty-three claimed that some people (for example, shamans) could do this, even if ordinary people could not.

But what of NDEs – are they also similar in other cultures? Recently a few researchers have started taking this question seriously. Following the consistency argument, they have wanted to know whether NDEs in India, Africa or Mesopotamia are just like the ones Moody reported in the US.

Here the evidence is scanty in the extreme. The largest study was carried out by Osis and Haraldsson who sent out questionnaires to 5,000 doctors and nurses in the US and interviewed about 700 medical personnel in India (155, 156). This was not strictly about NDEs but about the medical workers' recollections of the experiences told to them by people who were dying. Of course, all the stories were second-hand and often told many years after the events. None the less, the findings are very interesting. The most common visions were of dead people or religious figures: the former more common in the US and the latter in India. Americans most often visualized their mother but female figures were extremely rare among Indians, especially among males. Religious figures were, not surprisingly, in conformance with the person's own religion. No Hindu saw Jesus and no Christian saw a Hindu deity. Most of these figures had come to take the dying person away. Here another fascinating difference emerged – Americans were quite likely to go along happily with their dead relatives or visionary angels whereas Indians were more likely to put up a fight and refuse to go.

Why this difference? It appears to be based on religious teachings. In Hindu mythology Yamraj, the king of the dead, is a well-known figure, as are his messengers, the Yamdoots. Then there is Chitragupta, the man with the book. In this book are entered each person's deeds throughout their lives, implying, once again, the belief in a final judgement. In Christian mythology St Peter is waiting at the gate to heaven but there are no messengers to drag the unwilling soul away from life. The difference in experience could be due to such contrasting cultural and religious beliefs.

Of course, these were accounts from people who did die. So what happens to the ones who return from NDEs? Do they, like many Westerners, decide of their own accord that their children need them or that their life's work is not completed and they must 'come back'? Apparently not. NDE researchers Satwant Pasricha and Ian Stevenson reported sixteen cases of NDEs in India and a common theme was the story of mistaken identity (163).

A typical case is that of Chhajju Bania, interviewed in 1981 when he was about forty years old. Some six years before he had become ill with a fever and appeared dead so that his relatives began preparing his body for cremation. He recalled that four black messengers came and seated him near Yamraj. There was an old lady with a pen, and clerks with heaps of books in front of them. One of them said, 'We don't need Chhajju Bania (trader). We had asked for Chhajju Umhar (potter). Push him back and bring the other man. He has some life remaining.' The trader must have liked it there because he then requested some work to do and asked Yamraj, who had a white beard and was sitting on a high chair, whether he could stay, but in vain. He was pushed down again and revived.

Cases like this one seem dramatically different from the Moody-type NDE. There is no tunnel, no bright light and no out-of-body experience. There is no mystical insight and no reported transformation afterwards. Some have argued that this means NDEs are not universal. To test this I set about collecting more cases from India.

I put an advertisement in the *Times of India* in Bombay asking for accounts from people who had come close to death, but without saying anything about what I was looking for. Later I followed up their letters with a questionnaire. I received nineteen extensive accounts, including twelve who reported some kind of experience during their brush with death. Four had very strange dream-like or hallucinatory experiences, from a vision of a mother hen with chicks to a gruesome fight with a seven-foot monster, while eight reported at least some elements of the classic NDE. One man suffering a serious liver disease and thought unlikely to live 'travelled to a space of brilliant light where I was being loved ... I had a feeling that for hours together I was away from this world enjoying the light . . . I was beyond time and space.' A pop star, playing on an outdoor stage, was accidentally electrocuted and explains that 'I felt "myself" light as a feather, shooting upwards at an indescribable speed, which can never be measured by the words "speed" or "time" ... surrounding me on all sides were lights of all colours – shining spots.' In a third case, a woman who fell suddenly unconscious found herself travelling down a dark tunnel through complete blackness with the tingling sound of tiny bells in her ears.

Of the eight NDErs, one heard sweet music, three reported a tunnel or dark space, four saw bright light, four experienced joy or peace and three claimed effects on their lives or beliefs – in other words, though this was only a small study, the features were similar to those reported in the West.

For the consistency argument this is quite important. We find not a complete duplication of an identical experience but rather similar features appearing in different forms across times and cultures.

Some have argued that there is a kind of core experience that is common to all people and to all cultures but which is overlaid with cultural differences. This theory would account for the variations that occur with time and place but has its own problems. It is tempting to think that if we could somehow delve beneath the surface of the accounts people give we would find the invariant, true NDE underneath. But this is a vain hope. In fact it is the same kind of vain hope that affects many religious seekers and many people who have mystical experiences or NDEs. They think they have glimpsed some kind of truth. They tell the story to others, they try to remember it for themselves in images and words, but images and words cannot capture what it was, how it felt, the 'real thing'. If there *is* any 'real thing' it is as ineffable as a moment of bliss.

If there is a person there experiencing this 'thing' then that person is themselves a product of their culture, language and past experience. You cannot find the 'real thing' underneath by stripping all that away. If there is no one there, only the experience, then little can be said about it beyond dealing directly with the accounts of such experiences. So we should not seek to peel off layers of culture and find the core beneath. Rather we must accept that all the accounts come from real people living in different times and places and try to learn what we can of human nature as it expresses itself in these different but related experiences.

One last way of exploring the consistency of NDEs is by looking to children. If culture shapes or creates our experiences then those who have imbibed least of it may have the clearest stories to tell. So what do children have to say about coming close to death and returning to life?

CHILDREN FACING DEATH

The best known examples of childhood NDEs come from paediatrician and researcher Melvin Morse (136). One day, in the course of his work in the intensive care unit, he was struggling to resuscitate a nine-year-old girl named Katie who had been found floating face down in a swimming pool. She had massive swelling of the brain, no gag reflex and was kept breathing with an artificial lung. He estimated a 10 per cent chance of survival but three days later she was fully recovered. What surprised him most, though, and started him on his NDE research, was the story she told. To help decide on her treatment he wanted to find out what had happened in the pool. To his surprise she told him how a tunnel had opened up and through the tunnel came 'Elizabeth', with bright, golden hair. Elizabeth took Katie on to meet her dead grandfather, other spirits and the Heavenly Father who asked if she wanted to go home. Katie said she wanted to stay with him but when Jesus asked if she wanted to see her mother again she said, yes, she did, and awoke.

After that Morse began an eight-year project to research childhood NDEs. Many of his findings have contributed to our understanding of the NDE and I shall return to them later. For now I shall only note that from children recalling incidents that happened when they were as young as nine months old, there come stories of tunnels and lights, out-of-body experiences (OBEs) and travels to heaven. Here is another story from Dr Morse's collection, this time told by an eight-year-old girl called June who also nearly drowned when her hair became caught in the swimming-pool drain.

All I remember was my hair getting stuck in the drain and then blacking out. The next thing I knew, I floated out of my body. I could see myself under the water but I wasn't afraid. All of a sudden I started going up a tunnel, and before I could think about it, I found myself in heaven. I know it was heaven because everything was bright and everyone was cheerful.

A nice man asked me if I wanted to stay there. I thought about staying; I really did. But I said 'I want to be with my family.' Then I got to come back.

(136 p. 32)

Like many of the adults who have had NDEs these children seemed to be changed by their experiences. Some remarked on a new purpose for living; some seemed to change for the better. For them too this was no ordinary experience or dream. It was something special.

We may now return to our question: are NDEs universal and are they always the same? I think, with all the limitations of our research, we can even answer it. We have consistency but not invariance. Yes, the NDE is universal in the sense that something like the modern NDE has been reported in adults and children and in many ages and cultures. And 'no', it is not always the same but varies with the individual, the culture and the circumstances.

The big question, however, remains unanswered. Consistency we have, but why? Two possible answers still remain: either we all have a spirit or soul that survives death or we all have similar brains that die in similar ways.

2

The Stages of Dying

When June nearly died she went up a tunnel to heaven. Why?

If she had stayed a little longer in the water would she have also had a review of her life? Or not? If she had been pulled out sooner would she have come back through the tunnel? Or not? Had she been older or younger would the experience have been different? And have other little girls come as close to drowning and *not* had an NDE?

In trying to understand the origin of NDEs it may be useful to find out the answers to these kinds of questions. Part of what is at issue is the difference between what I have called the 'consistency argument' and the more restricted 'invariance hypothesis'. Consistency we certainly seem to have but, beyond that, is the NDE invariable? Does it always take the same form? If not, when and why not? By appropriate research we ought to be able to find out, but it is not an easy task.

A first step for many researchers has been to try to categorize NDEs or to develop some kind of typology or scheme of the stages involved. Ways of scoring NDEs have even been developed. All these make it easier to compare the experiences so as to answer the above questions.

Moody, from his collection of accounts, has made several lists of the typical features of the NDE (133, 134). In his first book he lists fifteen aspects of the NDE:

Ineffability (or being impossible to describe)
Hearing the news
Feelings of peace and quiet
The noise
The dark tunnel

Going out of the body (usually known as an out-of-body
    experience or OBE)
Meeting others
The review
The border or limit
Coming back
Telling others
The effects on people's lives
New views of death
Corroboration

This list was derived by Moody directly from the accounts.
Moody makes it clear that his is not a 'scientific' analysis, his
sampling is not random and he provided only a collection of
cases as he found them. He cannot give precise information on
who has which stages or which are most common and simply
notes that these are typical components of an NDE; no two
experiences are exactly the same and no one person in his collection reported every single component. Many reported eight or
more of the fifteen and a few up to twelve. In addition there was
no one essential element which every person recounted nor was
any component unique to one person.

The order is important though. Moody gives it, both in this
list and in his 'composite account' (see chapter 1, p. 7) as he
most often found it, but he adds that some people saw the being
of light before or at the same time as they left their body rather
than afterwards. Perhaps more important, he remarks that how
far someone gets into the experience seems to depend on whether
they actually experienced clinical death or not. As he puts it
'those who were "dead" for a longer period go deeper than those
who were "dead" for a shorter time' (133).

This is an important claim. It implies that there is more than
just a selection of experiences which people can have near death,
and that there is some kind of progression from the shallowest
to the deepest of NDEs. I say it is important because if there
were just a collection of possible experiences, any of which might
happen in any order near death and each individually could be

induced by stress, chemicals or whatever, then the case for a special experience would be weakened. On the other hand, if there is really a progression of stages as one gets further into dying, then we require an explanation of the whole unfolding experience, as well as separate accounts of all the parts.

THE DEPTH OF NDES: STAGES AND SCALES

It was Kenneth Ring who carried out the first research to explore this question properly (182). Ring is a psychologist at the University of Connecticut who was much impressed by Moody's findings and wanted to investigate the many unanswered questions. In 1977 he began to collect accounts systematically from adults who had come close to death through serious illness, accident or suicide attempt and who were recovered enough to be able to talk about it. There was no stipulation that they had to have had any 'experiences'.

Insufficient numbers of such people could be found through hospital referrals alone, but finally, through advertising and word of mouth, 102 people were included in the study. Of these, the vast majority were white and Christian. Half had nearly died as a result of a serious illness, about a quarter from accidents and the remainder from suicide attempts.

To many critics' surprise the interviews confirmed most of Moody's claims. Similar experiences were reported and Ring was able to describe what he called the 'Core Experience'. This consisted of five core features rather than Moody's fifteen:

Feelings of peace
Body separation (the OBE)
Entering the darkness (Moody's dark tunnel)
Seeing the light
Entering the light

Using this categorization it became clear that not only do these features usually occur in the above order, but that the earlier

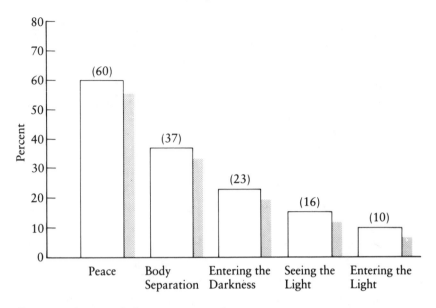

Figure 1. Stages of the NDE according to Ring (1980).

ones in the sequence are the most common. This is shown in Figure 1. A solid 60 per cent of his sample reported peace but only 10 per cent had an experience of entering the light.

Ring concludes that 'there is a consistent and remarkable experiential pattern that often unfolds when an individual is seemingly about to die. I will call this reliable near-death pattern the core experience' (182 p. 22). So Ring had apparently confirmed Moody's claim about the depth of the NDE.

From there Ring went further to develop a 'Weighted Core Experience Index' (often known as WCEI). The various components of the NDE were assigned different weights. These were the subjective sense of being dead, feelings of peace, bodily separation, entering a dark region, encountering a presence or hearing a voice, taking stock of one's life, seeing or being enveloped in light, seeing beautiful colours, entering into the light and encountering visible spirits. Each person's experience was scored for presence or absence of each feature. Multiplying by the weights and adding the points gives a total score in the range 0 to 29. Ring gives accounts of NDEs scoring anything from

6 to 18 (a few in the study attained even higher scores). He also divides people into deep experiencers, moderate experiencers and non-experiencers; a scheme which has been adopted by other researchers, as we shall see.

Some interesting differences from Moody's work also emerged. For example, Ring claims that people either meet their relatives or encounter a 'presence', but not both. He tries to give a functional account of this, suggesting that the purpose of both is to end the experience or to send the person back. Since both images are performing the same function there is no need of both.

Many questions remain. There is undoubtedly a certain arbitrariness about the way the components were divided up. Would a person from another culture or religion have divided them up this way? The order of components, though described, is never systematically investigated. The measure was never tested for reliability, as needs to be done for any new scale. However, this research was the first, and a very big, step towards convincing doubting scientists, doctors and critics, that there *was* some kind of consistent experience here to be explained and that it could be measured.

Someone else who initially disbelieved Moody's claims was cardiologist Michael Sabom from Atlanta, Georgia. When psychiatric social worker Sarah Kreutziger gave him Moody's book to read he thought it was all fiction and had no hesitation in saying so. He was sure he could confirm this by speaking to survivors of cardiac arrests in his wards but, much to his surprise, the third patient he spoke to described a near-death experience. From there he went on to research NDEs. He chose to categorize them into three types: autoscopic (or out of the body); transcendental; and combined NDEs (204, 205). However, this scheme was never thoroughly tested or turned into any kind of formal scale.

The first categorization based on statistical analysis was by two Iowa psychiatrists, Russell Noyes and Donald Slymen (154). Prior to this, Russell Noyes had argued that a common reaction of people faced with life-threatening danger is depersonalization;

a psychiatric syndrome characterized by a sense of the self being separate from the environment or unreal in some way (150). He had described three successive stages, resistance, life review and transcendence (148), but this scheme had not been thoroughly tested.

Noyes and Slymen now gave questionnaires to 189 people who had survived falls, drowning, car accidents, other accidents and serious illness. The questionnaire included twenty-six items about such subjective experiences as altered passage of time, thoughts speeding up, loss of emotion, strange bodily sensations, feelings of joy, great understanding or unreality. The results were then submitted to factor analysis; a statistical technique for revealing any underlying factors.

Three factors emerged (accounting for 41 per cent of the variance among the experiences):

1. A Mystical Factor, including feelings of great understanding, harmony, joy and revelation, as well as enhanced visual imagery and panoramic memory.
2. Depersonalization, including the self seeming strange or unreal or detached from the body, objects seeming far away, a wall between the self and emotions and altered passage of time.
3. Hyperalertness, including vivid or speeded up thoughts, and sharper vision and hearing.

The hyperalertness responses were the most common and the mystical ones the least common. Because of this Noyes and Slymen suggest that the mystical state of consciousness represents a more complete withdrawal from the extreme circumstances.

Depersonalization may be an adaptive response when the threat is less extreme. It seemed, from their findings, to be almost the opposite of the hyperalertness factor. But the combination of these two could make some sense as combining both higher arousal with a kind of dissociation from that arousal. Presumably the arousal or alertness might be useful in some circumstances to escape death while emotional separation might be necessary so as not to become swamped by the extreme emotions.

It is obvious that this approach is a departure from Ring's and Moody's. What are presumably the same kinds of experiences have been categorized in a totally different way. If nothing else, this should remind us (as we follow the research using Ring's approach) that the categories, features, items or whichever ways the experiences are divided up, are not fixed. To some extent any attempt to divide up a composite experience is theory-laden. There is no right way – but there may be more or less useful ways.

Ring's scale and the approaches that followed from it, have been the most widely used. For example Kohr (111) produced a simplified scale based on Ring's work from which people could be categorized by a list of six core features as light, moderate or deep experiencers. With this simpler scale he again confirmed Moody's speculation that the later features were also less common.

Bruce Greyson, an American psychiatrist and NDE researcher, pointed out some problems with Ring's scale (81). He argued that people could get a fairly high score with very few typical NDE experiences; for instance, a suicide attempter might have experienced a life review and feelings of peace or relief and get a score of seven, or if they also seemed to go through a region of darkness a score of eleven, without ever having any transcendental or out-of-body experiences. Therefore he tried to produce a more valid and reliable scale.

To do this Greyson solicited accounts of NDEs from among members of the Association for Near-Death Studies, an organization founded to further NDE research and to bring together experiencers and researchers. He initially listed eighty features, including emotional states, thought content (e.g. the life review), thought processes (e.g. thinking unusually fast), perceptual content (e.g. hearing music), perceptual processing, bodily sensations and other features such as the tunnel experience. These included all the main items from the previous scales. After a pilot study he reduced the list to thirty-three items with three-point scaled answers, and this was sent to the respondents. A cluster analysis led to a modified version of Ring's scale with a maximum score of 23 (compared to Ring's 29) from which the final scale was developed.

The final Near-Death Experience Scale consisted of sixteen questions grouped in four clusters. These four were concerned with emotions, cognition (or thinking), paranormal features and transcendental aspects. Some people were asked to complete the scale again later and the 'test–retest reliability' and internal consistency were high. Finally the scores people got correlated highly with the modified Ring scale (the transcendental component correlated the most highly) and the scores did not correlate with the person's age, sex or the circumstances of the close brush with death.

Some fascinating findings emerged from this work – including one that challenges many people's idea of a 'classic NDE'. First Greyson found that the depersonalization symptoms correlated only very weakly with the rest of the scale. So he concluded that the NDE is not just a non-specific stress response but a distinct syndrome (81 p. 57).

What then constitutes this distinct syndrome? Is it most people's idea of a classic NDE – leaving the body, going down a tunnel and having a mystical vision of another world? Are the most well-known or common features the crucial ones? It seems not. For example, the sense that time had stopped or become meaningless was very common (64 per cent reported it) yet it correlated very weakly with the rest of the scale so it cannot be specific to the NDE. On the other hand, visions of the world's future, which were relatively rare (16 per cent), were specific to the NDE.

Most surprising of all, though, was the tunnel. This must, above all, be the feature people think of as central to the NDE but Greyson found it was not. The tunnel experience was not significantly correlated with any other single NDE item, nor with the other thirty-two items together. He concludes, 'Although the tunnel experience may be a part of the NDE, its presence does not help differentiate depth of NDE, and therefore was not included in the quantitative NDE scale' (81 p. 58).

This is very strange. It certainly changes what we need to do in trying to understand the NDE. If the tunnel is independent of the rest of the NDE it probably occurs for a different reason and requires a different kind of explanation.

This also deals a blow to some quite popular claims about the tunnel: that it is the flow of 'vital force' leaving the body or that it is linked with the silver cord that is broken at death. Crookall (39) regards the tunnel as a symbol of shedding the physical body and it is commonly described as though it formed some kind of direct route to heaven. This research suggests it may not be connected with the heavenly experiences at all.

Drawing these researches together it now seems that there is more than one experience to be explained. For Noyes and Slymen there are three factors. For Greyson there is a distinct NDE syndrome which does not include either the tunnel or depersonalization. To understand the whole range of NDEs we may need to account for these factors separately. Perhaps they have different underlying causes.

We now have some scales with which to score people's NDEs. This is an important step in the research for it allows us to return to our questions with more tools for answering them. I had been wondering about little June's experience; whether nearly drowning inevitably leads to the kind of experience she had or whether she might equally have experienced something completely different. Perhaps we can now formalize this underlying question with a series of simpler questions about the NDE.

1. How common is the NDE?
2. Does everyone who comes close to death experience something?
3. If not, who has NDEs and who does not?
4. If the experience is not always the same, what factors influence its nature?
5. Do you have to be near death to have an NDE?

Dying to Live

Armed with ways of measuring the NDE, researchers have been able to make more progress with questions such as these. So let's see what answers have emerged.

HOW COMMON IS THE NDE?

In 1982 Gallup published a report on a 'look beyond the threshold of death'. He believed the most provocative question of all time to be 'Does life exist beyond death?' To answer it, the Gallup Poll organization conducted a series of national surveys of Americans' beliefs and experiences. Of course, as Gallup recognized, such a survey could never really answer the question. Nevertheless the thousands of interviews provided a lot of information and one of the questions asked was 'Have you yourself ever been on the verge of death or had a "close call" which involved any unusual experience at that time?' (69 p. 198). Overall 15 per cent of the population sampled said they had.

This very high figure is probably an overestimate. Many kinds of experience were included and none of the scales we have looked at were used. No attempt could be made to check whether the people really did come close to death. Also, of course, coming close to death may mean at least two totally different things. It can be having a near escape in which there is really no medical or clinical problem (such as narrowly missing being hit by a car or falling from a cliff and landing safely) or it may mean being medically close to death, being resuscitated from near-drowning or a cardiac arrest, for instance.

Another study with the same flaw asked the question 'Have you yourself ever had an experience during which you strongly felt you were going to die?' The claim that 'near-death experiences were reported by 28 per cent' (225 p. 35) seems quite unfair when the 28 per cent included a college student who thought she was going to die when the school bus nearly ran into a car in the school parking lot.

Other surveys have resolved these problems and typically found lower figures than Gallup's. Two psychologists from the

University of Kansas, Thomas Locke and Franklin Shontz (120) surveyed 1,000 university students. One hundred and seven said they had come close to death but half of these had only faced a potential danger which they had managed to avoid. These were excluded and the authors only used those who had suffered a period of unconsciousness. Thirty-two people had done so and of these just seven scored 6 or more points on Ring's scale; in other words, they could be considered to have had an NDE. This is just 0.7 per cent – a far cry from Gallup's 15 per cent.

Perhaps this question is unresolvable for the population at large, there are too many problems. In any case, it is probably not the most interesting question for our purposes. More relevant is a related question. Forget about the population at large and just consider those people who do come close to death in circumstances that sometimes produce NDEs. Of these people, how many report NDEs? This is tantamount to finding out whether coming close to death inevitably leads to an NDE.

DOES EVERYONE WHO COMES CLOSE TO DEATH HAVE AN NDE?

As we have seen in Locke and Shontz's study, their figure was seven out of thirty-two, or 22 per cent. By contrast Ring (182) had found that forty-eight, or almost half, of his 102 survivors of cardiac arrest reported NDEs. A similar figure of 44 per cent was reported by Kohr (111), although his was not a random sample.

Another researcher who has explored this issue is Michael Sabom. He and Sarah Kreutziger interviewed one hundred hospital patients who had come close to death and suffered complete loss of awareness of their surroundings (205). Of these, sixty-eight were collected from their regular hospital contacts regardless of whether the patients reported any experiences (the others were referred to them from elsewhere so could not be considered a random sample). Of this main group, 43 per cent recalled an

NDE. So we have figures ranging between 22 per cent and 48 per cent with, as yet, no very clear idea of why.

This uncertainty may reflect no more than the difficulties of knowing what counts as coming close to death or what counts as an NDE, even with the scales now available for measuring it. With such uncertainty we cannot answer the question with a precise figure but we can conclude this much: less than half of those who come close to death report an NDE.

WHO HAS NDES?

If some people who come close to death have an NDE and others do not, what is the reason? Ideally, research to answer this question should compare two groups of people, all of whom have come close to death but only some of whom claim to have had an NDE. There is very little research along these lines.

After a review of the literature, two British psychiatrists, Glenn Roberts and John Owen (191), concluded that there were no demographic differences between the people who did and did not have NDEs. In other words things like age, sex, educational achievement, marital status, occupation and socio-economic group or religious background did not influence the chances of having an NDE. Interestingly, one sex difference was found by Moody (though he did not have proper comparison groups). This was that men were more reluctant to talk about their NDE, presumably fearing ridicule more than women.

This irrelevance of demographic variables has recently been confirmed by Bruce Greyson (83) who contrasted the near-death encounters of 183 people who reported NDEs and 63 people who did not. They did not differ in age, gender or time elapsed since their close brush with death.

Perhaps then, a person's personality is more relevant to whether they have an NDE or not. This was investigated by Locke and Shontz (120) who compared nine people who had had NDEs with ten who had come close to death with a life-threatening illness or serious accident but did not recall any experiences. They found no significant differences in intelligence, extraversion, neuroticism or anxiety. However, the groups were very small so it might be worth noting that the people who did report an NDE were slightly more neurotic and more anxious than those who did not. If future research proves this to be a valid difference it might imply that the NDE represents some kind of resistance to dying or anxiety response to the threat of death which, as we shall see, is a theory preferred by many.

Most other studies which have looked at personality have not been able to make the direct comparisons Locke and Shontz made. One compared NDErs with people who had had OBEs in other circumstances and found that both groups were psychologically healthy. The only difference was that NDErs scored higher on a measure of 'absorption'; that is, how easily they can become immersed in imagination or such things as books or films (227). Another example is Greyson and Stevenson (86) who compared seventy-eight NDErs with the normal population and with a group of 354 non-NDErs and ninety-two psychiatric in-patients. The NDErs reported more prior experiences suggesting transcendence of death than the other groups; these included a mystical experience of unity or of God within, perception of people not present, memory of a past life and out-of-body experiences occurring when not close to death.

Richard Kohr, from Pennsylvania (111), carried out a large-scale survey of members of the Association for Research and Enlightenment, a group interested in the work of Edgar Cayce. He divided those who responded into three groups: 358 people who had never come close to death, 105 people who had come close to death but did not report an NDE and, finally, 84 who had had a 'deep, moving personal experience' and at least one of Ring's six features of the core experience.

He found that the experiencers tended to report more out-of-body and psi-related occurrences. He gave a composite score to each person based on these experiences and the score was significantly higher for the NDErs. Ability to control out-of-body experiences was also reported more often by the NDE group and scores were higher on another composite score for openness to dreams, past-life memories and meditative practices. These differences in psychic-related phenomena may seem odd but they will prove important when we come to consider the role of the temporal lobe in NDEs in chapter 10.

All this research seems very complicated and the results confusing. Some people have tried to summarize it, amongst them Roberts and Owen (191) who suggest an association between having (or recalling) an NDE and a cognitive style of openness and inner-directed attention. But they also point out that all this work is retrospective and the observed differences could be a *consequence* of the NDE rather than a cause.

There is one researcher, however, who believes it can all be drawn together to provide an account of the NDE-prone personality – none other than Kenneth Ring.

An NDE-Prone Personality?

Ever since his study of the 102 near-death survivors Ring had been perplexed as to what made those forty-eight have NDEs while the others did not. Rather than just hunting around for possible differences he began to think about what, in a person's childhood, might predispose them to having NDEs as adults. What he and a student of his found added a new dimension to the research (190). He suggested that it all has to do with the ways people learn, as children, to cope with the traumas of life.

To investigate this he developed a special battery of questionnaires to find out about fantasy-proneness, childhood experiences, home life and childhood abuse. These were given to seventy-four NDErs and fifty-four people who were interested in NDEs but had never had one.

A very interesting finding was that abuse and stress appeared to be significant factors. The people who had NDEs as adults were more likely to report that, as children, they had been abused, physically, mentally or sexually, had been frequently ill or had had a troubled home-life.

It has long been known that such troubled childhoods can

easily lead people to develop ways of coping or mentally escaping from their unhappiness. A common one is dissociation. Indeed, people with some of the most extreme kinds of dissociation – people who end up as multiple personalities – were often severely abused as children. It is as though they have to become someone else, or split off from what is happening, in order to cope at all. Perhaps something similar is happening here. Perhaps it is the people who have to escape from their childhood troubles by living in other worlds who end up as adults having NDEs. This received added confirmation when Ring and Rosing also found that the NDErs scored higher on a dissociation scale.

There is one fact that detracts from this research as an answer to our question: the control group were not people who had come close to death without having an NDE but people who were just interested in NDEs. To be sure what these findings mean the comparison needs to be made properly for groups of people all of whom have come close to death but only some of whom have had NDEs. Until that is done there is another perfectly reasonable possibility – that the people with traumatic childhoods or those who were often ill as children were just more likely to fall ill as adults and therefore to come close to death, and this is why they experienced NDEs more frequently; a much less exciting finding than that which Ring himself claims.

Ring also makes other claims that I cannot agree with.

He says that people's proneness to fantasy as children was not relevant to having NDEs, but their 'sensitivity to alternate realities' was. NDErs were more likely to agree with statements like: 'As a child, I was aware of non-physical beings while I was awake' or 'As a child, I was able to see into other realities that others didn't seem to be aware of' but not 'As a child, I had a very vivid imagination' or 'As a child my fantasy world was very rich.'

Ring concludes that the adults who report NDEs 'are not as children especially inclined toward involvement in a world of fantasy, but they are apparently already sensitive to non-ordinary realities' (190 pp. 218–19). He seems to be implying that this validates the status of the NDE as a glimpse into this 'non-ordinary reality' rather than as a kind of fantasy. The trouble with this conclusion is that it presupposes the very distinction Ring is trying to draw from it. If you assume there is a difference between fantasy and some 'real' other world of psychic events then you may be able to draw a line between the statements above. To me, however, there seems little difference between children with a rich fantasy world who play with imaginary playmates, and being aware of 'non-physical beings'. I would like to see independent evidence for this distinction before being able to draw the conclusions Ring draws.

With this in mind, we may consider Ring and Rosing's conclusion. They suggest that

> the core defining feature of the NDE-prone personality is the capacity to shift into states of consciousness that afford access to non-ordinary realities coupled with strong tendencies toward psychological absorption. That is, the person who is especially likely to register and recall an NDE is one whose awareness is easily able to transcend the sensory world and enter into focused attention to interior states.
>
> (190 p. 235)

They add that 'the mystery and numinous power of the NDE itself remains intact' (p. 236). Interesting as this is I think we need a little caution before accepting it.

So is there an NDE-prone personality? My own conclusion is no conclusion at all. There is so little research that uses the appropriate control groups that I think we cannot yet make a balanced judgement.

FACTORS AFFECTING THE NDE

We may now turn to asking what influences the *kind* of NDE a person has. In other words, returning to June and her narrow escape – was the *quality* of her experience affected by the kind of person she was or by the fact that she nearly drowned rather than coming close to death in some other way?

Once again demographic variables appear not to be particularly important (90, 191). One exception is that in their three-factor analysis Noyes and Slymen found that younger people were more likely to report mystical components to their NDE (154).

Other irrelevant variables seem to be strength of religious beliefs, previous knowledge of NDEs, personality, and the length of time intervening between the experience and reporting it (204, 225). For example, in developing his NDE scale, Greyson found that neither the whole scale nor any of its four components was significantly correlated with age, sex, time since the NDE or with the conditions of the close encounter with death. All this has been taken by some authors as support for the invariance hypothesis (90, 182).

I disagree. There is now accumulating evidence that the circumstances of the NDE *do* affect the nature of the experience and this is very important when we try to understand its causes.

For example, Michael Sabom (204) reported that people were most likely to have NDEs when they were in hospital, and unconscious for more than a minute, and likely to have been resuscitated. This implies that they would have had greater neurochemical imbalance (90), a point to which we shall return in considering what happens in the dying brain.

In their comparison of mystical, depersonalization and hyper-alertness features, Noyes and Slymen (154) found that mystical responses and the revival of memories were most common amongst the ill and in people who thought they were about to die. Indeed, those with serious illness reported about twice as many of most of the mystical items as did accident sufferers. People who nearly drowned reported more increased visual imagery and less depersonalization and those who were unconscious were more likely to feel detached from the body and from the world. Many interpretations of this are possible but one is that the mystical features occur when there is time to think about death and its implications.

Another way of exploring this question was pursued by Kansas psychiatrists Stuart Twemlow and Glen Gabbard (227). They advertised in a national newspaper for people who had had OBEs. They sent questionnaires to 700 people and got 339 replies. Of these, thirty-four, or 10 per cent, had had their experiences near death, including childbirth, accidents, illness and drugs. They applied a statistical technique to divide the NDErs into five groups according to their type of experience (228). The largest was the 'low-stress' cluster who had calm, relaxed responses to their experience whether it occurred in childbirth, an accident or illness. An 'emotional-stress cluster' were quite the opposite, not calm, relaxed or meditating; also not under drugs and with a wide variety of conditions. A small group were under the influence of narcotic drugs or alcohol and these experienced severe emotional stress. By contrast, the cardiac arrest cluster reported mainly a meditative state of mind with flying and dream-like qualities. Finally, those who had had anaesthetics had a dream-like experience.

They also found that cardiac arrest was more commonly associated with feelings of power and awareness of people who had already died, while anaesthetics were associated with brilliant light. Accidents produced more joy and less desire to return to the body (227). Perhaps most interesting was that the tunnel and brilliant light experiences were much more common in the anaesthetic and cardiac-arrest groups. We must remember this important finding when trying to understand the origin of the tunnel.

Another interesting issue is the effects of drugs. Some scientists have argued that the whole NDE is just a drug-induced series of hallucinations. If this were the case you might expect that the deepest and most vivid NDEs would happen to people who were taking drugs at the time. This is clearly not the case. Greyson and Stevenson (86) even suggest that drug-free NDEs diverge more from the normal state of consciousness than drug-inhibited NDEs. And Osis and Haraldsson (156) reported that drug intoxication during a close brush with death actually diminishes the chance of an NDE.

Returning to the work of Twemlow and colleagues, they

reported that the people who were under the influence of narcotics or alcohol formed a separate group and experienced severe
emotional stress rather than the calm and relaxed responses of
so many NDEs. Also, those under the influence of drugs were
more likely to report communicating beings, little sense of
awareness back in the body and more absorption, which they
suggest may indicate that drugs alter the NDE to become more
like depersonalization with hallucinatory features.

All this is relevant to the critical argument about drugs and
the NDE. Apparently drugs taken near death are more likely to
damp down the experience than bring it about.

Can we now answer our question? My own interpretation is
that the invariance hypothesis is not supported. The NDE varies
according to the conditions that set it off and the person having
it. Probably little June would have had a different experience if
she had been pulled out of the water sooner or had been a
different kind of girl.

We may now turn to the last of our five questions.

DO YOU HAVE TO BE NEAR DEATH TO HAVE AN NDE?

One motivation for asking this question is the 'just like hallucinations' argument. According to this view NDEs, drug-induced
hallucinations, out-of-body experiences occurring under normal
conditions and other kinds of hallucinations are all related. This
might lend support to theories trying to explain the features of
the NDE in medical, psychological or physiological terms and
go against theories involving a spirit or soul or heavenly realm.

There is lots of evidence for NDE-type experiences in people
who are not close to dying.

The experience of leaving the body has a long history and
surveys show that something like 10–20 per cent of people have
this experience at some time during their life (13, 67, 160). It
often occurs in times of stress, tiredness, deep relaxation or with
certain drugs but it can occur at almost any time. In the Western

occult tradition it is known as 'astral projection'; the 'astral body' separates from the physical and can travel around without it, temporarily in life and permanently at death (40, 140). In parapsychology (the scientific study of claimed paranormal phenomena) it is known as an out-of-body experience or OBE and many inconclusive experiments have been performed to try to find out whether anything really does leave or not (13).

Sometimes the OBE is associated with other features of the NDE such as the light, sounds or tunnel. Occasionally an entire NDE-type experience can occur. For example, the parapsychologist Scott Rogo (196) claimed that a full NDE could be induced from the lucid dreaming state. Similar effects can also be obtained in sensory deprivation. In the 1960s psychologists experimented with lying in completely dark, sound-proofed rooms, sometimes for days on end, until they experienced hallucinations, sensations of floating or pressed the 'panic button' to be let out (230). The modern version, used for short periods for recreation, is the flotation tank (99). That sensory deprivation might play a role in NDEs was suggested by Bruce Greyson and Ian Stevenson (86) who found that unusual visual phenomena were more common in NDEs at night when there was less sensory stimulation.

However, a far more common cause of NDE-type experiences is taking a variety of drugs, from hashish (217) or opium to Ketamine and other anaesthetics (195). Sometimes such drugs produce elements of the NDE in isolation – the tunnel is a common drug-induced hallucination as are out-of-body experiences. However, more interesting here is that sometimes an apparently complete NDE-type experience occurs under the influence of drugs.

Zaleski reports that in a classic Zoroastrian story, Viraz, a Persian priest, volunteers to take a narcotic and travel to the other world. After a seven-day coma he returns with stories of the Bridge of the Separator, the weighing of deeds, the place of the mixed, the heavenly stations and the dark pits of hell (239). Psychologists Siegel and Hirshman (217) report all the features of the Moody-type NDE appearing under the influence of hashish. My own experience confirms this too. Under conditions of extreme tiredness and smoking hashish I had an NDE-type experience complete with the tunnel and light, out-of-body travels, expansion and contraction of size, timelessness, a mystical experience and the decision to return; all occurring over a period of about two hours while I was sitting up and quite alive and healthy (13, 18). Hallucinogens such as LSD and the short-acting DMT can also do the trick.

This much seems to be clear: that all the NDE features have been reported from non-near-death conditions. In a well known paper entitled 'Do "Near-Death Experiences" occur only near death?' psychiatrists Glen Gabbard, Stuart Twemlow and Fowler Jones (68) give a definitive 'No' answer, at least as far as the individual features are concerned. They found that there were no characteristics which were unique to the NDE occurring near death. However, they went on to tackle a related and highly relevant question – can near-death NDEs be distinguished from other similar experiences? And here their answer was 'Yes'.

As already mentioned, they solicited letters from people who had had OBEs, receiving about 1,500 replies. Of these, 339 reported OBEs but only 10 per cent had actually occurred near death. They then compared the two types, finding that although no feature was unique to the near-death accounts, some were significantly more common in them. A person near death is more likely to hear noises during the early stage of the experience, is more likely to experience the tunnel and to see a brilliant light. They are more likely to see their physical body from a distance and to sense other non-physical beings, especially deceased friends.

The aftereffects are different too. NDErs are more likely to feel there was a purpose in the experience, that it had lasting benefit, that it was a spiritual or mystical experience and that their life has been changed by it. This appears to be a long list but notably there were no differences between NDEs and other OBEs in terms of the feelings of peace and serenity, the life review, encountering a border or barrier or even in the change in belief in life after death.

Finally, one more recent study in the medical journal *The Lancet* (158) reports on fifty-eight patients who believed they were near death during an illness or after injury and remembered unusual experiences happening at the time. In this case medical records were available and twenty-eight were judged to have been so close to death that they would have died without medical intervention. The other thirty were not in danger of dying even though most of them thought they were. The only differences between the groups were that the patients truly close to death more often reported enhanced perception of light and enhanced cognitive function such as greater speed and clarity of thought, clear and vivid colours and sounds, and control of their thinking.

The authors point out that these findings offer support for both sides of the argument. The similarity between the groups implies that just the belief one is near death is enough to set off the experience; in other words it can have a psychological origin. The differences imply that the physiological state has a role to play in triggering some features and not others. Yet the enhancement of cognitive powers seems to be evidence to support the afterlife hypothesis. The argument used by others reporting on this research goes like this: if the brain is responsible for thinking, then when it is dying one would expect thinking to become disordered or less clear. The evidence that it becomes clearer therefore implies that the brain is not responsible; that the soul or spirit is experiencing the clarity and may go on doing so after death.

This is one possible interpretation of the evidence, but it is not the only one. It is not obvious that the dying brain must produce either more or less clear perceptions and thoughts. An alternative is that as the brain dies, less thoughts are possible and so the few that remain seem clearer and simpler by comparison. To know which is more likely we need to know a lot more about what happens in the dying brain.

All this research may appear contradictory and confusing but I believe it is clear enough to tell us how to proceed. It does matter what conditions set off the experience. The noises, tunnel, bright light and other beings are more likely in conditions we would expect to directly affect the brain state, such as cardiac arrest and anaesthesia. The peace, mystical aspects, life review and positive aftereffects can occur when a person just believes they are going to die or has an OBE when they are perfectly well.

My conclusion from all of this is that we need to try to understand these different aspects of the NDE in quite different ways. The tunnel, bright lights, noises and so on need to be addressed by looking at the changed brain state caused by coming close to death. The other features and transformative property of the experiences need to be understood in some other way. Our next step is now clear, if not easy: to try to understand what happens in the dying brain.

3

Visions From the Dying Brain

Then by degrees I began to realize that I was the One, and the universe of which I was the principle was balancing itself into completeness.

The common experience (80 per cent of cases) is that of rushing into a dark tunnel. There is singing in the ears and a flashing of lights in the eyes.

(54 pp. 74, 75)

More NDEs? Not at all. These descriptions come from a study made nearly a century ago of the effects of ether. Ernest Dunbar, writing for the Society for Psychical Research, was studying the effects of chloroform, ether and cannabis and, like more modern writers after him, he found many effects that we now associate with the NDE.

Nitrous oxide is another of those strange drugs that has also been claimed to take people physically out of their bodies. As in the case of NDEs the claim is usually backed up by evidence of the 'I couldn't possibly have seen it otherwise' type. I remember being much affected by a story I heard long ago and cannot now find out whether it is purely apocryphal or ever had a basis in fact. Perhaps some readers may know. The story was that a man went to the dentist and while inhaling nitrous oxide floated out of his body and up to the ceiling. On coming round he told the dentist what had happened. The dentist's incredulity was transformed when the man said, 'If you don't believe me, look up on the top of that cupboard. You'll find an old penny lying there.' Of course, the story goes, the penny was there.

I think this illustrates the reluctance we have to accept that our experience, especially profound and personally meaningful experience, comes from our brain's activity and nothing else. It does not make a 'good story' to say 'I had some laughing gas and it gave me a profound insight.' That seems somehow to denigrate the insight – though logically I can see no reason why it should. Instead it seems to make a better, more tellable, story to say that 'I' was something other than my brain's activity. The 'real me' was propelled by the drug into leaving the body. The insight was because 'I' left that brain and travelled somewhere else. The role of the penny is to prove this point. It makes for a better story but it is not necessarily so.

Of course, the relationship between brain and mind has been a major – perhaps *the* major – philosophical issue. And the NDE brings up the problem in a very direct form.

BRAIN AND MIND

Are these profound experiences a direct correlate of changes in the brain's activity and nothing more, or are they experiences of a separate mind, soul, astral body or spirit? And how do we find out? The general working assumption of today's science says one thing yet most people, as we saw in chapter 1, say another – especially people who have had NDEs. Scientists for the most part assume some form of materialism; that mental phenomena depend upon, or are an aspect of, brain events. Most people in our culture believe that there is something more; mental events, or at least some mental events, depend on a 'me', a 'self', a special soul or something which thinks, is conscious and maybe can even survive death.

As we have seen, the very occurrence of NDEs is not proof either way. Yet, if we want to understand the NDE, this is the fundamental question. So how can we answer it? Some people believe that unless there is *very* strong evidence to the contrary we should accept the dying brain hypothesis. I take a different view. Science has, after all, made some colossal blunders in the past. It might be making one again now. Decades have passed in diligently pursuing quite false theories such as the explanation of fire by the theory of phlogiston in the eighteenth century or the famous ether which was thought to permeate all of space until the Michelson–Morley experiment in the 1880s. Our current materialism and its rejection of the idea of a spirit or soul might be just another great falsity. So I cannot just accept it without question. Instead I want to compare the two kinds of theory. This way I can ask which one better accounts for the data. I can compare how well they explain the specific features of the NDE and how well they can predict future findings about NDEs.

A good theory is not one that explains everything. Anyone can think up theories of this kind – like the angels that push the stars around the heavens or the vital spirit which 'explains' the difference between life and non-life. Nothing can be done with such theories, except to throw them out when something better comes along. Something better means a theory which explains why the world is this way rather than another. It excludes many possibilities and allows only a few – the ones that are actually found. It can therefore predict what we will find, not predict that 'anything can happen'.

In the case of the NDE, a good theory is one that explains why NDEs are like they are: why, for example, there is so often a tunnel and not a green square or a sea shore; why the tunnel is light and not dark at the far end; why OBErs look down from above and not up from the floor; why there are rushing and roaring sounds and not the squeaking of mice or the blasting of trumpets; and, perhaps most difficult of all, why the insight is so often that 'I' and my death are unimportant and not 'Get as much as I can for myself 'cos I haven't got long.' These are the real questions that any theory of the NDE must satisfy.

If the afterlife hypothesis can answer them best then I shall accept that and work with it as well as I can. If the dying brain hypothesis does better then I shall work with that.

One of the difficult facts we have to deal with is that NDEs are not unique to dying. Our task would be easy if NDEs were quite different to any other experience and happened only when a person was physically close to death. Then the job of pinning down the necessary conditions would be easier and progress probably swift. Instead, as we have seen, all the components of the NDE can occur under other conditions, under the influence of drugs, stress, or even during dreams. Yet the experiences near death do have a different pattern, so there must be something special happening when near to death.

Some writers have been quick to conclude that if NDEs can happen with drugs, it must be the drugs given to the dying that caused the NDE. This is easily refuted by the fact that many NDErs were given no drugs at all and still had the experience. Of course, it is then necessary to think about what drugs the dying brain can make for itself and so the argument becomes a bit more complex.

Others have jumped to the conclusion that since the dying brain is deprived of oxygen this must be the cause of the NDE. They are quickly countered by the fact that NDEs can occur under other conditions too. So it cannot just be the lack of oxygen. All too easily this turns into the conclusion that lack of oxygen (or cerebral anoxia) is irrelevant. This too is a false conclusion. Anoxia might be just one of the many factors that can set off the experiences.

I think we can sort out these issues, but only by understanding more about the brain. So let us begin there. What happens to the brain when a person approaches death?

BLOOD GASES AND CEREBRAL ANOXIA

A first approximation to an answer is simply to say that we do not know. It is perhaps odd that with all the advances in modern psychology and medicine we know very little about the dying brain, but maybe it is not so odd when you remember that the first priority when someone is dying is usually to save them, not to study the state of their brain.

Of course, it is important to medicine to understand what

happens in the brain close to death and especially how to prevent the damage that can occur from depriving the brain, even for a short time, of oxygen. For this reason there have been lots of experiments on animals. These have provided most of what we know about the dying brain but the problem is that in studying NDEs we are interested not only in the physiology and biochemistry but in the experiences. Those experimental animals, if they were travelling down a tunnel and meeting friendly rabbits in glorious green fields, could not tell their experimenters about it even if the experimenters were prepared to listen.

Nevertheless we can put together information from what we do know to give the beginnings of an idea.

There are thousands of ways to die but, whether death is from a mountain fall, a terminal illness or a cardiac arrest, at some point the brain will stop getting enough oxygen. This is called cerebral anoxia (no oxygen) or hypoxia (not enough oxygen). Since NDE research began anoxia has been considered a possible cause of the experience.

Since the anoxia argument has been quite complicated and heated, it is worth trying to sort it out. Several researchers (134, 156, 182, 204) have argued that anoxia cannot be responsible for triggering NDEs for four main reasons:

1. NDEs can occur in people who obviously do not have anoxia.
2. There is evidence of an NDE in one person with normal measured blood gases.
3. Anoxia causes effects quite unlike NDEs (such as tiredness or confusion).
4. No explanation of the anoxia type can explain true visions of events occurring at the time or knowledge acquired 'on the other side' (for example, about people who have died).

I am going to argue that anoxia *can* be the trigger to set off an NDE and that it can (like many other conditions) be responsible for the individual components of the NDE. Let me explain why I do not find the usual arguments against it compelling.

The final point, above, about paranormal visions, is a very general and important argument against any naturalistic account of the NDE. Because of this I shall deal with it later on in detail (in chapter 6). The other three arguments are more specific to anoxia.

1. *NDEs can occur in people who obviously do not have anoxia.* This is certainly true but is not a sound argument at all. As we have seen, there is clearly no one cause of the NDE. It is a varied experience or group of experiences and can be set off by many things. Anoxia may be one of them. The fact that NDEs can occur without anoxia is no argument against it sometimes being responsible for them. Other NDEs may be set off by something else. We may even find the common link which all these factors share.

2. *There is evidence of an NDE in one person with normal measured blood gases.* This often-quoted blood gases case, though extremely interesting, is not conclusive either. Michael Sabom reported on a sixty-year-old man who had a heart attack and cardiac arrest. As he told Sabom, '[the doctor] said I had to have blacked out, but I never really blacked out. It was just like I got up and moved.'

While he was watching from above their heads he saw what the medical staff were doing to him. Sabom asked 'The first thing they did was put the pads on your chest?'

'No. They gave me those shots first in the groin down there somewhere. It appeared to me they were putting a shot in there. My right side' (204 pp. 148–9).

In fact the doctor had removed some blood from the femoral artery to be sent to the laboratory for analysis. It would not be surprising that the man confused being given a 'shot' with having a blood sample taken. Since the man apparently observed this procedure from above it seems likely that the blood was actually taken during the out-of-body experience. And the blood gases were found to be relatively normal, in fact with elevated oxygen ($pO^2 = 138$) and lower than normal carbon dioxide ($pCO^2 = 28$, pH = 7.46).

This might seem to be evidence against cerebral anoxia but

certainly it is not. Gliksman and Kellehear (74) point out that peripheral blood measures are not reliable indicators of cerebral blood gases and cite evidence from animal and human studies. In any case, this is obvious when you consider the cause of (near) death. If the heart stops pumping blood then blood in the arteries is not reaching the tissues or cells which will use it and therefore oxygen levels in those arteries will only fall very slowly. If extra oxygen is given as well, which is common during cardiac arrest, then the arterial levels may actually rise. By contrast, blood in the veins will not have much oxygen left because it is in contact with the tissues and therefore loses oxygen. Since the brain uses a lot of oxygen, levels in the cerebral veins will fall fast and the brain quickly run out of the oxygen it needs. Sabom's patient had arterial blood tested and so we cannot conclude that he was not suffering from cerebral anoxia.

3. *Anoxia causes effects quite unlike NDEs.* To deal with this third argument we need to know a bit more about the effects of anoxia. In the first place, there are several types of anoxia which come about in different ways.

Stagnant anoxia is when the blood flow is reduced so that not enough oxygen reaches the tissues. This happens, for example, in cardiac insufficiency (when blood flow is reduced), cardiac arrest (because the heart has stopped pumping altogether), and also in shock. This is the type that, presumably, Sabom's patient was suffering from.

Anoxic anoxia occurs when not enough oxygen is supplied from the air to the blood. This happens in pneumonia, drowning and paralysis of the respiratory muscles or from breathing gases without enough oxygen, such as at high altitudes. In this case the blood keeps on circulating but does not contain enough oxygen.

Anaemic anoxia is when the blood itself cannot carry enough oxygen, such as in anaemia or haemorrhage or poisoning with carbon monoxide.

Finally, histotoxic anoxia is when the tissue cells are unable to use the oxygen that is available. Alcohol, narcotics and some poisons such as cyanide produce this condition. There is still enough oxygen in the blood but it cannot be used properly.

If anoxia is, at least on some occasions, responsible for NDEs then we might expect all these different conditions to be associated with NDEs. However, the effects of anoxia are very variable depending not only on the type of anoxia but how quickly it sets in and how far it gets before the oxygen supply is returned. If the anoxia occurs very fast the person may become unconscious without realizing anything is amiss and if the oxygen supply is restored again as rapidly may even deny having been unconscious.

This can happen in cardiac arrest.

If the anoxia develops a little more slowly, various odd reactions can occur such as pleasant feelings of well-being and power, unstable emotions and judgement, muscular incoordination and loss of vision and memory – effects sometimes likened to alcoholic intoxication. People are often noted for carrying on doing remarkably dangerous or pointless things in this state even when they might be able to escape the situation by doing something quite simple. They become weak and helpless, suffer nausea and vomiting and may finally collapse, sometimes with convulsions.

Finally, if the anoxia is very slight and slow, as at high altitudes, or living with a leaky gas appliance, then the body compensates to some extent and the symptoms may be relatively slight, such as lassitude, constant tiredness and loss of appetite.

Linked with anoxia there may also be a build up of carbon dioxide, or hypercarbia. This occurs because the cells using up oxygen produce carbon dioxide in the process. The blood has to transport carbon dioxide out through the lungs just as it brings oxygen in. Sabom has argued that the psychological impairment of oxygen lack is nothing like the NDE but that hypercarbia can produce NDE-like symptoms.

THE EFFECTS OF CARBON DIOXIDE

In the 1950s a psychiatrist at the University of Illinois, L.J.Meduna, experimented with giving psychiatric patients and normal control subjects various mixtures of oxygen and carbon dioxide. Some of these people saw bright lights, had out-of-body experiences and relived past memories. Some faced terror and some ecstasy, some cosmic understanding and universal love. One described everything as 'so real and simple' and another reported 'complete understanding and harmony with God.' One called it 'a wonderful feeling, as if I was out in space' (130 p. 24).

There was a 'bright light, like the sun' and many reports of vibrant colours. Some who breathed the carbon dioxide saw circles which pulled out into a straight tube or funnel. A 29-year-old nurse first described a rush of colours and continued

Then the colors left and I felt myself being separated; my soul drawing apart from the physical being was drawn upward, seemingly to leave the earth and to go upward where it reached a greater Spirit with Whom there was a communion, producing a remarkable, new relaxation and deep security.

(130 p. 28)

Sabom admits that there is a great similarity between NDEs and the effects of hypercarbia. Even so, he uses his famous case of the measured blood gases to refute the suggestion that the NDE can be explained this way: 'Thus, in this one documented case, neither a low oxygen level (hypoxia) nor a high carbon dioxide level (hypercarbia) was present to explain the NDE!' (204 p. 244).

I cannot agree with his conclusion. As we have seen, in this special case it was quite likely that the man's brain, though not his arterial blood, was suffering hypoxia or hypercarbia. To me the similarity between NDEs and these other experiences points to some underlying explanation for them all. It is this underlying factor that we need to track down. It must be something that can be produced by anoxia or hypercarbia as well as by other triggers.

How, then, does what we know about anoxia and hypercarbia relate to NDEs?

We have very little information to go on here but I think two pieces of evidence are relevant. First, as we saw in the last chapter, there is evidence that NDEs occur more often to people who are in hospital, have been resuscitated and unconscious for more than a minute (90, 204). These would be very likely to be suffering cardiac arrest (if they were resuscitated) and some form of anoxia and hypercarbia would be associated with being unconscious for a long time. We may, at least tentatively, infer that longer anoxia is more likely to produce an NDE.

Second, there is the fact that anoxia can come about in different ways and at different speeds. All types of anoxia have been associated with NDEs with the possible exception of histotoxic anoxia. Alcohol and barbiturates produce delusionary and confused mental states, not the clarity so characteristic of many NDEs. Indeed, these drugs are implicated in damping down NDEs near death rather than causing them.

The speed of oxygen loss may be most relevant. Very fast onset of anoxia is rather like alcoholic intoxication and can also lead to sudden black-out with no experience. On the other hand, very slow anoxia produces confusion and lassitude quite unlike NDEs. This leads to the possibility that NDEs come about with intermediate speeds of oxygen decline. Drowning is one example and is a common trigger for NDEs. With the heart still working for a while and some oxygen still available in the circulating blood, the anoxia will not be as fast as with sudden cardiac arrest.

If I am right then NDEs should be less likely if the cardiac arrest is very sudden and more likely if it is preceded by a period (even relatively short) of cardiac insufficiency. There are many cases like this on record but to date no one has made this important comparison.

Can this approach be tested in any other ways? The most direct and obvious way would be to subject people to various speeds and types of anoxia and then resuscitate them and ask them what they experienced. This certainly makes for good fiction but could it really be done?

VOLUNTEERS FOR UNCONSCIOUSNESS

In the film *Flatliners* a group of young medical students dare
each other to venture ever deeper and deeper into a brain-dead
state, the electroencephalogram registering their brain waves
fading to a flat line. Their adventures in facing up to the consequences of their own past deeds make a good moralistic story
but are not enlightening on the topic of NDEs.

In the novel *Twilight* Peter James creates a crazed scientist
whose mission in life is to prove survival after death – to the
world and to a pretty young journalist who finds herself alone
with him, locked in his basement laboratory . . .

> 'I can prove it, you see, Kate.' He pointed at the wire mesh.
> 'I don't imagine you've ever seen one of these before.'
> He pulled a latch and swung the end section open. It
> was like a miniature operating theatre, with a padded steel
> table, an anaesthetics machine with a drip stand, gas and
> oxygen cylinders, a ventilator and a battery of wires and
> gauges . . .
>
> He removed a vial from the wrapping and held it up to the
> light. 'The rules have changed. Religion used to make the
> rules, now science makes them. Science has ruled if someone
> is brain dead, they are dead. But you know that isn't true,
> don't you? . . . So what we have to do is fool God. Create a
> state of death so convincing He believes it.'
> 'Fool God?'
> He drew the fluid out of the vial, filling the syringe. 'Yes.'
>
> (105 pp. 297–9)

You might think such experiments have to be confined to the
realms of fiction. But not so. Unconsciousness is a common problem in aerospace medicine. Fighter pilots in particular are often
subjected to intense gravitational or acceleration forces, especially during fast manoeuvres. Then the heart is unable to pump
the blood against the high G forces and the lack of blood to the
brain leads to unconsciousness or G-LOC ($+G_z$-induced Loss

of Consciousness or Acceleration-induced LOC). Although the unconsciousness itself is unlikely to kill the pilot and recovery is usually swift and leaves no lasting damage, the consequences of even a few seconds unconsciousness can be serious in a fast-flying plane. To try to reduce the losses of aircraft and pilots, research on G-LOC has meant sending volunteers into unconsciousness.

These intrepid explorers are apparently willing to go into a human centrifuge which simulates the acceleration of the aircraft and induces unconsciousness again and again. James Whinnery at the Naval Air Development Center in Pennsylvania has made a special study of such episodes. He points out that you cannot die unless you lose consciousness so LOC should be of interest to us all. He himself has endured this kind of 'death' about ten times in fifteen minutes – the maximum researchers have dared in experiments on volunteers. One might well wonder why. Apparently it is not just in the name of science but because the experience itself can be pleasurable. Whinnery (233) even likens it to the auto-erotic effect some people induce by partially hanging themselves. So it seems that, like NDEs, G-LOC includes pleasant emotions.

The comparison with NDEs makes an interesting case. In G-LOC, unlike most NDEs, there is always anoxia and (by definition) unconsciousness but there are no other symptoms of illness since the volunteers have to be extremely healthy pilots, aircrew or other medically vetted personnel. There is no expectation of dying or hospital environment and the episodes are very brief. Therefore by comparing G-LOC and NDEs which actually take place near death we may find out which phenomena of the NDE are likely to be associated with the anoxia and which with the other factors that are present when a person is near death.

Whinnery reports on a series of over 500 reports of G-LOC episodes over a period of twelve years (233, 234). The length of unconsciousness varied between 2 and 38 seconds with a mean of 12 seconds and the episodes were all video-taped. The volunteers typically had a short period of total incapacitation followed by a second period of confusion or relative incapacitation, the total time being dependent on the strength and length of the deliberate insult to the brain. In 70 per cent of the cases they had convulsions and made flailing movements which stopped when they regained consciousness. They were interviewed immediately afterwards and several times in the following months.

A noticeable reaction was denial. Until the subjects were able to see the video showing they had collapsed they would often maintain that they had not lost consciousness. Others filled in the void by confabulating or inventing events to fill it. They sometimes showed embarrassment, euphoria, anxiety or antagonism.

I have not said much about denial so far, mainly because it does not appear in most of the modern typologies of the NDE. Ring, Moody and Sabom have little to say about it and it is not a part of any of the NDE scales discussed in the last chapter. Nevertheless, it is sometimes reported with NDEs. Interestingly, the reports of survivors of cardiac arrest that predate Moody and the popularity of the NDE seem to include more instances of denial. These could well be ones suffering sudden cardiac arrest more comparable to G-LOC.

For example, in 1967 (Moody's first book came out in 1975) Druss and Kornfeld reported on ten survivors of cardiac arrest: 'Not a single patient could face the full implications of the arrest and called forth various defense mechanisms to control the anxiety evoked' (53 p. 291). The most common defence mechanisms were denial and isolation – that is, an isolation of their emotions.

Some authors have used the concept of denial as an explanation of the entire NDE and especially of the OBE. In a classic book Ernest Becker (9) explores our tendency to deny our own mortality, and it is true that our society evades death in every aspect. Menz builds on this to argue that the OBE is just another mechanism for denying our own death. As he puts it, 'OBEs are merely defense mechanisms against the anxiety of death' (131 p. 324). Whether this is a helpful theory of the OBE I shall consider later on but for now we need only note that there is evidence of denial in both G-LOC and survivors of cardiac arrest.

This is perhaps a minor point of comparison. More pertinent are other reactions to G-LOC: dissociation, seeing one's own body from outside and a sense of floating were frequently reported and at least two subjects had an OBE. In fact, Whinnery had one himself (235). These followed multiple G-LOC episodes and Whinnery concludes that a severe insult to the brain is required to induce the OBE as compared with the sensations of floating which are far more common.

Another interesting effect is paralysis and inability to communicate – reminiscent of the struggle experienced by our Indian warrior chief and the traveller of Lithuanian folklore. Barney Dlin, a psychiatrist from Philadelphia, worked with coronary and open-heart patients for twenty years and interviewed many survivors of cardiac arrests: 'One patient recalled thinking, "I'm trying to signal you that I'm alive," and feeling a tremendous sense of desperation because "my lips wouldn't move . . . I couldn't even move my hand." ' Dlin goes on 'The futility of this feeling defies description' (48 p. 63).

By comparison, one of Whinnery's volunteers felt himself being propelled by something like a magic carpet. He could not make any purposeful movement, or even turn his head, which was terribly frustrating since he could hear the G-LOC warning tone in the centrifuge and couldn't turn it off even though his consciousness was returning. Whinnery concludes that sensory function (vision and hearing) returned before the return of motor function.

This is most important for the NDE. It implies that there may be a phase, at least in patients who have been unconscious, when they are immobile and unresponsive, so that the medical staff will assume they are unconscious when in fact consciousness is returning. During this state they might be able to hear what was going on around them and so build up a clear mental picture of what was happening. There would be nothing paranormal about this even if the picture proved relatively accurate and the person appeared completely unconscious.

G-LOC subjects also report 'dreams'. They are referred to as dreams because the volunteers consider them to be such. However, they do not involve the rapid eye movements typical of night-time dreams. They are in many ways similar to NDE visions, at least in that they include radiantly bright colours and sights, beautiful surroundings and loved ones appearing to meet them. One volunteer went home and saw his mother and brother – 'We were outdoors, it was wild! . . . I got to go home without taking leave!' (233 p. 9).

Another sounds reminiscent of the tunnel: 'I was in a dark closet, and there was a red light at the very top . . . I was confused but unafraid' (64). This might be a little far-fetched as an example of a tunnel but in one of his own experiences Whinnery found himself in the frozen food section of a local grocery store. 'The trouble was that I couldn't move my hands or turn my head to look into the freezer. In the meantime, I was being uncontrollably propelled down the aisle' (236).

The tunnel experience is not a major feature of G-LOC, although the pilots often report tunnel vision in which they lose peripheral vision in a kind of grey-out. However, among NDEs tunnels, noises and lights are most common in cardiac arrest and other extreme events involving a fast drop in the amount of oxygen in the brain. Drab (52) also found that tunnels are more often triggered by a sudden change in physiological state and do not occur in slow illness. With G-LOC being the most sudden and illness the slowest, it suggests that the tunnel, lights and noises are intermediate.

Conspicuously absent features in the G-LOC research are the mystical insights, life review and subsequent transformations. No G-LOC subjects reported anything like this.

To sum up, it seems that anoxia and unconsciousness, without the proximity of death, can provoke floating, euphoria, failure to move or communicate, vivid beautiful visions and (with repetition) OBEs but not mystical experiences or a panoramic life review. Once again it seems these features need a different explanation. To understand this better we might compare the effects of sudden unconsciousness with its complete opposite: examples of people who have been threatened with death but not been seriously hurt or ever unconscious.

THE THREAT OF DEATH

Few threats could be as terrifying as finding yourself falling from a mountainside. A study by Iowa psychiatrist Russell Noyes and psychologist Roy Kletti includes many examples of this type. They report first on the work of Albert Heim, in 1892, who collected accounts of more than thirty survivors of falls in the Alps. He described their experience as involving no despair or pain but acceptance, mental quickness and objective clarity. 'In many cases there followed a sudden review of the individual's entire past; and finally the person falling often heard beautiful music and fell in a superbly blue heaven containing roseate cloudlets' (149 pp. 46–7).

Noyes and Kletti go on to describe 114 cases of their own collected by advertisements in mountaineering journals and personal contacts. One mountaineer, losing his footing during a descent, found himself exposed to a 2,000-foot drop and reported, 'I felt intense fear; my thoughts speeded up; time slowed down; and my attention was redirected toward survival and deeply imbedded memories' (150 p. 21). Another found that when he gave in to his presumed fate he felt no more fear, 'in fact, at that moment I became elated' (150 p. 23).

Noyes and Kletti include other causes of near death in their analysis. For almost all the experiences listed, the people who thought they were near death were more likely to have them. These included detachment from the body, great understanding, harmony or unity, colours, visions, voices and sounds, but the biggest difference was in having vivid mental images and a life review. Life reviews most often occurred in people who suddenly expected to die.

This is most interesting when compared to the findings of Bruce Greyson (82). He found that experiences like the life review, thought acceleration and sudden understanding rarely

occurred when the person had *long* been expecting death, but
only when it threatened suddenly. He concluded that people who
have been ill for some time may have worked through much of
their thinking about death and no longer need all these transformative experiences.

From this evidence I would now like to try to piece together an
idea of which experiences should occur under which conditions.
The evidence is pitifully inadequate at the moment and I am
unable to disentangle the effects of the suddenness of the anoxia
from its duration and many other factors. Nevertheless, I think
I can say this much: the very sudden anoxia and unconsciousness
of G-LOC is associated with positive emotions, visions, sensations of floating and inability to communicate. The slightly
slower anoxia with cardiac arrest and other serious conditions
is also associated with the tunnel, bright lights and noises. The
fear or expectation of dying, even without being physiologically
close to death, is associated with mystical elements of harmony
and understanding, very vivid images and the life review.

The invariance hypothesis is not sustainable. The NDE is not
always the same and we need to try to understand its different
elements in different ways. Some elements depend on a person's
state of mind. Others appear according to the depth and rapidity
of anoxia.

Most important here is to remember that anoxia is not an
explanation in itself. It can only be one of the many possible
triggers to the NDE. We now need to go on with our search for
the underlying cause. To find this we must discover what anoxia
does to the brain cells.

UNDERSTANDING ANOXIA

All brain cells, all neurons, require oxygen. It is needed to provide the energy on which the cell operates. Without energy, cells
cannot maintain the differences in chemical concentrations
across their membranes and the electrical potentials which make

firing and signalling to each other possible. They need it all the time and without it they very rapidly stop functioning.

Oxygen is supplied by the blood vessels which course through the brain. These blood vessels range from large arteries bringing large quantities of blood, to tiny capillaries barely big enough to let a red blood cell through. There is a very fine network of capillaries but still it is not fine enough to reach every cell. As the oxygen supply in the arteries fails it will take a different length of time to affect the neurons closer and further away from the blood vessels. The most vulnerable areas are the so-called 'watershed' regions of the cortex which are the furthest from the arteries. The most resistant are the areas concerned with autonomic functions. These can keep the body functioning for some time after unconsciousness sets in.

From knowing which areas are most rapidly affected we might be able to make general predictions about the nature of the NDE. Studies of brain damage after hypoxia are also relevant and show that memory is the function most often impaired. The hippocampus has been found to be easily damaged and this area is crucial to memory (162). This will become most relevant when we consider the origin of the life review.

Other important factors are the level of each cell's activity and the size of the brain cells. Active, rapidly firing, cells use oxygen much more quickly than quiescent cells and so they will be affected by the anoxia first. This means that the effect of a heart attack, near-drowning or any other event which reduces the brain's oxygen supply may depend on which cells were firing at the time. In other words, the person's state of mind, or the task they were engaged on, or what they were thinking about at the time may affect their experience. That this does happen was noted by Bruce Greyson (82) who concludes 'that psychological set may influence the type of experience'.

It is certainly dangerous to speculate about specific mental processes on the basis of global brain processes. However, bearing in mind this is pure speculation, an interesting possibility arises. If those cells that are active at the time of the oxygen deprivation are the first to stop firing then we might expect that whatever areas were being used most actively at the time would be the first ones to be affected and vice versa. So a person actively looking around and therefore doing a lot of visual processing would find visual experience affected first. By contrast, someone with eyes closed but still listening might find hearing interfered with first.

On an even more speculative level, since a person threatened with death, under stress or in fear, is likely to be preoccupied with negative thoughts we could predict that these will rapidly cease and this might give rise to a sense of relief or even comparative happiness and joy. Possibly this is related to the finding of a greater sense of power and energy in cases of anaesthesia and cardiac arrest (228).

This might even imply a kind of see-saw effect, as successive groups of cells fail. Is there, then, any way of meeting death that avoids this thrashing from one idea to another? One way would be to approach the end without any fixed ideas, with indifference to whatever arose and accepting whatever came along. If this were the case, I imagine, the whole brain might more gently settle down into inactivity. This might well be a good way to approach life as well as death. I wonder whether some Tibetan Buddhist traditions are aiming at this in warning the dying person of the lights, sights, sounds and illusory experiences one will meet in death. None are to be clung to. Liberation comes only through letting go.

But that is enough speculation, and it may be entirely unwarranted given the complications of the brain and the many other interacting variables. We need now to consider a better understood effect of anoxia.

I have talked about which cells will be affected first without saying how they will be affected. One might imagine that anoxic cells would simply stop firing, but it does not work that way. There is now evidence that what actually happens is a shift in the balance between excitation and inhibition (202).

Inhibitory connections between brain cells are very important for normal functioning. Neurons interact with each other by sending chemical signals across the fine gaps, or synapses, between them. The effects are of two main kinds, either to excite the next cell or to inhibit it. This has a function in complex computations and also serves to keep global levels of activity damped down. To a large extent the stability of brain activity is controlled by inhibition.

Studies of rat brain cells have shown that in anoxia inhibitory potentials are abolished before excitatory ones (66). If this can be generalized to the living brain we would expect to find inhibition becoming less effective. This 'disinhibition' would mean that a lot of cells that should not be firing would start to fire. Or more likely, since all cells tend to fire at some fairly low baseline rate, they would start firing faster. With anoxia affecting large areas of the brain we would therefore expect to get general or global disinhibition and hence random excitation of whole brain areas.

This also means we can understand the effects of different speeds and depths of anoxia better. If anoxia is sudden and deep the phase of disinhibition will be very short, possibly too short to give rise to any noticeable experiences. If it is very slow the brain might compensate gradually for the effects. It is only with the intermediate speeds of onset of anoxia that we would expect a fairly long phase of disinhibition and consequent activity. This is therefore the key phase for the NDE.

If this is correct it means we know where to look to understand the NDE better. The key is not in anoxia itself but in the disinhibition and consequent excitation it can produce. It may well be this kind of disorganized activation that is the common thread running through *all* the experiences we are considering.

To understand why certain other conditions can set off an NDE we need to find out which conditions produce a similar disinhibition or excitation. It turns out that these include drugs, epilepsy and certain chemicals the brain itself makes. Hallucinations are known to occur in all sorts of states of central nervous system excitation and arousal. Siegel (215) lists psychedelic drugs, surgical anaesthetics, fever, exhausting diseases, certain injuries and accidents, as well as the emotional and physiological processes involved in dying. I shall return to some of these in considering the tunnel, the 'realness' of experiences and the nature of the NDE world. For now, it seems we have found the underlying common thread we were looking for – cortical excitation.

Why, though, should disinhibition and random excitation produce NDEs? A simple example might be the strange rushing, roaring or tinkling noises sometimes heard. There are at least two reasons to expect anoxia to produce these. The cochlear region of the ear is especially sensitive to anoxia and random activity here would produce jumbled sounds (170). Also, as Scottish psychiatrist James McHarg (129) has pointed out, there is a part of the brain's temporal lobe in which sound is represented according to pitch, something like on a keyboard. Disinhibition or overactivity here would produce strange noises and a suppression of activity might produce a 'hush' that could help to create certain feelings of peace.

It might be relatively easy to explain how noises could be produced but is it not far-fetched to suppose that something as specific as a tunnel could be produced by disinhibition or random firing of brain cells? In fact, it is not. I think this is precisely what we would expect. So let us have a closer look at that tunnel.

4

The Light at the End of the Tunnel

I became less and less able to see and feel. Presently I was going down a long black tunnel with a tremendous alive sort of light bursting in at the far end. I shot out of the tunnel into this light. I was the light, I was part of it, and I knew everything.

(52 p. 126)

This account comes from a 27-year-old woman with heart failure and is reported by Kevin Drab, a Canadian researcher who made a special study of the tunnel experience.

Here is another: 'I seemed to see a bright white light at the end of a long tunnel, and had an intense feeling that it would be wonderful if I could only reach it. I couldn't get to it before the effects of the gas wore off' (101 p. 157).

The gas was carbon dioxide. Tunnel experiences are not confined to dangerous or near-death situations. In fact they appear in a bewildering variety of conditions and are one of the commonest forms of hallucination.

FORMS OF HALLUCINATION

One of the earliest studies of hallucinations was carried out in the 1850s by a Frenchman, Brierre de Boismont, who found that hallucinations, whether caused by delirium, drugs, dreams or ecstasy, were all characterized by excitation and the production of images from memory and imagination. Another Frenchman, Jacques Moreau, described hallucinations as like dreams in which the events seem to be real; he thought they depended on excitation of the brain, an idea much in advance of the physiological findings of the time. Moreau learned a great deal about these hallucinations by taking hashish, a method that became popular with many nineteenth-century artists and writers who even formed the Club des Haschichins to explore the mental spaces this drug could reveal to them.

They learned what many explorers of altered states have learned before and since: that the imagination can be made to produce realistic images that can take up the entire mental space, or be projected outward as though a part of the perceived world. Although there is no limit to the forms hallucinations can take, there are, none the less, some that keep constantly reappearing. Paintings on shamans' drums, cave paintings and clothing from many cultures show persistent forms – spirals, concentric patterns, wavy lines and bright colours. The mandala pattern, consisting of variations on the circular theme, is common in Buddhist and Hindu tradition as an aid to meditation (see Figure 2) and the psychologist Carl Jung included it as one of the archetypal forms in the collective unconscious. The similarity to the tunnel is clear. These drug-induced hallucinations with their familiar forms have been used as magical symbols, both in divination and as inspiration for art and literature in primitive cultures and in our own.

They have also been studied systematically. In 1926 Heinrich Kluver, at the University of Chicago, began a series of investigations into the effects of mescaline, a drug extracted from the cactus, peyote, and one of the most potent producers of visual hallucinations (112, 113). He found that the imagery produced was extremely bright and vivid and the colours highly saturated. They appeared whether the eyes were open or closed. Most importantly, he found that the images tended to take on certain repeated forms.

He called these the 'form constants' and described four types. They were:

Figure 2. Circular patterns are very common in mandalas or, as here, in this Tibetan Buddhist tanka.

1 gratings, lattices, fretworks and honeycombs
2 tunnels, funnels, alleys, cones and vessels
3 spirals
4 cobwebs

Since then other researchers have found the form constants again
and again, induced by drugs, fever, migraine and epilepsy, and
in hypnagogic imagery just before sleep. They even appear in
the imagery of synaesthetes, those people who habitually see
sounds, smell shapes or hear colours. Like NDEs, the images in
synaesthesia are memorable and emotional. Interestingly, they
are now known to be accompanied by a reduction of blood flow
in the relevant brain area (42).

The 1960s saw an explosion in the popularity of hallucinogenic drugs and the start of research into their effects. This
rapidly became impossible when the drugs were made illegal.
However, much was found out in the early days. Psychologists
Lindsley and Leary devised an 'experiential typewriter' on which
volunteers could use special keys to report rapidly on what they
saw in experimental drug trips. American psychologist Ron Siegel has studied many hallucinogenic drugs and his subjects have
described, drawn and painted the tunnel in a dazzling variety of
versions (214, 219). It seems that the tunnel form is ubiquitous
in hallucinations (see Figures 3 and 4).

Among the best known attempts to understand hallucinations
is the 'perceptual release' theory. In the 1930s the British neurol-
ogist Hughlings Jackson suggested that memories and internally
generated images are inhibited by the flow of information from
the senses (219, 220). If the mechanism controlling this is disrupted or there is no sensory information coming in although
awareness remains, then hallucinations will result.

This fits with the drugs effects and also with the results of
sensory deprivation.

Coming close to death often involves sensory deprivation, if
only because the eyes are usually closed, so these effects are
highly relevant. After many hours in flotation tanks in the silent
darkness people experience complex, dynamic and often realistic

hallucinations. This happens also in real-life situations, such as when two miners were trapped 300 feet underground in total darkness for six days. They experienced strange lights and saw doorways, marble stairs, women with radiant bodies and a beautiful garden (35).

Other theories emphasize that in hallucinations people mistake their own internally generated imagery for external events (220). Siegel refers to hallucinations as false perceptions which 'have their roots in excitation of the central nervous system' (214 p. 132). Since we have found that a temporary excitation is what we might expect in the dying brain it seems possible that an explanation of the tunnel is to be found this way.

However, it is not enough just to say that a near-death tunnel experience is a hallucination like all these others. It may well be a hallucination but our explanation must go much further than

Figure 3.

Figure 4. A drug-induced tunnel with complex memory images (from 'Hallucinations', R.K. Siegel, © *1977 by* Scientific American, inc. *All rights reserved).*

that. Near-death tunnels are not just bland circular forms. The light is bright and alluring, its warmth seems almost personal and can indeed become like a presence in the tunnel, a meeting of minds. Going down the tunnel feels like much more than just seeing a tunnel form in the abstract and many NDErs can never forget the experience. An explanation of the tunnel of death cannot ignore all this.

Another odd point is that the tunnel is only one of the form constants. What about the others? The spiral could be thought of as similar, but the grating, lattice or cobweb? To my knowledge NDErs do not report bursting through cobwebs or flying into lattices and gratings. Why not? An adequate explanation must deal with this too.

EXPLAINING THE TUNNEL

The similarity with other hallucinations is an important starting point. If the tunnel is a hallucination caused by the physiological effects of nearly dying we would expect to find that it appears more often in serious conditions. This is exactly what is found. Canadian psychologist Kevin Drab collected well over a thousand accounts of 'other world' experiences and seventy-one of them included a tunnel. These occurred in cases of cardiac arrest, severe stress (such as near-drowning, coma, severe blood loss, serious illness or traumatic shock), mild stress (he included here minor injuries and pain, fear, fatigue, mild fever and migraines) and normal conditions (including relaxation, sleep, meditation and hypnosis). Although tunnels could occur in conditions that were obviously not near death, he did find that they were more common in serious medical conditions than non-serious ones. He says, 'extreme physiological stress may be especially conducive to tunnel experiences' (52 p. 130).

When the experience occurred under what he termed normal conditions, Drab found the tunnels were often associated with out-of-body experiences. This association is well known (13). In their book *With the Eyes of the Mind* psychiatrists Glen Gabbard and Stuart Twemlow (67) explore the out-of-body experience and recount many examples in which a tunnel preceded or accompanied the OBE. Here is one example from a woman under emotional stress but otherwise in excellent health.

> I found myself rushing through a tunnel as if pulled by a pneumatic device, or a magnet. It was very fast . . . It was very frightening, in retrospect, but at the time, was only a matter-of-fact awareness. Then I was literally spewed out into a place of light, and a huge female figure, on a golden throne, looked down at me.
>
> (67 p. 140)

Gabbard and Twemlow conclude that although 'NDE features may occur in OBEs not associated with life-threatening illness or injury, they are much more common in the context of a brush with death.' We have here the familiar finding that is true of the NDE as a whole. While tunnels can occur to people who are quite well, they are more common near death. Any explanation of the tunnel must account for this.

What more do we know of the tunnel that needs to be explained? Drab, whose study must be the most comprehensive, found that the tunnels were usually dark or dimly lit (only 10 per cent were brightly lit), none of the experiencers reported touching the sides, although these varied widely and included scintillating darkness, luminous vapour with fine lines and bricks with a cobblestone floor. In my own experiences I have been in tunnels made of leaves, varying textures and swirling colours or just bands of darker and lighter grey.

Nearly half of Drab's cases reported a light at the end of the tunnel. Three-quarters of these described it as becoming larger in their field of vision or they were moving towards it. Many said the light was extremely bright and some even commented that it did not seem to hurt their eyes. The colour varied but many people had positive feelings towards the light and some saw other beings in it.

Almost all of Drab's experiencers described moving through

their tunnels; most went through, some up and some down, but only eight cases described coming back through the tunnel. It is not clear from Drab's description whether they came backwards through the tunnel or turned round and moved forwards in the (as it were) opposite direction. About a quarter of his experiencers heard sounds, several felt warmth and most felt calm, with some experiencing joy, happiness and peace.

These, then, are some of the features of the tunnel that any explanation has to deal with.

In the last chapter I built up a picture of what we would expect to be happening in the brain under stress or near death and I want to see how far this can get us in understanding the tunnel. But first there are many other theories that have been offered for the tunnel. When considering these we need to bear in mind what makes a good theory.

A good theory is not one that can explain absolutely anything. A good theory is specific. In this case, it should be one that explains why there is specifically a tunnel near death and not something else. Why not a door, for example, why not a staircase, or a ring of fire? A good theory needs to explain the form of the tunnel and light, its colour and appearance. Something like 'it's just a hallucination' is not good enough. I would only ask why *this* hallucination and not another? Why the deep emotional feelings? Why the associations with certain conditions and not others?

Secondly, a good theory does not just invent 'other worlds' or extra 'forces' or 'vibrations' *ad hoc*. There may be other worlds and so far undiscovered energies that we may need to understand one day, but before we start invoking them we need good evidence. Generally speaking a theory that uses known and well-understood principles is to be preferred to one that just invents a new 'force' or 'plane' to account for any findings that come along.

And thirdly, a good theory is one that makes testable predictions. It is easy to come up with any number of theories that will account for the facts at a given time. What distinguishes the useful theories from the useless ones is whether the predictions they make come true. A theory that makes no predictions is useless, a theory that makes true predictions is better than one that makes false predictions. Bearing all this in mind we can consider the four explanations commonly offered for the tunnel experience.

There is a 'Real' Tunnel

In his book about children's NDEs, *Closer to the Light*, Melvin Morse asks whether NDEs 'prove the existence of the soul, a part of us that leaves the body, flies up that tunnel, and, well, goes to heaven?' (136 p. 96). From this I get the impression that he believes in an actual tunnel. Whether he means a physical tunnel, a tunnel in some 'other plane' or whatever, I do not know. But the implication is that the tunnel is actually there for us to travel along.

He is obviously not alone. Another NDE researcher explains that 'persons on the verge of death have begun to pass through a tunnel of mental energy into another dimension' (8). Similarly in some occult systems of belief the tunnel is said to lead from one plane to another. In the Theosophical tradition there is a silver cord connecting the astral body to the physical and the tunnel is then seen as the flow of 'vital force' out through the cord.

There are many serious problems with such a theory. If the other worlds are a part of this world then they cannot really account for the afterlife. I do not imagine many people believe in heaven or hell as a literal place to go to through physical space. If they did then some predictions should be obvious. Something should be seen leaving the body and going to the tunnel. The tunnel itself would be present in physical space and we should be able to measure it or in some way detect its presence. Attempts to do this have certainly been made but have notably failed (13).

Not surprisingly, a more popular interpretation is that the tunnel goes to a non-physical world in some 'other dimension' or different 'plane'. Now the problems are different. If these planes and dimensions are not part of the physical world then all the problems of brain—mind dualism are raised. How can anything be said to pass from one world to another? Positing a tunnel between them certainly does not help. It is a bit like Descartes himself postulating that the pineal gland (a small gland deep in the brain) mediated between the world of matter and the world of mind, or like the spiritualists' contention that ectoplasm aids in the task of communicating between spirits and living beings. If two worlds are fundamentally incommensurable there cannot be anything that goes from one to the other.

Still, we should not reject such theories out of hand just because they seem senseless. It is better to apply some criteria to them and see how they fare. Is this theory specific? No, not at all. The tunnels described are all different in precise form and this theory can say nothing about what forms they should or should not take. Presumably if there is a 'real' tunnel then it should have one form and all the rest must be seen as inaccurate perceptions of that real tunnel. This theory also has nothing to say about the precise occurrence of tunnels, what conditions set them off and so on.

Does it require unobservable 'other worlds'? Yes, it does, and these are often backed up by evidence of spirit communication, descriptions of heaven and hell and evidence of paranormal events. We shall see later on whether these claims are strong enough to require the assumption of other worlds or not.

Finally, does it make any predictions that can be tested? Not really. The assumption of a tunnel to another world does not prescribe who should go there, under what conditions or how the tunnel should vary with circumstances. I can think of no specific predictions that follow from such a theory. For these reasons I reject this theory as any use in understanding the tunnel.

Representations of Transition

Perhaps in recognition of the problems of the 'real' tunnel theory, many prefer to see the tunnel as symbolic – of the transition from one state of consciousness to another, for example. Robert Crookall was the author of many books interpreting OBEs in terms of 'astral projection'. He claimed that there are at least three 'deaths' as first the physical, then the soul and finally the spiritual body are shed to unveil the Eternal Self. The tunnel is a blacking out of consciousness as the self passes from one state to another (41).

British psychical researcher Celia Green suggested that the tunnel is a representation of a long journey (75) and Kenneth Ring considers it a psychological phenomenon through which the mind shifts from its normal state of consciousness to a holographic or four-dimensional consciousness of pure frequencies. It is 'the mind's experience of transition through states of consciousness' (182 p. 238).

This idea escapes the obvious problems of 'real' tunnels and allows for more flexibility. But in the process it loses any possible power as an explanation. It simply begs the question 'Why the tunnel?' Why shouldn't something else be used as a symbol of transition? There could be gates, doorways, arches, chasms or the great river Styx. In fact these other forms do occur later on in NDEs, in the stage of worlds beyond, but it is the tunnel that appears regularly, in predictable forms and, as we have seen, in numerous different circumstances. We understand this ubiquitous tunnel no better by saying that it is symbolic of something else.

Birth Relived

An extremely popular theory is that the NDE entails reliving one's birth and that the tunnel is the birth canal down which we travelled at the start of life (97, 206). Carol Zaleski (239) tells of a physician early this century who watched the death of one of his patients and saw the correspondence between the birth of a child into this world and the birth of our spirit from this world into a higher world; even down to the umbilical cord represented by a 'thread of electricity' connecting the material and spiritual selves.

More recently, astronomer Carl Sagan has promoted a similar idea in his book *Broca's Brain*, in gripping language.

> The only alternative, so far as I can see, is that every human being, without exception, has already shared an experience like that of those travellers who return from the land of death: the sensation of flight; the emergence from darkness into light; an experience in which, at least sometimes, a heroic figure can be dimly perceived, bathed in radiance and glory. There is only one common experience that matches this description. It is called birth.
>
> (207 p. 143)

The idea that we return to birth in death has an obvious appeal and a superficial plausibility. I do not believe it has any more than this.

Carl Becker, a philosopher living in Japan, has thoroughly criticized the idea, as have others (6). One problem is that it is implausible to suppose that the infant would perceive the world in a way which could be later recalled by an adult who has totally different perceptual capabilities. Perhaps more obviously, the birth canal is nothing like a tunnel with a light at the end and the foetus does not float gracefully nor rush rapidly down the middle of it. It is an extremely tight fit, squashed to a very short length, and the foetus is pushed out with the top of its head usually emerging first, not its eyes. It takes a vast leap of the imagination to make the two comparable and yet this theory has produced a welter of 'New Age' ideas and techniques.

One virtue of this kind of theory is that, at least in some forms, it can be tested. If the tunnel experience is reliving birth then the kind of birth should make a difference. In particular, people born by Caesarean section have never been along the birth canal and so, presumably, should not be able to relive it. I carried out a survey of 254 people, of whom 36 had been born by Caesarean section. These 36 did not report more or less tunnel experiences than the others. In fact, the proportions were just about identical: 36 per cent in each group (14).

This seems to refute the birth idea, but to get around the difficulty parapsychologist Scott Rogo (193) argued that the tunnel is not actually a reliving of one's birth but is a kind of symbolic representation of birth in general. He also suggested that people who had a difficult birth would have more negative OBEs than people who had an easy birth. This means the theory can still be tested to some extent but as far as I know this idea has not yet been investigated. If it proves to be the case, the theory will have some evidence to support it. Beyond that it becomes equivalent to the previous kind of theory and is no more helpful.

I would add one last point on death and birth. I am sure the birth theory does not help us explain the tunnel but that does not mean that there is nothing at all in the birth–death comparison. As Sagan points out, the mother in labour produces powerful internal hallucinogens and if these affect the baby they could well be the basis for a similarity in the experiences at each end of life.

It also does not mean that there is nothing of value in techniques like 'rebirthing' or experiencing birth fantasies with drugs or in therapy. We can get so tied up in our anger, resentment, fear and material possessions that it is terribly hard to let go. An experience of seeming to be reborn can sometimes help in imagining we have a new start and in dropping the attachments. So we need not throw out all potential value of the birth image just because it does not help us to understand the near-death tunnel.

Just Imagination

'The orthodox view of NDEs is that they are just hallucinations,' claims Michael Talbot in a popular account of the *Holographic Universe* (223 p. 241). He has a point. A lot of commentators seem to like the idea that the tunnel is 'just imagination'. I think this dismisses the experiences rather than explaining them (22). The experiences almost certainly involve the imagination and they may well be hallucinations but this alone is no explanation. We need to take it further. Again we must remember the criteria for a useful theory. A good theory must account for the specific features of the tunnel. Why the dark tunnel with a light at the end and not a green gate with a ditch in front of it? 'Just imagination' gives us no answer to this question. The 'just imagination' theory does not involve any *ad hoc* 'other worlds' or powers but can it be tested? As it stands, no. We need to take it much further and ask just what sort of imagination, or just what sort of hallucinations, are involved and why. This we can only do by understanding more about what happens in the dying brain.

DISINHIBITION AND THE DYING BRAIN

As we have seen, one of the effects of anoxia is to cause disinhibition leading to generalized excitation. But why should this general excitation produce something as specific as the tunnel experience, with its characteristic form and movement and its bright light and colours? Some research on the effects of disinhibition in the visual cortex may provide the answers we need.

First, why should we look to the cortex for an answer? We are considering the visual impression of a tunnel first and this could presumably be created anywhere in the visual system. The answer comes from drug studies. Anoxia affects the eyes as well as the brain but there are good reasons for thinking the drug-induced tunnel is created specifically in the visual cortex, the part of the brain's cortex devoted to processing visual information.

Hallucinatory tunnels found in drug experiences do not move with the eyes, so they cannot be after-images or other effects on the retina. Similar tunnels can be produced by pressure on the eyes, it is true. If you press gently on both eyes for a few seconds you will find that various forms start to appear and the tunnel is a common one (although this can be bad for the retina and is not recommended!). In this case the images do move with the eyes but they can only be produced by pressing on both eyes at once. This suggests that the tunnel is produced in the brain after the information from the two eyes is combined.

An American researcher, Jack Cowan, has made a special study of how the hallucinatory form constants come about in the visual cortex (38). His argument involves the relationship between the outside world, or its representation on the retina, and the way the information is mapped in the visual cortex. This mapping is well understood from studies of both monkeys and humans (43), and from this, he argued, we should be able to calculate the cortical form that corresponds to any hallucination.

Using this mapping he showed that concentric rings on the retina (or in the visual world) correspond to straight lines in the visual cortex. Straight lines at right angles to those map into radiating lines; straight lines at other angles into spirals. If the lines move the spirals or rings would expand and contract. Expanding concentric rings will produce the impression of moving through a tunnel. This relationship is shown in Figure 5.

This theory suggests that if ever you get stripes of activity moving across the cortex then a tunnel, spiral or indeed any of the four form constants will be seen.

But why should there be moving stripes across the visual cortex? Cowan argues that this is exactly what you would expect when the cortex is disinhibited and the normally uniform state is disrupted. He makes an analogy with thermodynamics. When a fluid is heated from below it is often found that either hexagonal patterns or stripes of rising and falling fluid are produced. He concludes that a similar process takes place in the cortex and gives rise to the four form constants. This may seem a far distant process to compare with neural activity but Cowan argues that it is found widely in nature. There are also other states in which waves of activity pass across the cortex, such as in epileptic seizures. Cowan's theory makes it very clear why we would expect tunnels and not gates, doors or rivers, when the visual cortex is disinhibited. In this sense it is a great advance on any of the previous theories.

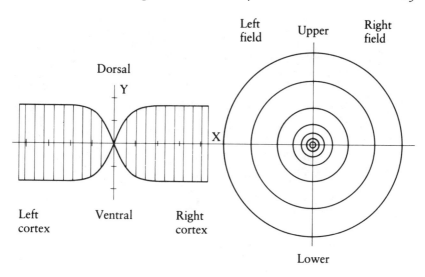

Figure 5. The transformation from eye to cortex. The visual field is shown on the right and the corresponding cortical images on the left. Stripes of activity in the cortex will appear like concentric rings in the visual field (Cowan, 38).

However, it does seem to have some problems. First, it does not account for the fact that NDEs include tunnels but not cobwebs and lattices. To do this it would have to explain why the stripes of activity in the cortex appear in some directions and not in others.

It also does not explain why people usually seem to move forwards through tunnels but rarely backwards. Again it would have to explain why the stripes move in one direction and not another. An extension of this theory might be able to do this but no further work has been done on this so far.

DOWN TO THE DETAILS

In view of these problems I suggested a simpler theory. Perhaps no stripes are needed at all. When the visual cortex is disinhibited

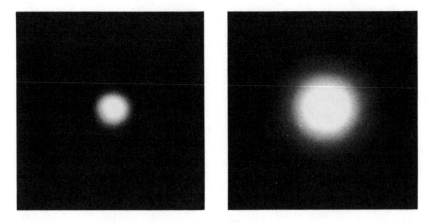

Figure 6. A computer simulation of the near-death tunnel. The proportion of cells firing gradually increases and the bright light at the centre gets bigger and bigger.

the cells will be firing randomly, producing neural 'noise'. We can use the same retino-cortical mapping to imagine what this would look like. An important feature of this mapping is that far more cells are devoted to the centre of the visual field than to the edges. In other words, if all the cells start firing randomly then there will be more in the middle, gradually fading towards the outside and with hardly any at all far out at the limits of where we can normally see. I imagined the effect would appear like a flickering speckled world which gets brighter and brighter towards the centre. Again, this is like a tunnel form.

To test whether such a simple pattern really could look like a tunnel we created a computer simulation based on the known retina-to-cortex mapping and displayed it on a screen. It does indeed appear like a tunnel (25) (see Figure 6).

Near-death tunnels are not just static though. Why should it be that we seem to move forwards? One possibility is that it is simply due to the brain's bias towards forwards movement. For example, it is known that the visual system is biased towards movements in an outward direction (71). In addition, movement that you see, especially in the absence of any static reference, is

easily interpreted as self movement. The classic example of this is the feeling that your train is moving backwards when another train pulls out of the station. Put these two together and it might explain why this scintillating speckled world of neural noise could appear to be a tunnel expanding outwards from a brighter centre.

Bristol vision researcher Tom Troscianko made a different suggestion to account for the movement in this tunnel (25). If you started with very little neural noise and it gradually increased, the effect would be of a light at the centre getting larger and larger and hence closer and closer. To make this clearer he uses the analogy of the lights turning on in London as night falls. If you watched from above you would probably see the first few lights come on in the city centre where there is a higher concentration of people, streets and buildings. Others would gradually appear dotted about but the centre would always keep ahead, with more lights coming on there than anywhere else. In a similar way the tunnel would appear to move as the noise levels increased and the central light got larger and larger. Developing the computer simulation he showed that when the proportion of cells firing increases it does indeed give the impression of moving down a tunnel towards a light (see Figure 6).

And what next? If the whole cortex became so noisy that all the cells were firing fast, the whole area would appear light. In other words, one would have entered the light. It could get no brighter. It might appear to be brighter than anything you have ever seen because the stimulation in the cortex could be stronger than any that visual experience could actually produce.

This might explain a common claim made by NDErs, that the bright light did not hurt their eyes. One man recalled what happened during surgery.

> Here comes this white light. It didn't blind me. It was just the whitest white and the total area was filled with it . . . It was just like you looked out into a total universe and there was nothing but a white light. The most brilliant thing in the world, and it was not the kind of white that hurt a person's eyes like looking at a light bulb.
>
> (204 p. 111)

Naturally, it would not hurt your eyes because your eyes are not involved in any way.

According to this theory the tunnel would usually come to an end with all the cells finally ceasing to fire. Alternatively, if the oxygen supply happened to return before this stage was reached, the inhibition would resume, the light dim, and the movement reverse. In this case one would presumably have the sensation of going back down the tunnel.

These, then, are three physiological theories to account for the tunnel experience. They have some advantages in common. They explain why there is a tunnel rather than any other symbol of passage to another world. They explain how the light can be extremely bright but does not hurt the eyes. They all explain some of Drab's findings, that the tunnel occurs with more serious medical conditions and that it does not occur with slow progressive disease.

How do these theories measure up to the criteria we have been using? Certainly they are very specific in dealing with the form of the tunnel and the conditions that elicit it. They do not involve any other worlds, strange vibrations or non-physical phenomena. They also make many testable predictions by which their value can be judged.

In some ways the three differ in their predictions. Cowan's theory requires stripes of activity passing across the cortex. This might be related to 'cortical spreading depression' which is thought to be implicated in migraine. This is a suppression of activity that spreads at a rate of about 2–3 mm per minute (116). By contrast Cowan claims that tunnel hallucinations fill up the visual field in about 2.5 milliseconds, which corresponds to a rate of spreading of 10 or 20 mm per second. However, he gives no data or reference for this claim and this is clearly something to be investigated further.

If Cowan is right we could expect that the tunnel would always be travelled at roughly the same speed. This is not the case in NDEs. Some people claim to float gently down tunnels while others rush at a tremendous rate. Drab (52) reports sixty-seven cases describing movement and of these twelve said they were moving at a 'slow' to 'moderate' speed while twenty-four were moving very fast.

By comparison, my own theory makes no stipulation about speed. If the movement is induced merely by the speckled noise then it depends on the amount of noise. The more noise, the greater the speed. But this in turn implies that faster movement be associated with a larger central white area. As far as I know, this has not been tested. Another prediction is that a flickering tunnel form should always induce apparent movement even if the flickering is random. Gavin Brelstaff, at Bristol University, has tested this using a high resolution graphics system and, although a clear tunnel is seen, the movement appears to be random. It seems that an increasing light is needed to get the impression of movement (see Figure 7).

The final theory makes another clear prediction. If the movement is created by the expansion of the central white area then the speed itself is not restricted but the overall change in the tunnel is. In other words, you can only move from a tiny white light to a completely enveloping one. The faster you move through the tunnel, the quicker the experience will end. This has never been tested but could be by collecting appropriate descriptions of tunnel experiences.

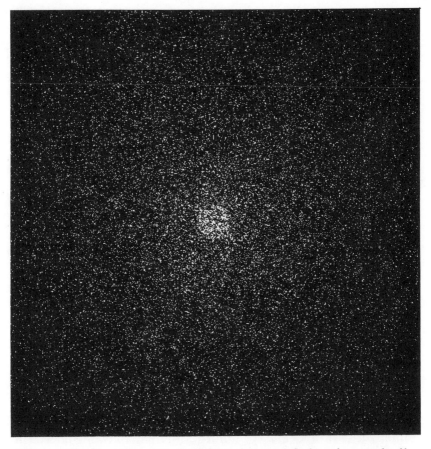

Figure 7. In this computer simulation the spots flickered on and off at random. A tunnel was seen but with no movement towards the light.

At least these differences provide a way of testing the various theories. All three of them are specific, testable and build on what we already know about the dying brain.

DRUGS AND THE TUNNEL

There are some other more general predictions made by these three theories. If the key to the tunnel is cortical disinhibition then the drugs that produce tunnels should all be those that reduce inhibition. This certainly appears to be the case, the major hallucinogens being the best example.

The mechanism of action of LSD is still not entirely understood. However, it has a similar chemical structure to one of the major brain neurotransmitters, serotonin or 5HT (5-hydroxy tryptamine). Serotonin is found in the Raphe system in the brain stem which is involved in the control of dreaming, leading to speculations that LSD hallucinations are like released dreams. From this area, connecting neurons go to many midbrain areas, to the hippocampus which is important in memory and to the cortex. It is the Raphe nucleus that controls the excitability of the cortex (38) and so LSD's action may be to increase excitability – just like anoxia.

On the other hand, some drugs increase inhibition, including the minor tranquillizers such as Valium. This is relevant to cases of drug overdose and attempted suicide. Kenneth Ring reports on a man who took a cocktail of Librium, Demerol, Valium and Dilantin and remained unconscious for four days. He reported the richest of all Ring's (usually rather muted) suicide experiences but it was still a long way from the full core NDE. He experienced a lot of greyness and even the music he heard seemed hollow and metallic. He did hear a voice and have sensations of movement: 'it was a soothing voice. I kind of remember that with the grayness – her voice kind of calling, my moving toward it . . . Like that was the place to be.' Eventually he began falling. 'The thing I remember most is a falling feeling. Like I was coming down really fast and then hit. And then I woke up with a jolt' (182 p. 123). But, like so many suicide attempters, he reported no tunnel and no light. This is just what we would expect from our knowledge of the drugs he had taken.

I would like now to return to the question of why tunnels occur when they do. With the major hallucinogenic drugs tunnels are common but so are lattices, spirals, cobwebs and other simple forms. Near death the tunnel seems to have a special place in the experience. Why is this?

As far as I can tell, Cowan's theory provides no answer. If the disinhibition is the same regardless of its immediate cause, then the patterns produced should be the same. On the other hand, both the other theories can only produce tunnel forms and not the other form constants. In particular, Troscianko's theory suggests that the tunnel occurs when there is a fairly rapid increase in cortical noise, as would be expected in cardiopulmonary failure or an accident or sudden severe stress.

This provides a possible answer. Cowan's effects would be expected whether disinhibition were due to a drug or to nearly dying. However, the rapid effects of sudden anoxia would be more likely to produce the moving tunnel. We can now explain the common finding that the tunnel (like other NDE features) can occur in all sorts of conditions but is more common in serious cases and when death is really near. It is only in these conditions that the light will be bright and increasing. If Troscianko's theory is correct it also explains why drug tunnels sometimes move in both directions but NDErs rarely come back down their tunnels.

In addition, all these theories can account for Drab's apparently odd finding that there were no tunnels reported by stroke victims. They all require a normal and intact visual cortex and if that were damaged by a stroke the tunnel could not be seen. A further prediction is related to this. If the tunnel is of cortical origin then anyone with a damaged visual cortex should not experience it. So, for example, people blind through disease or damage to the eye should have tunnel experiences just like anyone else but those with cortical blindness should not. This, too, awaits testing.

These physiological approaches to the tunnel experience already account for many of the previous findings and they provide numerous ways of testing them for the future. In this respect they are quite different from all the previous theories I have considered.

THE LIGHT AT THE END

The three physiological theories can all account for there being a light at the end of the tunnel but the NDE light may be more than just a brighter area appearing up ahead. It is often described as warm and loving, or bright, or golden. I shall discuss the emotional impact of it later on, but what about the colour? Can any theory successfully predict what colour the light should be?

I do not think any of the early theories can. If the tunnel is a gateway to another world we need to know what colour that other world is, but as far as I know it is unspecified or extremely variable. So the light at the end should be similarly variable which is not a lot of help.

If the tunnel is the birth canal then the light should presumably be the colour of the room or space into which the person was born. In modern hospital settings at least this would usually be white. In addition one might expect there to be red in the tunnel or even at the end if there was much blood already in the birth canal. White light shining through bloody membranes would appear red.

According to the 'just imagination' theory the light could be any colour one can imagine. It is only with a specific comparison with certain kinds of hallucination that something more specific can be predicted. The idea of random excitation of the cortex implies that the cells' coding for colour should be randomly excited. This gives the clear prediction of white light since this consists of all colours mixed together. Whether other colours would be predicted depends on a more detailed understanding of the way colour is processed in the brain and this is not entirely understood. In the eye there are three types of cones, red, green and blue sensitive. There are least of the blue, which might imply the other colours would be predominant. There is also an opponent system in which cells signal for red versus green or yellow versus blue, with the former type being more common. If all cells are randomly stimulated then this might imply a greater mixture of red and green, in other words yellow. This is all very speculative but does suggest that the light at the end of the tunnel is most likely to be white or yellow.

Another interesting comparison is with drug effects. We have already seen that the drugs likely to produce similar effects to near death are the hallucinogens. In a study of drug effects Siegel and Jarvik (218) compared colour reports from subjects having a placebo, barbiturate, amphetamine and various hallucinogens. For the first two types of drug (which do not produce effects anything like NDEs) and the placebo the most common colours reported were blue and violet. For the hallucinogens they were yellow, orange and red.

In Drab's study of tunnels the few colours reported varied from white or golden to red or bluish, but of course these were not all near death. How does this compare with the colours in the NDE?

In his original collection Moody includes many bright lights: 'A very very brilliant light' (133 p. 62); 'It was a bright yellowish white – more white. It was tremendously bright' (p. 63). And Ring's are similar: 'a brilliant golden light' (182 p. 57); 'I saw this beautiful, golden light, way, way small, down the tunnel. I said, "That's a funny light. It doesn't even look like gold and yet it is gold and it isn't yellow"' (182 p. 57).

Another example comes from a case reported in 1971, before NDEs were generally heard of: 'My next sensation was of floating in a bright, pale yellow light – a very delightful feeling' (124). And it has even been painted this colour. In Hieronymus Bosch's famous painting *The Ascent into the Empyrean*, in the Doge's Palace in Venice, the souls of the dead are seen floating through a tunnel towards a very yellow light.

Zaleski summarizes the light as 'clear, white, orange, golden or yellow in hue' (239 p. 124). But perhaps most helpful here is a recent survey by London neuropsychologist Peter Fenwick. He has reported preliminary findings from about 300 questionnaires on NDEs, which may, when it is completed, make it the largest survey of NDEs in the world. He reports 'the colour of the light that is seen by our experiencers is either white or yellow. Other coloured lights are very rare' (61 p. 1).

I have occasionally come across other colours. For example, the famous British philosopher and committed atheist A.J.Ayer (3) recently reported his own NDE, much to many people's surprise. He choked on a piece of smoked salmon, having rejected the hospital food he would otherwise have had to eat, and his heart stopped, apparently for about four minutes. He described a bright red light but since there was no tunnel this might be a different kind of experience. Clearly the white or yellow lights are the most common and are just what would be predicted from the physiological theories. It seems that they, and not the other theories, can account very well for a simple detail like the colour of the light.

Nevertheless, I know that many people will not be satisfied by such an explanation. 'But the tunnel is real', they will argue, 'The light was warm and meaningful and changed my life', 'It was a light of joy, peace and love.' And this impression is not to be ignored. No explanation of the NDE is worthwhile unless it can explain why it feels the way it does.

5

Peace, Joy and Bliss

It was one of the most intense and happiest moments of my entire life which a quarter of a century has not erased or diminished.'

(192 p. 64)

I felt embraced by such feelings of bliss, that there are no words to describe the feeling. The nearest I can come to it in human terms is to recall the rapture of being 'in love', the emotion one feels when one's first born is put into one's arms for the first time, the transcendence of spirit that can sometimes occur when one is at a concert of classical music, the peace and grandeur of mountains, forests and lakes or other beauties of nature that can move one to tears of joy. Unite all these together and magnify a thousand times and you get a glimpse of the 'state of being' that one is in.

(79 p. xiv)

While travelling in India, in 1976, Margot Grey was struck down by a strange illness and hovered on the brink of death with a raging fever for three weeks. As she floated against the ceiling of the room she was surprised to find herself quite unperturbed by the idea of dying in a strange country, far from home, family and friends. She felt happy to discard that body which had served her well, and accept death. The feelings were, as she says, bliss. She went on to devote herself to the study of NDEs and wrote a book, *Return from Death*, about their transforming and spiritual quality.

I am, of course, going to argue that the direct cause of such blissful feelings is to be found in the physical processes of the dying brain. Is this to denigrate a spiritually transforming experience? This depends on whether you think it destroys the value of any experience to understand its origins. I do not think it does.

Evolutionary theory was rejected by many people in Darwin's time because it seemed to undermine their spiritual nature and deprive them of their unique position in creation. It made them only 'glorified apes'. Nowadays most people can happily accept their evolutionary origins without conflict. Similarly, some people may now think that understanding the physiological basis of spiritual experience would detract from the experience itself and from their own quest for spiritual development. I see no reason why it should, unless it is too unpalatable an idea to suggest that there is no lasting spirit or soul which 'has' these experiences. It could even be quite the reverse, that understanding their physical origin might lead to clearer insight and a way out of our illusions. In any case it is worth examining the evidence, and there is plenty of it, that suggests that feelings of bliss, love and peace are engendered by specific chemicals acting in specific parts of the brain.

But first: are all NDEs blissful and happy, or is such delight the privilege of a few?

SUBLIME AND JOYOUS MOMENTS

The popular story seems to be that almost all NDEs are pleasant and peaceful. Moody's prototypical NDE includes 'intense feelings of joy, love, and peace' (133 p. 22). Peace is the first stage of Ring's 'core experience' and the most common one, being reported by 60 per cent of his sample (181). Many of his respondents never got past this stage and for them these feelings of peace and calm *were* their near-death experience. Of those who went deeper, qualifying them as 'core experiencers', about 70 per cent explicitly describe peace or calm and many more used related words to describe their feelings. So positive emotions are a key part of the modern NDE.

This surprisingly positive response was also reported a hundred years ago. It may seem odd that, confronted with the fearful prospect of dying, most people are calm and happy. This probably seemed even more surprising to Albert Heim in 1892 than it does to us today, now that NDEs are widely talked about. Heim collected accounts of people who had nearly died in mountaineering falls. His account (translated by Kletti) begins

> I intend to present neither a series of terrifying stories, describing agonies, nor an enumeration of misfortunes. Let us apply ourselves rather to the scientific study of a horrible event. The subject may thereby lose a portion of its ghastliness. Sometimes, to be sure, a fall is dreadful for the survivor [the friends or relatives of the victim] . . . He thinks of these last seconds as containing extreme desperation, great pain, and fearful anguish, and he seeks to read in the countenances of the disfigured dead signs of anxious distortion. But it is not so!

He goes on to explain that it is something quite different for the victim himself. Whether the fall is from a cliff, mountain or scaffolding, or even into water, near drowning, the result is the same. The people he talked to did not report the sort of paralysing fright that occurs in less extreme situations. Rather, they reported a 'rather calm seriousness, profound acceptance, and a dominant mental quickness and sense of surety' (149 p. 46). He pointed out how often this calmness saved them by allowing them to act very fast to avert disaster.

More recently, although still before Moody's book appeared, another American physician observed the reactions of patients hours or days after cardiac arrest and was especially impressed by their outward calm (48).

Of course, this kind of calm acceptance is not quite the 'delightful bliss' of the modern stories and has been likened to the stunned calm of soldiers in battle (1). Could it be that the popularity of Moody's and Ring's work has led to exaggerated claims and a tendency for people to report their feelings as even more dramatically pleasant than they really were?

I think not. Certainly there are accounts from before Moody that sound just as enthusiastic. For instance, in 1971 two Canadian physicians, MacMillan and Brown, reported on a 68-year-old man who had been admitted to hospital with chest pain and suffered a cardiac arrest in the coronary unit. He recalled a dual sensation of both experiencing things and seeing himself experience them. He seemed to leave his body through the head and shoulders and then took a fantastic journey at great speed. 'My next sensation was of floating in a bright, pale yellow light – a very delightful feeling ... I had never experienced such a delightful sensation and have no words to describe it' (124 p. 890).

After this experience the man could offer comfort to others:

> If death comes to a heart patient in this manner, no one has cause to worry about it. I felt no pain ... The floating part of my sensation was so strangely beautiful that I said to a doctor later that night, 'If I go out again, don't bring me back – it's so beautiful out there,' and at that time I meant it.
>
> (124 p. 890)

Heim used his stories to offer consolation to the families of the victims of mountain climbing accidents. I have also found that the bereaved can be helped to know that the last experiences of the people they have lost were probably not painful or horrifying but calm and even joyful; the dying were probably not adding up all the wrongs done them by friends and relatives but joyfully accepting life as it had been and death as it was.

The same response is found in other cultures too. One of my Indian respondents, Mr M.G.Hyder, wrote

> I experienced as though I was being flown away and up by two winged creatures (angels or fairies?) towards the higher skies. Each one of them was holding one of my hands and

proceeding smoothly up and up! It was an extremely exhilarating journey for my body and soul and I was fully enjoying . . . such sublime and joyous moments.

And another speaks of 'that indescribable peace of mind state which somehow I regretted having left when I became conscious'.

So it does seem that the feelings of extraordinary peace and happiness are more than a modern invention of our own time and culture. But wouldn't we still expect some unpleasant ones?

JOURNEYS TO HELL

Moody has often been asked whether he ever hears tales of people going to hell but says that 'no one has ever described to me a state like the archetypal hell' (133 p. 36). Similarly, Ring (182) and Sabom (204) report no hellish experiences. This seems surprising given the horrifying tales reported throughout history and religious traditions of retribution in the afterlife for wrong deeds in this life.

If religious expectation has anything to do with it we might find that Christians, with expectations of heaven and hell, might more often report both. David Royce gave a questionnaire to 174 Christian clergy. Almost three-quarters of them said that parishioners or others had shared an account of coming close to death with them. Of all these experiences hardly any were 'hellish' in tone and the people reporting them apparently became more religious and less afraid of death. They generally found the experience uplifting and positive. None ended up fearing they would go to hell when they died (201).

Nevertheless, there have been a few 'hellish' experiences reported. The most well known come from Maurice Rawlings who is convinced, from the accounts he has been given, that there is a hell and that people have been there and come back to describe it (178). Rawlings's research has caused an extraordinary controversy among NDE researchers.

A postman had a cardiac arrest while undergoing testing and Rawlings resuscitated him. Each time the man started breathing again he yelled that he was in hell and whenever Rawlings paused in his attempts the man complained that he was slipping back there. As if his yells were not convincing enough, the doctor could see the expression of terror on the man's face.

Another of Rawling's patients found herself in a gloomy room inhabited by elves and imps and a huge giant with a grotesque face. The giant beckoned her to go outside where she found herself in darkness with people moaning all around her and things moving about her feet. Another went down a tunnel, not to a brilliant light, but to a hideous cave filled with the rancid smell of decay and half-human creatures mocking one another. These seem hellish indeed and more reminiscent of the medieval tales collected by Zaleski than what we nowadays think of as an NDE.

Margot Grey, who had a blissful experience herself, also reported some hellish ones. She interviewed forty-one people, most of them English. Thirty-eight had had a 'core experience' and of these just five (12 per cent) had had a terrifying experience. In one case a woman was working in a nursing home when she was overcome by the heat from the Aga cookers. She recounts her story:

> I rushed outside the back door feeling faint and sick. I remember going down three or four steps. I don't remember falling, but the next thing that happened was that I had this experience. I found myself in a place surrounded by mist. I felt I was in hell. There was a big pit with vapour coming out and there were arms and hands coming out trying to grab mine . . . I was terrified that these hands were going to claw hold of me and pull me into the pit with them.

(79 p. 63)

More recently Bruce Greyson collected fifty accounts of distressing experiences (84). Some were prototypical NDEs complete with tunnels, lights and other familiar features but with the difference that the person was terrified. In some cases the experience turned pleasant and even blissful when they gave in or stopped fighting against it. Many occurred during childbirth with anaesthetics and these tended to be horrific experiences of being suspended in a frightful vacuum, naked in nothingness – no religion, no heaven or hell, just nothingness for eternity. This negation of everything personal or familiar was hell at its worst for some people. Finally, there were a few cases with chattering demons, black pits, people chained and tormented and other traditional symbols of hell. However, it was not clear what was responsible for any of these distressing experiences.

Why should Rawlings, Grey and Greyson find all these nasty experiences when Moody, Ring and Sabom found none? Have the latter been concealing their findings? Or have their respondents been hiding their true experiences from the researchers? Rawlings's own answer came to him from that first patient. After his visits to hell the postman went on to have a peaceful NDE but the extraordinary thing was that later on he recalled only the pleasant parts; his experiences in hell seemed completely forgotten. This, says Rawlings, is the answer. The other researchers only interviewed people days, months or even years after the experience, whereas he was there at the time and talked to people the moment they regained consciousness, before their trips to hell were forgotten.

These other researchers were quick to fight back. Sabom (203) criticized Rawlings for giving no data to support his claim. In his book there are twenty-one examples of 'ascending to heaven' followed by twelve examples of 'descending to hell' but Rawlings does not clearly state which were interviewed immediately after the event and which later on. Even worse, says Sabom, these tales are sometimes from sources other than Rawlings's own interviews and the hellish ones even include some published in the nineteenth century.

The same problem is evident in Grey's work. She claims to have 'found evidence to support the claim that negative experiences are most likely to be obtained immediately after the event'

(79 p. 56) but does not substantiate this. She mentions one cardiologist who found people unwilling to disclose their bad experiences because they felt ashamed of them or embarrassed about them. But, like Rawlings, she gives no breakdown of which experiences came from people interviewed at different lengths of time after their brush with death and in any case she only has five 'hellish' cases to go on. As far as I know this relationship has yet to be investigated properly.

A more tricky accusation is that Rawlings's work is biased by his own beliefs. He is a 'born-again' Christian and a believer in a literal heaven and hell. Has he then fabricated or distorted the stories to fit his own beliefs? Ring (182) calls his book a 'proselytizing Christian tract' that tries to persuade people that the only way to avoid these hellish experiences and ensure a heavenly death is to turn to Jesus. This is not science, says Ring, and therefore cannot be taken as evidence.

But perhaps we should not be too greatly influenced by this issue. More important is whether Rawlings's suggestion really does stand up scientifically. Ring thinks not. He points out that both Sabom and Moody have occasionally interviewed people immediately after a cardiac arrest and have still never found a hellish experience. He also compares the recall of NDEs with the recall of LSD trips. LSD can induce experiences ranging from blissful and mystical visions with joyful acceptance and peace to truly hellish, terrifying journeys with horrific hallucinations and intense fear. However, all these are remembered afterwards. The hellish ones are not selectively repressed.

Delightful experiences can be forgotten too. Melvin Morse and his colleagues, collecting accounts of childhood NDEs, sometimes found that the parents could tell of experiences, both pleasant and unpleasant, which the child had since forgotten. One 16-year-old boy with chronic renal failure underwent an exploratory operation and suffered severe complications requiring several minutes of resuscitation. After the operation he told both his parents, 'I have a wonderful secret to tell you. I have been half-way to heaven.' He said the experience 'felt wonderful and peaceful. I was on a dark staircase and I climbed upwards'

(138 p. 597). However, when he was interviewed four years later he said he had no memory at all of the operation.

From all this evidence it seems that the case for selective repression is almost totally unsupported. If repression is not the answer we still do not know why it is that Rawlings and Grey find hellish experiences and practically no one else does. All we can do for now is accept that some NDEs are negative in tone and contain elements comparable with traditional tales of hell. However, they are clearly in the minority. Most NDEs are pleasant and a large majority peaceful.

SUICIDE

What about those people who actually choose to die? Many religions treat suicide as a mortal sin, deserving of terrible punishment. Do suicide attempters also experience peace, bliss and joy as they come close to death? Or do they form the majority of those who go to hell?

The answer is clear. In one study people who jumped off the bridges in San Francisco Bay were interviewed. The Golden Gate Bridge is the number one location for suicides in the world and jumps from it are almost always fatal, with only one per cent surviving. The drop from the mid-point to the water is 250 feet and it takes about three to four seconds to fall at speeds of up to 75 miles per hour (47). In the early 1970s, California neuropsychiatrist David Rosen sought out the ten known survivors and managed to track down seven of them.

One survivor said, 'It was a good feeling – no screaming. It was the most pleasant feeling I've ever had. I saw the horizon and the blue sky and I thought how beautiful it was' (199 p. 291). All seven reported peaceful or tranquil feelings during their jumps and all experienced transcendence and spiritual rebirth.

In their well-known books both Moody and Ring describe NDEs in suicide attempts (133, 182). Ring found that NDEs were shorter or somehow truncated in these cases but still many included positive emotions. In interviews with a further thirty-six suicide attempters he found that nearly half had had Moody-type experiences (189). He specifically notes that the emotional tone of all of them was extremely positive and that most descriptions emphasized the peace, beauty and sense of perfection accompanying the experience. None described any negative experiences.

It might seem logical to assume that these depressed or frightened people would want to get back to that blissful feeling again; wouldn't this only encourage them to try again and next time to succeed? This is quite the reverse of what actually happens. Moody notes that some of his respondents did not want to come back from death but even so denounced suicide as a way of returning there. When asked whether he would try again one man answered,

> No. I would not do that again. I will die naturally next time, because one thing I realized at that time is that our life here is just such a small period of time and there is so much which needs to be done while you're here. And when you die it's eternity.
>
> (133 p. 46)

Of all those seven who survived a jump, none had gone on to commit suicide at the time of Rosen's study (199). There is even evidence that the positive emotions themselves are linked to changing one's mind about suicide. Greyson and Stevenson (86) asked a group of thirty-eight NDErs about their attitudes to suicide after their experience. Most claimed that they had become more negative towards it and none had become more positive. Interestingly this change against suicide was more likely in those who had feelings of peacefulness or contentment during their NDE. It seems that threats of hell are less persuasive than a positive experience.

Where does this leave us now? It seems there are some hellish NDEs but a careful look at these reveals a possible asymmetry between the wonderful experiences and the hellish ones. Positive NDEs include beautiful visions but more often the bliss and peace seem to be free-floating, to be felt in their own right rather than as a reaction to what is seen. Many positive NDEs begin with nothing but this sense of peace and love and some never get further than this. By contrast, going by the limited reports of hellish NDEs, it seems that the fear is usually engendered by the sight of arms crawling out of pits, boiling hot lakes or terrifying creatures. One possible interpretation is that the hallucinations people have and the places they visit can potentially take on almost any form and will have emotions to match, but in most NDEs there is a free-floating peace and joy which comes right at the start and is over and above the specific content of the visions.

HEAVEN TURNS TO HELL

One of the nastiest experiences I have ever read also begins with this peace and happiness. A patient suffering from cancer, described by his doctors as a 72-year-old eminent literary gentleman, was found in a coma with lowered breathing rate and blood pressure. He was immediately given an injection of naloxone and awoke, looking extremely frightened, struggling to remove a cannula and drip from his arm, and repeating the words 'This is evil, this is evil'. Afterwards he wrote a long account of a truly devilish experience. He had found himself a living being on a high plateau standing in the shadow of a rock. He was in a state of bliss and utter rightness when a group of beings appeared. They had kind and compassionate faces but he knew they were in the wrong place at the wrong time.

> Alarm deepens into panic as they close in upon me. I beg them to go away. To my horror, they lay hands upon me and try to pull me out of shape. The pain is unbearable . . . please, please let me alone. You are destroying me. O please, why do you do this to me?
>
> (109 p. 561)

The creatures tried to abduct and manipulate him against his will and he began to despair. Then came a powerful rhythm or vibration and a cloying, astringent, all-pervading odour more abhorrent than the pulsing rhythm. He goes on

> I am lying on a bed, looking up into the eyes of the two beings who have been and are still 'manipulating' me. The scene has changed, moving from the sandy outdoor landscape with its great rock to this small room with its curtained door through which there are agitated comings and goings.

And he was back in the world of doctors, nurses and drips; still struggling and still afraid.

Perhaps the transformation of the creatures from benign to evil was forced by the doctors' interventions. This fits with parapsychologist Scott Rogo's idea that the hellish aspects of the NDE are hallucinations brought about by the violent physical ordeals which are part and parcel of normal resuscitation techniques (197).

The strange thing is that even this experience began with the kind of peace we have come to associate with the NDE. While still by his rock the man relates, 'I am a living being, and my life is bliss and utter rightness, but a greater bliss and discovery of being are imminent. I rest in and open myself to the power which is within and about me.'

Could it be that all NDEs begin with this pleasant and even mystical tone and only some of them later turn nasty? Australian psychologist Harvey Irwin and one of his students report a case in which a 50-year-old woman, Vera, had a car crash and was unconscious for many hours (104). Her experience began in calm and peace, free from worry about the physical accident or anything else. She floated in spiral fashion through a very large tunnel and came to a 'beautiful place'. It was very light with a blue sky and very green trees. But once she entered a church everything changed. The pews were filled with hooded figures and then the devil appeared, looked her straight in the eye and told her to pick up a goblet. As he began pouring something into it she saw it was fire. She screamed, dropped the goblet and ran.

Irwin and Bramwell are clearly confused by this mixed experience for it has elements of the typical NDE for all its devilish horror. They speculate that perhaps different phases of the NDE have different determinants and therefore different factors can make some parts pleasant and others unpleasant.

I would take this speculation a little further. Indeed, on the theory I have begun to develop here I think it is just what we would expect. To see why, we must extend our understanding of the dying brain a little further.

THE BRAIN'S OWN DRUGS

I have explained how I think it is that the ND-specific experiences of the tunnel, light and noises come about. These are the phenomena most often associated with actual proximity to death and therefore probably caused by hypoxia and other direct threats to the brain.

The peace and positive emotions, however, are not specifically associated with being close to death. They occur in association with other experiences as well. For example, psychologists Gabbard, Twemlow and Jones found that peace was part of the general pattern of out-of-body experiences and was not specific to the near-death situation (68). It also occurs in almost all NDEs, including falls that result in no injury, or NDEs occurring during extreme stress and fear but without any physical harm. Confirming this, Owens, Cook and Stevenson found that positive emotions occurred roughly equally in NDErs close to death and those who were not (158).

Clearly these powerful emotions are part of a general pattern of experience and do not depend specifically on being close to death. We might therefore guess that (unlike the tunnel and noises) they do not depend on cerebral anoxia but on something that occurs more generally in times of stress to produce feelings of peace, happiness and well-being. That something is probably the endorphins.

The word endorphin comes from a contraction of endogenous (meaning internally produced) and morphine. Endorphins are peptides synthesized in the brain to have a variety of effects. They seem to act as neurotransmitters, as neuromodulators (interacting with and affecting the action of various other neurotransmitters) and as hormones (231, 118). There are two main classes of these neuropeptides, the enkephalins and the endorphins, though often both types are referred to collectively as endorphins.

It has long been known that morphine and heroin produce a state described as the ultimate pleasure by many users and often sought after to the exclusion of food, sex and every other pleasure. However, what they do to the brain and why they are so highly addictive was a mystery. It was therefore considered a great discovery in the early 1970s when opiate receptors were found in the brain: that is, cells that respond specifically to these chemicals. This discovery meant that the effects were probably created by the drugs mimicking the naturally pleasurable effects of a chemical made by the brain itself. The reason for having such a chemical would presumably be reinforcement of behaviour and the addiction would be due to interference with the natural balance of the chemicals and receptors. It was not long before the chemicals themselves were identified; first the smaller enkephalins and then the endorphins.

The endorphins are now known to be synthesized in the brain and released into the cerebro-spinal fluid, which bathes the cells of the brain and spinal cord. They are released during stress, sexual activity and fighting in many animals. One of their many probable functions is to reduce pain and induce pleasant sensations so that animals will keep on mating or fighting in spite of injury, and respond to stress in ways most likely to help their survival. They are also involved in regulating rewards and pleasure. Like the opiates they resemble, the endorphins have a variety of effects including analgesia, or elimination of pain, and the induction of intense pleasure, peace and calm. The most powerful narcotic among them is beta-endorphin.

These endorphins therefore appear to be capable of inducing just the kind of state we find in NDEs. Are they, then, released under those circumstances in which NDEs occur?

The first researcher to try to account for NDEs in terms of endorphins was Daniel Carr, an instructor of medicine at Harvard Medical School (29, 30). He reviewed the evidence available in 1982 and made a compelling case for the role of endorphins in NDEs.

Research to investigate their function was initially hampered by the difficulty of detecting the endorphins. However, it was soon found that beta-endorphin is synthesized along with a hormone called ACTH or adrenocorticotrophic hormone. This is released by the pituitary in the brain and acts to stimulate the adrenal cortex. This in turn produces the corticosteroids which play such an important part in the stress response. Subsequently it was confirmed that endorphins are released during stress just as ACTH is (95). This was important because a lot of research had already been done on stress and ACTH and could be relevant to understanding the newly discovered endorphins. It was subsequently confirmed that beta-endorphin is released in many of those same circumstances that provoke a stress response, including infection, hypoxia, hypoglycemia (low blood sugar) and various kinds of psychological stress; in fact, just those conditions that so often give rise to NDEs.

Carr also pointed out that the adrenal steroids are known to be elevated in patients shortly before death, regardless of their diagnosis. Since there is such a close association between beta-endorphin and stimulation of the adrenal cortex this is at least indirect evidence that endorphins are always released near death, regardless of the immediate cause of coming close to death. Interestingly, beta-endorphin is also released in response to ether and, as we have seen, ether induces a state quite comparable to the NDE. It seems that the endorphins are just what we have been looking for.

There may now be evidence to piece together most of the puzzle. Endorphins cause just the kinds of emotional response, including pleasure, joy, calmness and freedom from pain, that occur during NDEs. They are thought to be released in all those circumstances in which NDEs occur, including illness and stress as well as actual proximity to death.

One last point. The association between ACTH and endorphins has another consequence. As Carr pointed out, hypotension (or lowered blood pressure) causes the release of ACTH and presumably of beta-endorphin. Since morphine reduces blood pressure, beta-endorphin might also lower blood pressure during shock and so make things worse. A suitable treatment would therefore be a morphine antagonist. This appeared to work. A potent antagonist is naloxone; this was successfully used to treat hypovolemic shock and was found to raise blood pressure and improve the chances of survival.

Now this is presumably why the 72-year-old cancer patient studied by Judson and Wiltshaw was given naloxone to get him out of his coma. And what happened? His initially pleasurable NDE, in a world inhabited by kind and compassionate creatures, suddenly turned to a horrible world. The creatures were found to be evil and manipulating him and finally turned into the doctors who were treating him. As he puts it himself, 'Bliss is replaced by an alien rhythm which sends shock waves surging through my being' (109 p. 561).

Interestingly, the horror came for this poor man before his visions ceased. Indeed, the visions kept going for some time even though they turned from pleasant to horrific. I shall later explain the reason why endorphins can cause visions; it is related to their ability to cause electrical seizures in certain parts of the brain. What is interesting for this case is that naloxone can block the pain-killing and pleasurable effects of endorphins more easily than these seizures (65). So the change in this man's experience is exactly what we would expect if it was caused by his own endorphins and destroyed by the naloxone.

We shall never know what he might have experienced if he had been left to die or had come out of his coma naturally but my guess is that he would have continued with the blissful NDE. The bliss was induced by his own brain's high levels of endorphins; the despair and horror were induced by the injection of naloxone.

Before uncritically accepting this as the answer, there is one researcher who has argued against the role of endorphins in the NDE. Melvin Morse has made a special study of childhood NDEs. He and his colleagues interviewed eleven children who had survived critical illnesses including cardiac arrest and profound coma (137). Seven of them reported NDEs including most of the major features that adults report: OBEs, the tunnel, bright lights and the decision to return. They did not, however, report a life review or transcendent feelings. Their emotional reactions were mixed and their accounts were more fragmentary than adult narratives. The basis of his argument against the role of endorphins is that he compared these children with twenty-nine age-matched survivors of illnesses who required similar treatment: intubation, narcotics and admission to an intensive care unit. Even though these children had narcotics, which are similar to endorphins, none of them had any memories of the time they were unconscious.

Is this sound evidence against the endorphin theory of the NDE? That depends on how we see the role of the endorphins. I have argued that the tunnel and lights are induced by the disinhibitory effects of anoxia. Since these children did not have cardiac arrests or coma they might have had no tunnels because they had no anoxia. The role of endorphins is more important in inducing the positive emotions, the life review and the other worlds visited. However, Morse's NDEr children did not report these aspects of the NDE, so it is not nearly so surprising that the control group did not either. That leaves only the OBE. I shall argue later on that the OBE requires a combination of sensory deprivation and disruption of the body image and perhaps the control subjects did not have those conditions. So, although Morse's evidence is very interesting and more such evidence would be extremely helpful, it cannot be seen as demolishing the theory that endorphins are involved in the NDE.

A CHALLENGE TO THE THEORY

I have been developing a theory of the NDE that tries to explain it completely in terms of processes in the dying brain. Before I go any further with it I know that many people will object. 'It's too reductionist,' they will say. 'You can't explain everything with brain cells and physiology.' They are likely to use two very important kinds of objection.

The first is a direct challenge to any physiological or naturalistic theory of the NDE. It is simply this: that some NDErs claim they could accurately see events from outside their bodies. In other words, they claim paranormal powers. And paranormal powers, by definition, cannot be explained in terms of 'normal' theories.

The second objection often comes from people who have had NDEs or other kinds of mystical experiences. You are wrong, they say, this feeling of bliss is nothing like a chemically induced high. It is a spiritual joy; an experience of the soul; a transcendence of ordinary pleasure and pain. Drug induced joy is a sham; not the real thing at all. The 'real thing' comes from God, from another plane, from something way beyond complex molecules interacting with brain cells.

Well, does it? Of course I think not. It is my contention that this 'real thing' – NDES, mystical experiences and indeed everything encountered on the spiritual path – are products of a brain and the universe of which it is a part. For there is nothing else. It is our longing for something more that leads us astray. It is an illusion that we can find 'true spirituality' by looking outside of ourselves. It is all here, now, in the creatures we are, as we are. And as far as I can tell we are creatures who feel intense pleasure when endorphins are released inside our brains.

That is not to say that injecting a chemical from outside can duplicate spiritual joy. In the first place, the route of administration of any drug makes an enormous difference to its effects. This is why cocaine and crack offer quite different temptations and different problems even though they are essentially the same drug. This is why narcotics in a sleeping mixture have different effects from the same substances injected directly into the blood.

Then there is the difference in motivation. A drug taken to induce pleasure encourages lethargy, dependence and an attitude that happiness comes from outside, not from within. The joy that comes from a spiritual discipline, patiently practised, encourages composure, acceptance and an attitude that happiness is there all the time, waiting only to be uncovered. Yet both, in all probability, occur when certain molecules bind to the opiate receptors in the brain. I shall return to this issue but for now I shall just concur with Kenneth Ring – 'Paradise is paradise, however it is gained.' (185 p. 145).

My conclusion so far is that the release of endorphins as a response to stress is what causes the delightful, joyful and peaceful feelings so characteristic of the NDE, whether close to death or not. But what about the rest of that cluster of experiences, the life review and those strange and beautiful worlds visited in OBEs and NDEs? I shall return to these soon but first I must face that other challenge – what about that evidence for the paranormal?

6

But I Saw the Colour of Her Dress

The three of them were standing there – my wife, my oldest son and my oldest daughter and the doctor . . . There was no way, being out, that I could have seen anybody.

(204 p. 155)

The man's account . . . described in procedural detail how the CPR had been performed. His description is extremely accurate.

(204 p. 128)

I told my father who had dragged my body out of the building, and even what color clothes that person had on, and how they got me out, and even about all the conversation that had been going on in the area.

(133 p. 100)

Some very strong claims are made. The implication is always the same; that people during NDEs have actually seen the events occurring from a location outside their bodies. 'They' have left their bodies and that is why they can accurately see what is going on.

If these claims are valid then the theory I am developing is wrong – or, to be more accurate, inadequate. There could still be paranormal powers in addition to the other effects. I could still argue that most of the phenomena could be accounted for physiologically except for some paranormal events which need a special explanation. However, this would really miss the point of any physiological theory of the NDE.

I want to be quite clear. It is my contention that there is no soul, spirit, astral body or anything at all that leaves the body during NDEs and survives after death. These, like the very idea of a persisting self, are all illusions and the NDE can be accounted for without recourse to any of them. If so, then we should not expect people during NDEs to have access to any information other than that already available to them through perfectly normal means.

So do they?

One way of trying to find out is to gather together accounts that claim paranormal vision during NDEs. There are many of them. Sabom, Moody, Ring and in fact all the major investigators have presented cases of this kind. By their very numbers these claims provide the appearance of solidity. However, in very few is any kind of independent corroboration given.

Often the details described as correct are not the kind that can easily be checked later. For example, NDErs often describe what a particular person was wearing in a distant room or who was standing where and talking to whom. Such details cannot be confirmed for certain later on except by reference to people's memories and presumably at the time of near-death crises such details would not be in the forefront of their minds.

Moody is quite open about the problem. He explains that in a few cases he has been able to get independent testimony but in most cases the event itself is attested to only by the dying person himself and by at most a couple of close friends and acquaintances. He concludes that such corroborating stories, collected after the fact, cannot constitute proof (133).

There is no doubt that people describe, reasonably accurately, events that have occurred around them during their NDE. However, this need not be because they have used paranormal powers or left their bodies. Before reaching this conclusion we must consider all the other ways in which they could have known what was going on.

IMAGERY

The first thing to remember is that if the brain is still functioning, even very poorly, it will be capable of sustaining imagery. Later on I shall examine how that imagery comes to seem real in an NDE. But the main question here is where does the information come from to construct these images?

The answers include prior knowledge, fantasy and lucky guesses and the remaining operating senses of hearing and touch. Add to this the way memory works to recall accurate items and forget the wrong ones, and we have the basis for an alternative account of why people are able to 'see' what is going on. We may consider what each of these can contribute.

MEMORY

Our memories are fantastic in recording information for decades and being able to reconstruct events that took place yesterday or fifty years ago. However, reconstruct is what they do. Memory does not somehow burn into the brain exact details of everything that happens. Rather, as we go through life experiencing more and more, the neural networks are constantly developing, changing and growing in complexity. Old learning is subtly altered by the new.

When we retell an old story, the version we tell takes its place in memory as well as the version we originally recalled. The more often a story is retold the more distantly recallable becomes our initial response to the events. And, since we are all human, the version we tell is likely to be just that little bit more interesting or poignant than it might have been. Also, when we tell stories to others together with a friend, or as a couple, social pressures act to encourage both people to tell the same story. You don't always correct your friend who exaggerates the tale just that little bit over a pint in the pub. You may enjoy participating in the slightly exaggerated recollections of a trip you all took together last weekend. And why not? At the very least friends and couples may talk about the bits they agree on and often forget to mention the bits they don't.

So imagine two people talking about their recollections after a hospital resuscitation. The patient says, 'I could see you there, down the hall, you were wearing that green coat and skirt and your favourite pearl necklace. You were talking to George and he was waving a newspaper about. You looked terribly pale.' What if she was wearing the coat, but not the skirt and necklace, and she, not George, had a grip on the newspaper? She would be caring more for accuracy and less for the sick patient if she bothered to go into detail on all of this. More likely she would just confirm the correct details and forget the rest. In both their minds these correct details would be the ones retold and remembered by everyone.

This may sound destructive and doubting – an exercise in debunking. But my intention is not to debunk so much as to assess the alternatives. We are presented with cases that sound like evidence of paranormal perception during NDEs. If they are it matters crucially to our understanding of life, death and human nature in all its complexity. Yet the way we tell stories and the way our memories work can easily provide us with stories that sound like evidence but really are not.

PRIOR KNOWLEDGE AND EXPECTATION

Many people can imagine what happens in an operating theatre, in a hospital ward, at the scene of a car crash or whatever. Anyone who comes close to death is likely to have some prior information about the situation they are going into before they become unconscious. From what they know up to this time they may be able to build up a fairly accurate picture of what will follow. As they lose touch with sensory reality and their internal imagery takes over as real, their expectations will come to life. It may, then, not be so remarkable that afterwards they give a fairly good account of where they were, who else was there and what happened.

Take, for example, a person who nearly drowns in a swimming pool. Before they become unconscious they will certainly know where they are, the layout of the pool, the rough numbers and locations of other people and where the pool is in relation to the neighbourhood. They will be able to visualize the scene not only from where they are but also from above. If you doubt this, try an experiment on yourself. Shut your eyes now and try to imagine where you are but from above, first from a few feet up and then from much higher. You may be surprised at how much you can 'see' but this is just a reflection of how information is stored in our memories. This sort of information goes quite a long way towards providing the information needed for a realistic bird's eye view of events.

This argument, in various forms, has often been used but proponents of the paranormal view have argued that it cannot possibly account for the findings. Most important among these are cases where patients have described in detail the hospital procedures used to resuscitate them from cardiac arrest. They describe specific and purely visual details which, it is argued, they could not possibly have guessed correctly.

Sabom gives several such cases. For example, a retired air force pilot from northern Florida had a massive heart attack and cardiac arrest. He was interviewed by Sabom five years later when he was 44 years old. Sabom reproduces large parts of the interview with this man in which he describes in great detail the procedure which went on. Here is just a small part of it.

S: I remember them pulling over the cart, the defibrillator, the thing with the paddles on it. I remember they asked for so many watt-seconds or something on the thing, and they gave me a jolt with it.

A: Did you notice any of the details of the machine itself or the cart it was sitting on?

S: I remember it had a meter on the face. I assume it read the voltage, or current, or watt-seconds, or whatever they program the thing for.

A: Did you notice how the meter looked?

S: It was square and had two needles on there, one fixed and one which moved.

A: How did it move?

S: It seemed to come up rather slowly, really. It didn't just pop up like an ammeter or a volt-meter or something registering.

(204 p. 141)

He went on to describe in detail how the fixed needle moved and then stayed still while the other needle moved up. As Sabom puts it, 'This man's autoscopic report of his resuscitation accurately describes what would be expected during a CPR procedure performed by highly trained personnel in an intensive care unit setting.' Sabom was particularly impressed by his description of the behaviour of the needles and also by the fact that meters of the type described were commonly in use in 1973, at the time of the man's cardiac arrest, but are not found on more recent defibrillators (204 p. 145). The man denied having ever seen this CPR procedure being carried out and Sabom was convinced this was the truth.

Is this compelling evidence that he actually, paranormally, 'saw' what was going on? He may have done so, but this is not strong evidence. Sabom naturally checked the medical records which confirmed that the man had had a cardiac arrest in the critical care unit during the early morning hours and was successfully defibrillated. Other specifics of the CPR procedure were not available. This is perfectly normal. It is not usual to write down in medical records exactly what was done since anyone using those records would assume most of it from the bare facts stated. However, it is important from our point of view. From these records we have no knowledge of just what kind of apparatus was used, whether the needles did move in exactly this way at the right time and so on. Yes, the man gives a plausible account and it seems unexpected given his lack of knowledge, but without access to complete details of what happened (and these can never be obtained) we cannot know just how closely it really did fit the facts at the time.

We also have no clear idea of how much the man could have learned later, recovering in hospital or after he left. He might have been told more about the procedures afterwards. He might have become more interested in cardiac resuscitation after his own close brush with death and paid particular attention to books, television programmes or films about it. Without consciously intending to he might have incorporated small details from such later knowledge into his memory images, so adding to their plausibility. Five years later he could not be expected to remember where he got the information from. Some NDErs are interviewed immediately after their NDE but with many, like this one, it is years before they tell their story. Interesting as they are, we can get no further with cases like this.

The apparent power of this case rests, as for so many others, on whether we would expect the man to put together in his own imagination such a plausible view of the procedure or not. This is very hard to assess indeed.

It is hard, but there are ways the problem can be approached and Sabom himself has tried one of them. He compared descriptions of CPR from NDErs who had actually experienced it with descriptions by people who only imagined that they were being resuscitated. To do this he interviewed twenty-five control cardiac patients. None had had an NDE but their medical backgrounds were similar to those who had. Sabom found that 80 per cent of them made at least one major error in trying to describe the procedure; errors not found to that extent in the real NDErs. He also points out that the NDErs gave details specific to their own case and not to resuscitation in general. For example, one described only cardiac defibrillation while another describes several additional procedures including a 'shot in the groin'. Both correctly fitted their own case but not each other's. Sabom concludes that the CPR descriptions from NDEs could not have been based solely on the person's prior knowledge of CPR.

I cannot agree with his conclusion. At least, I can agree that the NDE accounts were not based solely on prior expectation, but this does not imply that they were paranormal. The real patients and the control patients differed in a much more important respect, one which Sabom does not mention. That is, the real NDErs actually went through the procedure. If they had had any residual sensory ability they might have heard things and felt things that were going on and this would allow them, in their vivid imaginations, to piece together the procedure much more accurately. Sabom's control group was not really a control at all because they did not have access to anything like as much information as the real patients.

This brings us on to the issue of how much relevant information can be obtained from what is left of the senses when someone is apparently unconscious.

BUT SHE WAS UNCONSCIOUS

Unconsciousness is not an all-or-nothing phenomenon. A person may appear unresponsive but still be able to hear. They may not react to surgical procedures or painful stimuli but still know what is going on.

The way consciousness is lost has been much studied because of its importance in anaesthesia. Some anaesthetics are non-specific, like the traditional gases we have already considered. They tend to produce their effects in a regular order. With the lowest dose analgesia, or insensitivity to pain, begins, then with a higher dose amnesia sets in, or the inability to remember the events afterwards. Only at a still higher dose does the patient become immobile and it is not entirely clear at what point we should say that they have lost consciousness.

Modern anaesthetics present a more complicated picture. Instead of giving one chemical to do all these jobs, several are typically given. The main component is a narcotic, or sleep-inducer, which binds to the opiate receptors in the brain. This alone can render a patient motionless and unresponsive to surgical procedures but patients may still respond to verbal instructions, such as 'raise your finger if you can hear me' and may remember some of the events afterwards. Increasing the dose could be potentially dangerous and there are many advantages to light anaesthesia. So instead these problems are solved by using other agents: tranquillizers which abolish the memory and curare-like agents which paralyse the patient. This way the muscles are well relaxed, the patient is unresponsive and cannot remember anything afterwards. That is, if all goes well. However, mistakes can occur.

> I came out of the anaesthesia and couldn't understand why I wasn't in the ward. I could see the surgeons at the end of the operating table and I thought, 'O my God, they're going to operate on me and I'm awake.' I tried to tell them but couldn't speak – couldn't move . . .
>
> (56 p. 190)

This man, being operated on for a hernia, described it as 'the worst experience of my life'. A woman with an ectopic pregnancy told of 'a nightmare to end all nightmares'.

Such cases were dismissed as fantasy when they were first reported but now are taken seriously, and attempts are being made to find ways to measure unconsciousness more accurately so as to prevent them (200, 115). It is also now common practice to speak about the patient as though they might be able to hear. Medical personnel in operating theatres are trained not to discuss the patient's illness or possible demise as though they were a lump of inanimate flesh but to realize that they might hear what is going on.

In the same vein, friends and relatives who sit with the dying, or those in a coma, are encouraged to speak to them as though they can hear. There are many accounts of people awakening from comas grateful for the human contact and friendship offered when, to any observer, they had appeared completely inert.

To return to the NDE, it is quite clear that people sometimes have quite a lot of sensory information about what is going on around them when they are in states we might call unconscious.

SENSORY INFORMATION

There are five main senses, vision, hearing, smell, taste and touch, plus proprioception which detects internal stimuli and allows a good body image to be built up. From these we construct our world.

During unconsciousness the senses are not all lost at once. As we saw in the experiments on G-LOC, a person may be able to hear and feel even when they are totally unable to move. In studies of awareness during anaesthesia it has been found that hearing is the most common sense remaining. In one study 85 per cent of the patients recalled hearing noises or conversation, only about 40 per cent felt pain and a third recalled seeing something (56). Most NDErs would probably have their eyes closed and have little chance of seeing much. Even so, like the failed anaesthesia cases who glimpsed the green gowns or looming faces of the people around them, they might glean a little useful information this way. However, the most important remaining sense is probably hearing.

From hearing alone we can construct extremely convincing visual pictures. One of my great failings, at least according to my family, is that I like to listen to radio's endless tale of farming life, *The Archers*. I know what Grey Gables looks like, I know the layout of the village green and shop. I can imagine driving into Home Farm or the Grundys' yard and I am intimate with the decor in Nelson's Wine Bar. Of course, I probably have all these things wrong, at least in as much as there is any correct version. But this does not matter for my enjoyment of the programme. For most people it is impossible (and no fun at all) to listen to stories or descriptions of events without building up a corresponding visual picture.

This is clear from experiments on imagery. When told a story about a cat crossing the path in front of them as they walk through the woods, people do not construct in their minds some kind of abstract representation of a cat or woods. They imagine concrete details. It is a black cat, or a silver tabby. The woods are dark or sun streaked. Abstraction is a difficult process. We start with the specific.

This tendency to make concrete images from little information has all sorts of consequences – some of them far-reaching. I would like to illustrate this with a story.

A man was driving his son to school one day when their car was in collision with a lorry. The man was killed, the boy was injured and the lorry driver drove them to the hospital. When they arrived the surgeon looked at the little boy and said, 'Oh, my God, that's my son.' And it was.

Do you have trouble understanding this story? Do you start wondering about uncles and grandfathers? About step-fathers and surgeon's relatives? If so, you are not alone. This is a typical reaction. Would it help you to know that this story was first told in an early feminist magazine and would it shock you to realize that it still seems to have as much power to confuse people as it did all those years ago? The answer is, of course, that the surgeon was the boy's mother. There really is no problem with the story. We create the problem for ourselves.

The reason is probably not that we are all ardent male chauvinist pigs, but that imagination works with concrete images. Most surgeons still are men, both in real life and in fiction, and we naturally tend to imagine the surgeon in our story as a man.

The implications for society aside, there are also implications for NDEs. Lying barely conscious at a pool side, on a hospital operating table, in the road by a crashed car, when we hear the voices of people around, or the sounds of objects moving, being lifted or put down, we will naturally construct a concrete visual image of what is happening. This is the way our minds work. The details may not all be correct but many will be and the picture will be most convincing.

So what kinds of information can we pick up from what we hear? Speech is probably the most important. The surgeon may issue instructions for the resuscitation, ask for instruments to be passed, or even start chatting to other people present; nurses may confer over procedures, check doses, ask for equipment;

anaesthetists may offer information on the patient's state, or even pronounce the patient close to death. Potentially, any of this may be heard by the patient.

It does not take much information from such sounds for a person to piece together a very convincing and realistic visual impression of what is going on. This will provide the best model they have and seem perfectly real. They may have no idea that the model was constructed primarily from things that they heard.

NDE researchers have not ignored this possibility. Sabom deals with it in some detail and points out that perhaps autoscopic NDEs could be explained

> as the piecing together of verbal information into an accurate visual image of what actually transpired. In the foregoing six cases, however, several of the autoscopically perceived events were of a non-auditory nature (e.g., the pattern of movement of the needles on the face of the defibrillator). Moreover, the interpretations of some of the autoscopic details indicate that the perception of the detail was visual, not auditory. For example, the man in Case 5 described 'a shot in the groin . . . It appeared to me they were putting a shot in there . . .'
>
> (204 p. 160)

Sabom goes on to explain that the procedure the man underwent was not an injection but the withdrawal of blood from the femoral artery for the test of blood gases. This is the case I have already mentioned in which blood gases were determined for someone having an NDE. It is an important case since this has so rarely been done. Sabom explains that if the man's description had been based solely on remarks overheard then he would not have made the confusion between having an injection, and having blood withdrawn. He continues

> such a misinterpretation could easily be understood if the man had watched it from a distance, as he claims; for the 'shot in

the groin' would then have been a logical conclusion based on the visual observation of the insertion of a small needle and syringe.

(204 p. 160)

However, I suggest it would also be a logical conclusion based on what the man could *feel* happening to his body. Hearing is not the only sense that can remain in semi-consciousness. He could have had residual sense of touch or pain and felt that needle going in. This applies also to cases where patients correctly recall where on their chest the defibrillator pads were placed, or which side of their chest injections were given. We would expect them to get such details right not because they saw them but because they felt them.

It is very hard to assess just how much information any patient would have available. We can only remember the general point that people who appear unconscious may still be aware of some of the things going on around them and they can easily build these up into a good visual picture of what was happening.

How can we get round this problem? There are two final approaches through which we might find convincing evidence. One is to search for details that could not possibly have been detected by any of the senses and the second is to look for NDEs in the blind.

DISTANT VISION

If the use of hearing, touch and proprioception are to be ruled out we need to look for cases where none of the senses could account for details correctly reported. Because this issue is so important I have long been on the lookout for any cases that seem to present potentially verifiable information of this kind. When I hear of one I often write to the author to ask for further information. Some never reply, while others are extremely helpful.

William Serdahely recently published some cases of NDEs in children (210, 211). One seemed to provide a possible detail that could be corroborated. A 7-year-old boy, Pat, was fishing with a friend from a stone bridge when he fell off, dropped nine or ten feet and hit his head on a rock. He was under the water for five to ten minutes before a police officer rescued him. After an ambulance ride to the local hospital and resuscitation he was shipped by helicopter to a larger hospital for specialized care.

He was in a coma all that day and the next, regaining consciousness briefly the next day. Eight days after the accident he was discharged from hospital.

Afterwards the little boy described how he had seen himself entangled in the fishing line, the police officer coming to rescue him, the ambulance ride and the trip in a blue, orange and white helicopter with three persons on board besides himself. Later he went into a dark, black timeless tunnel and met with his dog and cat, both of whom had died when he was only three years old. This fitted with Serdahely's finding that when children have NDEs and all their loved ones are alive, they tend to have animals or other alternative beings to meet them. It also fits with Ring's suggestion that you don't need both the 'presence' and dead relatives because both serve the same function of sending the traveller back. In this case it was the family dog who sent Pat back (211).

Pat was in a coma when transported to the hospital and therefore if he had the details of the helicopter colours and the people on board correct it would be most interesting. Serdahely has been trying to contact the boy's mother for confirmation of these details but has received no replies. This is just one of many cases that may or may not be potential evidence but, frustratingly, we cannot find out.

Serdahely has, however, had more success with another case, that of Ben Bray, a little boy of six.

'I Went to Heaven and Talked to God' says the headline in the tabloid paper, the *Globe*; 'Boy, 6, snaps out of coma and bares startling proof.' Ben Bray had to have a heart transplant for an inherited heart defect, from which his older brother had already died. Ben was able to describe his journey to a beautiful, light and happy place with angels in white robes and a 'big, bright, yellow light far ahead, down a long, long, white room'. During his experience he met his brother Matthew and his two dead grandfathers, one with black hair and the other with brown. Ben's mother explained that he had only seen his grand-fathers – whether in real life or in pictures – with grey hair, so it was surprising that he had these details right. Or, as it puts it in the paper, 'It just absolutely stunned us that he got the color of their hair right and that he pinpointed which was which.'

Dr Serdahely wrote to Ben's mother and she replied that the article had exaggerated the story in most parts but confirmed that Ben recalled the colour of his grandfathers' hair. Of course, brown and black are both descriptions that could cover a wide variety of hair colours and the probability of getting them right by chance is quite high. The case is hardly the 'startling proof' of the popular headline.

I mention this case mainly because it is typical of the sort of account that gets embellished in the popular press and gives the impression that yet more proof is forthcoming. If cases like this were the weaker ones just adding bulk to a large body of properly corroborated and stronger cases then this would not matter. As it is, it seems to be typical of the problem we have in finding evidence of anything paranormal going on.

Of course, there are some very well-known cases that appear to be excellent evidence. Probably the most widely quoted is the case of Maria and the tennis shoe, reported by social worker Kimberly Clark (33). Maria was brought into hospital in Seattle after a severe heart attack and then suffered a cardiac arrest. She later told Clark that she had been looking down from the ceiling. Clark was not impressed by this, but took more notice when Maria described the view from outside the emergency room, since she had arrived at night inside an ambulance. Maria then explained that she had been distracted by the sight of something on the third floor ledge at the north end of the building. She had gone up close and found that it was a tennis shoe with a worn patch by the little toe and the lace stuck under the heel. She wanted someone to go and see if it was there. With mixed emotions Clark went outside and looked but could see little. It was only by trying many patients' rooms and looking out of the windows that she finally found and retrieved the now-famous shoe.

Clark explains that this story served to legitimize Maria's experience, as if without it the experience was somehow invalid but with it the experience was 'real'. Of course, NDEs should not need such legitimization for they are valid in themselves, as experiences. But this case underlines all too clearly how people use claims of the paranormal to convince themselves and others that what they experienced was *real* and that they are not going crazy. And if the need is so strong there is always the suspicion that the claims may be exaggerated or even invented. The problem is that claims like this are extremely important if they are true. So is it true? This is, sadly, one of those cases for which I have been unable to get any further information. Perhaps it may yet be possible but until then I can only consider it as fascinating but unsubstantiated.

The suspicion must be, rightly or wrongly, that there may be no properly corroborated cases that cannot be accounted for by the perfectly normal processes of imagination, memory, chance and the use of the remaining senses.

Of course, the use of the senses is easier to rule out for a person who does not have them. This is why stories of vision in blind NDErs assume a special significance.

NDES IN THE BLIND

Elisabeth Kubler-Ross, famous for her pioneering work with the dying and bereaved, is sure that NDErs can see the world correctly, even if they are totally blind.

> We asked them to share with us what it was like when they had this near-death experience. If it was just a dream fulfilment those people would not be able to share with us the colour of

the sweater we wear, the design of a tie, or minute details of shape, colours and designs of the people's clothing. We have questioned several totally blind people who were able to share with us in their near-death experience and they were not only able to tell us who came into the room first, who worked on the resuscitation, but they were able to give minute details of the attire and the clothing of all the people present, something a totally blind person would never be able to do.

(114 p. 130)

But as British commentator Ian Wilson puts it, 'Regrettably, Dr Kubler-Ross has tended to be too committed to her patients to spend time publishing these cases in the proper depth to prove her point' (114 p. 130).

One can easily imagine how wonderful it would be for a blind person to find that they are able to see again. This sense of joy is suggested, for example, by one of Kenneth Ring's cases where a woman who was very near-sighted said, 'my very first thought was, "Jesus, I can see! I can't believe it, I can see!" I could read the numbers on the machine behind my head and I was just so thrilled' (183 p. 42).

Exciting as this sounds, clear vision again after years of hazy blur is really not surprising. Our imagination can be extraordinarily clear and vivid, more so than our limited sight and hearing. The short-sighted and the newly blind do not dream in blurred vision, nor do they imagine objects as hazy and dim. Just like anyone else, they can imagine things vividly. The real question is, were the numbers on the machine just any old numbers, picked at random from imagination, or recalled from some previous experience, or were they the actual numbers showing at the time?

The patient herself claimed to have returned to the operating theatre to check up on this and other details of what she saw. She claimed that she had indeed been correct. However, she had since lost track of the anaesthetist concerned and so Ring himself was unable to get independent corroboration.

Aside from the corroboration of specific details, another exciting possibility is that people who have been blind from birth might be able to 'see' again during an NDE. A person who has had normal sight for much of their life will still have normal imagery. Although they may gradually come to rely more on other senses, such as hearing, touch and smell, they can still recall the differences between colours and the visual qualities of shape and texture. They can conjure up these things in their minds. Someone born blind has quite different imagery. They have never seen colours or shapes or textures. All they know comes from hearing, touch and so on. We should not expect them to describe visual qualities at all. If they do, something very strange is happening. Perhaps we might need to postulate an astral body which has perfect vision in spite of the defects of the physical eyes, or a kind of spirit vision which does not make use of either normal vision or normal imagery. Such cases would be very significant for a supernatural theory of the NDE.

Harvey Irwin, the Australian OBE researcher, has tried to find cases of visual OBEs in the congenitally blind. His search, so far, has not turned up any. In a sample of twenty-one blind people, three had had OBEs, which is roughly comparable to the incidence in sighted people. Two of them had become blind late in life and the third, though affected since birth, had residual vision of 40 degrees and so would be expected to have relatively normal visual imagery. Irwin concluded that a critical case has yet to be found (103).

In the Autumn 1989 issue of *Revitalised Signs* I noticed an advertisement from a researcher, Dr Emil Mueller, asking for accounts of NDEs from the deaf and blind. Hoping that he might be kind enough to share such accounts with me, or at least let me see some of his findings from such a survey, I wrote to ask. He was happy to share his findings with me and sent me one account of an OBE. But apart from that he could give me only the disappointing news that, much as he would like to help, from this and other advertisements he had received not one single report of an NDE in the blind.

It was therefore with great excitement that I read an account of just the type of case that sounded convincing. It was in a book called *Recovering the Soul* by physician Larry Dossey.

He begins by recounting the drama of a gallstone operation that seemed to go smoothly until the last moment when, as the surgeon was closing the incision, the patient's heart stopped beating. Defibrillation was successful and the patient recovered,

> Yet Sarah had something else to show for her surgery . . . that amazed her and the rest of the surgery team as well – a clear, detailed memory of the frantic conversation of the surgeons and nurses during her cardiac arrest; the OR layout; the scribbles on the surgery schedule board in the hall outside; the color of the sheets covering the operating table; the hairstyle of the head scrub nurse; the names of the surgeons in the doctors' lounge down the corridor who were waiting for her case to be concluded; and even the trivial fact that her anesthesiologist that day was wearing unmatched socks. All this she knew even though she had been fully anesthetized and unconscious during the surgery and the cardiac arrest.
>
> But what made Sarah's vision even more momentous was the fact that, since birth, she had been blind.
>
> (50 p. 18)

As soon as I read of this case I wanted to learn more about it. Like so many other cases before, this one stirred in me the thought that I might indeed be quite wrong. I could not ignore such potential evidence against my theories – I needed to find out if it were true. I therefore wrote to Dr Dossey in March 1991 and asked him whether I could possibly contact the woman herself, or whether he had any statements by her, the nurses, doctors or anaesthetist involved that I could see.

I soon received a very helpful reply but its contents were not at all what I had expected. Dr Dossey explained to me that

> 'Sarah's' story was a composite – the only composite story in the entire book, *Recovering the Soul*. My reasons for composing her were to dramatically illustrate the key features of non-local ways of knowing – ways that seem (to me) fully

documented in the experiences of diverse numbers of human beings. The 'fact' that Sarah was congenitally blind was a way of illustrating that non-local ways of gaining information bypass the senses and are ultimately independent of the brain.

(51)

He went on to explain that Kenneth Ring had also written to him about Sarah and had wanted to interview her. He had written to Ring, as to me, to explain that she did not exist. He believed that Ring had heard of cases of blind patients who had had near-death experiences much like Sarah's, suggesting that Sarah's case was largely true-to-life.

I very much appreciated Dossey's candid reply. It seems that he had read and heard enough of similar real cases that he believed there was nothing misleading in inventing one more to illustrate what can actually happen. Unfortunately I know, from comments made and letters I have received, that many people have been convinced by Dossey's 'Sarah'. So can it actually happen? Has it ever actually happened? Where are these real cases on which this invention was based?

The obvious person to ask was Kenneth Ring who, like me, had a special interest in these cases albeit from a totally different perspective. Just like Dossey, he believed in the ability of the human mind to reach beyond the limitations of the normal senses. He would probably have access to such cases if anyone did.

Ring also replied very quickly, dropping much other work to help me out, as he has so often done before. And his response, like Dossey's, was not what I had expected. He offered to tell me all that he knew about NDEs in the blind. It was a fascinating story.

First of all he confirmed that he had, like me, contacted Dossey as soon as he heard of his work. Like me, he had learned that Sarah was an invention but concurred with Dossey that he had heard of seemingly genuine cases. He proceeded to tell me about those.

First there was the work of Kubler-Ross, but as far as he knew she had never published detailed cases on this and, in his opinion, even if she did she would be unlikely to provide anything that would allow for an independent assessment. He had then heard of several other cases reported second-hand, for example at conferences, but had never been able to get further data on any of them.

Perhaps most promising was the work of Fred Schoonmaker, a cardiologist in Denver, Colorado, who claimed to have three such cases among his former patients, including at least one congenitally blind person. Ring telephoned him and the cardiologist confirmed that he did have such cases, describing one of them in some detail.

The woman in question, who was congenitally blind, had had an OBE during surgery and had correctly identified the number of people in the room (fourteen) and could describe the medical procedures (as some of Sabom's patients claimed to have done). She could not, however, distinguish colours but could see forms and activities going on. Ring urged Schoonmaker to publish this and his other cases but he never did. As Ring put it, 'Another intriguing, but in the end, useless anecdote. And so it goes' (187).

The only case Ring did find published was of a blind woman who had an OBE in bed, but she was not near death and there was no independent corroboration of what she saw. From this long attempt to find the genuine cases underlying the stories Ring concluded thus:

In short, as much as this is the lore of NDEs, there has never, to my knowledge, been a case of a blind NDEr reported in the literature where there was clear-cut or documented evidence of accurate visual perception during an alleged OBE. (And you can quote me.) I wish there were such a case – we'd all love it. I'm sure that's why people like you and me wrote to Dossey with such alacrity. It *seemed* exactly what we'd been looking for . . .

WHY THE LORE?

As Ring put it, it is 'the lore of NDEs' that these things happen. But it may not be the truth. If it is not true, why would so many people be wrongly convinced that they had paranormal vision? Why are so many books full of accounts of people seeing at a distance while out of their bodies? I think there is a simple answer to this.

When things seem real we expect them to correspond to an external shared reality. The NDE, like many other altered states of consciousness, is an exception to this rule. In the NDE things seem real when in fact they are constructed by imagination. No wonder people are led astray.

Also the things that affect us most are also usually 'real' things. We would feel rather silly to admit that we had been deeply affected by a dream or by a fantasy we happened to have one day. We might pride ourselves on making our decisions on the basis of things we can see and hear and touch; down-to-earth things. NDEs affect people profoundly. They may be a person's only spiritual or mystical experience and can change their lives in most important ways. In a culture so wedded to the objectively verifiable it may be hard to admit that we have been much affected by something 'in my own mind'. It is understandable that people want to proclaim their experiences 'real' and the things they saw as correct so as to avoid the suspicion that they allowed themselves to be deeply influenced by something imaginary.

Finally, many people have a strong desire to believe in a life after death and, even more so, in a self that persists through life. Evidence that what they saw was correct may seem to back up the idea that they, themselves, do have a separate existence and might survive. This desire in itself can fuel the exaggeration of claims, the distortions of memory, the wild newspaper headlines and the tendency to make a big story out of a very weak case.

For all these reasons I think it would not be surprising if there were many claims of paranormal perception in NDEs even if it never happened. It is my impression that it probably never does happen. Certainly I have found no evidence, yet, that convinces me that it does. I may still find it. However, for the moment at least, these claims present no real challenge to a scientific account of the NDE.

7

Realer Than Real

It was a day of sunlight and passing clouds, and at that moment the sun came out (or so I assume) and the oak leaves took on that brilliant translucent green that young oak leaves have in sunlight. That was normal enough, but the light went on brightening until it reached an 'impossible' degree of brilliance. It really seemed impossible that such light could be, and yet it did not dazzle my eyes. And it was speaking to me; yet not in words, for it was itself a word, and the word was 'Yes'. It was agreeing to the condition on which I was prepared to die. The light then faded to the ordinary brightness of sunlight on young oak leaves. I had no more anxiety or fear . . . I have never been tempted to interpret that event, either in religious, psychological or mechanistic terms. This is because it had for me a quality of what I can only call 'primary' reality. It was an absolute, and for me its authority was absolute.

This young woman, faced with the threat of cancer, wrote to me about an experience that seemed, for her, completely real. Others make the same point about the 'reality' of their experience. Many investigators have commented on this impression of reality (72) and Raymond Moody describes the life review as 'incredibly vivid and real'. One of his patients said, 'The whole thing was really odd. I was there; I was actually seeing these flashbacks; I was actually walking through them' (133 p. 68).

A man with a congenital heart defect wrote to me to describe his experience when his heart stopped:

For many years, it was the most real thing that ever happened to me. Yes, far more real and vivid than any real-life incident. It was so real, detailed and so vivid and consistent (except for the wood smoke); in fact, so totally un-dream-like!

So – it is quite clear that the NDE feels real. But is it *actually* real?

Asking the question in this form makes it obvious that there is a problem in talking about 'reality'. It is a problem that is often ignored. If you join IANDS, the International Association for Near-Death Studies, you will be sent a little leaflet asking three or four key questions about the NDE – including, of course, 'Is it real?' The implication seems to be that it is.

A recent issue of their newsletter *Vital Signs* ends with a quote – 'What becomes clear is the inescapable conclusion that a near-death experience is a very real phenomenon' (September 1991 p. 6). By contrast, any theorist who talks about hallucinations is taken to be implying that the NDE is 'not real'. Such comments as 'the near-death experience is a complex hallucinatory phenomenon in people who perceive death as imminent' (1) or Siegel's conclusion that 'the experience of life after death doesn't lead to a "real" other world' (216 p. 75) are taken as implying that the NDE is 'not real' and thereby denigrating it. Investigator of children's NDEs, Melvin Morse, says of a fellow researcher, 'It was finally clear to me that he had missed the most obvious explanation of all – NDEs are real' (223 p. 243).

But what do these people mean by asking whether the NDE is 'real'? There are at least three distinctions they might be making.

Firstly, there is the question whether an individual person really did have such and such an experience. This is difficult to answer for any particular case because of course people can make things up or exaggerate them. However, with all the many stories now accumulated from across different ages and cultures it is clear that many people do have NDEs. In general we can answer this question 'Yes'.

Secondly, there is the question whether the experiences felt real, or were experienced as though they were real. For this, too, we have numerous descriptions like those above and again the answer must be 'Yes'.

Finally, there is the question of whether the things seen and events experienced during the NDE were part of an objective measurable world or whether they were products of the individual and private to them. This means contrasting 'real' with 'imaginary'. It is this that causes all the problems.

The problems lie not in making the distinction itself. After all, it is a distinction we have to make all the time to survive. The problem seems to be this: in our culture at least, the 'real' is associated with reliable, understandable, measurable, interesting and worthwhile while the 'imaginary' is associated with unreliable, illogical, crazy and worthless. An experience is only seen to be valid if it is real.

Children do not make such value judgements. I sometimes think we underestimate the insight of young children into the nature of fantasy and imagination. One day 3-year-old Emily was playing tea-time with some of her dollies and earnestly discussing whether Rosie would prefer orange juice or blackcurrant. 'Shall I fetch some from the kitchen?' I offered, thinking some real juice would be helpful. Emily looked at me with something close to contempt. 'Don't be stupid, Mummy,' she said. 'She's only a dolly.'

I used to enjoy the frequent discussions about God and heaven with my children and their friends. 'Well, it's not exactly in the sky,' they would say. 'It's not really anywhere.' 'Well, you can go there' or the logical 'If God made the world he'd have to have made himself first, wouldn't he!' While they are still too young to appreciate how seriously adults take their religion, children can still laugh at each other for believing the ridiculous and half believe it too. At five or six years old they can enter whole-heartedly into fantasy play and quite appreciate the folly of heaven as a place where you go when you are obviously dead and buried in the ground. They can entertain real, unreal and half-real worlds and play in all of them. That is, until they learn that only 'real' things are important.

NDEs are experienced as valuable, insightful and realistic and so to justify their obvious importance adults think they must be objectively 'real'. In other words they answer 'Yes' to the first two kinds of question and then think they must answer 'Yes' to the last as well. I think NDEs are real in the first two senses: they happen to people and they seem as real or more real than any experience. I think they are 'unreal' in the third sense; though still valid and life-changing.

To see how this helps us understand the NDE we need to ask quite a different question: what makes anything ever seem real? It is a difficult but not intractable question and one that will lead us on to the nature of consciousness and what happens to it near death.

But first, what do people usually mean when they say the NDE is real? Not often this, I trust . . .

REALITY IN OUTER SPACE

'Church Leaders Stunned' proclaimed a cutting in a recent Sunday magazine, 'Spacecraft Takes Photos of Heaven'. Lambeth Palace was apparently astounded by the fantastic photos taken by a Soviet space ship probing life on Pluto. Instead of craters and gases the photos showed a 'tremendous tunnel of light, billions of miles from Earth.' People who saw the pictures burst into tears at the sight of heaven and some were even left temporarily blinded by 'the fantastic frames that prove Heaven is for real'.

Locating heaven at a distance from earth is not just the stuff of cheap journalism but sometimes appears in occult lore too. Dr Douglas Baker, a British lecturer and teacher of 'astral projection' claims that after death we all inhabit the astral planes which stretch 200,000 miles from the surface of the planet. Worrying that this confined space might fill up with all the souls of the dead awaiting reincarnation, he claims that waiting times are getting shorter and shorter as the planet's population rises (4).

In these forms the ridiculous is obvious but it is harder to assess the more sophisticated theories of alternate realities.

ALTERNATE REALITIES

There are cosmic realms and dream-times, parallel universes and many other derivations from physics and psychology. All these are held to be 'other realities' that people can travel to in altered states of consciousness. To avoid the obvious problems of making these into concrete other places a slightly more subtle step is sometimes taken. This is to argue that the distinction into 'real' and 'imaginary' is false and that there is some third additional category. One author argues that we wrongly divide experiences into either real ones or 'products of fantasy, delusion, hoax or hallucination' (all words denigrating the imagination!) and offers instead a third 'imaginal' realm that 'in some sense truly exists outside time and space' (188). Such imaginal realms are found in many other fascinating accounts, such as the explorations and drug experiences of Carlos in his meetings with the Indian sorcerer Don Juan (31).

However, they are not really a third category at all. Any theory of this kind is asserting that the NDE is real in all three senses.

If we believe the proponents of any of these views then it makes sense to talk about experiences in 'another reality'. The job of the various theories is then to describe that reality and explain NDEs in terms of it. If they succeed they can end up concluding 'There you are, you see, the experiences were real.' Often they will add to this 'and the scientific establishment was wrong all along!'

I don't think it works and I don't think it is necessary to denigrate the private world of imagination this way. I have read many theories offering some kind of alternative reality where NDErs go. I don't think any of them makes any sense or can do the job of explaining the NDE.

This is a wide and sweeping dismissal but I believe it is justified, not least because all these theories start from confused assumptions about the difference between reality and imagination. Even so, many of these theories *are* fascinating and lead us into important questions about life and death. So I shall begin with one very popular example, the Holographic Universe.

THE HOLOGRAPHIC UNIVERSE

Foremost among holographic theorists is Kenneth Ring, whose early research on NDEs confirmed the nature of the core experience and began scientific exploration of the NDE. Ring contends that 'holographic theory may turn out to be one of the most significant intellectual developments in the history of modern thought' because it brings together science and mysticism in a common vision of the nature of the universe (182 p. 235). To understand why he says this we need to know more about holograms and their relevance to human memory.

A hologram is a way of making a three-dimensional image. When any object is illuminated the light is scattered off in different directions. It can be thought of as ripples spreading out in all directions. These ripples interfere with each other in ways that depend on the shape of the object and the wavelengths of the light. These patterns are extremely complex but are simpler if the object is illuminated by a laser.

It was the invention of the laser that made holograms possible. Lasers emit light that is coherent; that is, all vibrating in the same direction at once. To make a hologram of an object, say a face, it is illuminated with a laser beam. The beam is split into two; one half is bounced off the face and the other half is reflected back to meet it. The two beams then make interference patterns that can be stored on a photographic plate. The trick is that when the same laser light (or in some cases ordinary mixed light) is shone through the plate, the three-dimensional image is reconstituted and the face seems to appear again in space.

Holograms have some interesting properties. For example, if part of a normal photograph is cut away that part of the image is lost and the rest remains intact. You do not see a whole face any more. By contrast, if part of a hologram is cut away the image remains whole. It becomes fuzzy because information has been lost but it is degraded all over rather than in just one part. It may be a blurred face but it is still a whole face.

The comparison of a photograph with a hologram is analogous to the comparison of computer memory with human memory. In most types of digital computer, information is stored in discrete bits in specified locations. To call the information up you have to specify the location in which it is stored. If that part of the memory, in that location, is lost then the information in it is gone for ever but other information remains intact. When all the locations are used no more information can be stored.

Human memory, however, does not appear to work that way. For a start it appears to be enormous and never to 'fill up' even though it may become harder to learn things. Memories do not seem to be saved in specific locations at all but distributed all over the brain. When we forget it is as though the memories become weaker or more confused than they were before, rather than some being lost and others retained. Experiments with rats and other animals have revealed that removing part of the brain only weakens learned associations, it does not remove some and leave others intact.

Psychologists have long been puzzled about this. The search for the magic molecule that stored the information never led anywhere, though many scientists in the 1960s and early 1970s expected to find it. Meanwhile other ideas were tried.

One was the holographic theory of memory originally proposed by Karl Pribram, a neurosurgeon and neurophysiologist at Stanford University in California. Pribram suggested that the brain operates by analysing frequencies and storing their interference patterns much as a hologram does. He argued that this could help understand how human memory operates in a way that the digital computer analogy could not (174).

The appeal for psychologists was obvious but short-lived. Many felt that it was no more than a superficial analogy and it did not seem to solve the problems they had. Meanwhile, research into artificial intelligence, neuropsychology and physiology was progressing and soon took some important steps into what are now called neural networks.

The basic principle is that networks of interconnected neurons can store information in response to learning by changing the strengths of the connections between them. Rather than one neuron, or molecule, or part of a neuron, storing one bit of information, it is the whole network that changes. No one piece of information is stored in any one location and damage to the network results in a weakening of the associations learned rather than a loss of specific bits of information. In addition, the same network can store many different associations.

Research on neural networks now involves simulating them on digital computers as well as investigating brain function. Much of this work is still speculative but it appears to be the way that the study of memory is going. It seems to solve the problems about the associative nature of memory and the way it is distributed throughout the brain and is much more than just a nice analogy. So much so that it is already leading to important developments in artificial intelligence such as teaching robots to walk around unfamiliar places or handle objects. Artificial neural networks can learn associations and develop their own ways of discriminating different objects, and some think it may even lead to them learning natural languages – all skills thought impossible for computers until very recently. Pribram's holographic theory of memory has produced nothing like this.

Now what has this to do with NDEs? The answer is that the holographic theory appeals not to psychologists trying to understand memory but to people who want to explain the tunnel, the light, the OBE and the worlds beyond.

Mystics, as well as NDErs, often speak of time and space disappearing and of everything being a matter of light and different frequencies. Occult theories are often based on notions of 'higher' and 'purer' frequencies of vibration. The analogy with the light used in holograms forms a basis for the comparison with mystical experiences and from here Ring builds his holographic theory of the NDE. He argues that the NDE is a mystical experience that ushers one into the holographic domain. It is a new state of consciousness in a new order of reality. One is working in the frequency domain and in the frequency domain only densities of occurrences are important. Time and space are collapsed; locations irrelevant. The act of dying, according to Ring's new theory, 'involves a gradual shift of consciousness from the ordinary world of appearances to a holographic reality of pure frequencies. In this new reality, however, consciousness still functions holographically (without a brain, I must assume) to interpret these frequencies' (his parenthesis) (182 p. 237).

This may seem plausible at first glance and the analogy with mystical experiences is appealing. But there are two really fundamental errors.

The first is to misunderstand the term 'frequency domain'. This is a term used, for example, by visual scientists to refer to the range of frequencies to which cells respond. Some cells are responsive to spatial or temporal frequencies, and in talking about their behaviour visual scientists might refer to responses 'in the frequency domain'. Similarly they might speak about responses in the 'orientation domain' when cells respond to stimuli at different orientations. To give an analogy, we might talk about a painting in terms of its colours by saying we are analysing it in the colour domain. We could ignore all the spatial detail in the picture and simply concentrate on the colours it used. Space and time would therefore be irrelevant.

The frequency domain is more like an alternative way of describing something; an alternative view of the same world. It is *not* a different place or a separate world. It is not justified to base on it the idea of a separate 'holographic reality' or 'new order of reality' in the way Ring does.

The second error is to suggest that consciousness can function in this other reality without the brain. This not only implies that consciousness *goes* somewhere else, it also stretches the holographic model a very long way from its origins. It began as a theory about brain function; a theory that suggested the brain operated on frequency analysis and holographic storage. It is an extreme, and as far as I can see quite unwarranted, leap to say that consciousness is something separate and can function without the brain that is supposed to be doing all this holographic analysis and storage.

Ring concludes that in the NDE access to the holographic reality becomes experientially available because consciousness is freed from its dependence on the physical body. Only close to death does one experience it directly. As he puts it himself, 'That is why core experiencers (and mystics generally) speak about their visions with such certitude and conviction, while those who haven't experienced this realm for themselves are left feeling skeptical or even indifferent' (182 p. 237). In other words, it is this that makes the NDE 'real'.

My dismissal of the holographic theories might still seem cavalier, especially since they seem to provide an insight into mystical experience generally. So a useful check is to measure up Ring's theory against our familiar criteria.

Does it account specifically for the features of the NDE? Not really. It provides no special reason why you should have a tunnel. The bright light is presumably 'explained' by analogy with the light used in holograms but nothing specific about its colour or appearance is accounted for. The OBE is 'explained' in the statement that consciousness is freed from its normal restraint but this accounts for none of the details of what OBEs are like. Paranormal aspects of the NDE are supposedly explained because consciousness has left the brain behind but this idea is not even a direct consequence of understanding the world or brain function as a hologram. The worlds beyond are presumably the worlds seen in the 'frequency domain' but this idea neither makes sense nor specifies what this domain should be like. I do not think this approach deals specifically with the details of the core experience. Its main claim is to explain why it seems real and even this it does not do effectively.

Does it have to invent new worlds ad hoc? Yes, it does; the 'holographic reality of pure frequencies'.

Does it make any testable predictions? Ring does not discuss this directly but I do not think it does.

I conclude that the holographic theory does not do the job demanded of it. It has not proved itself useful in psychology and it is nothing more than a superficially pleasing analogy when it comes to understanding the NDE.

THE MYSTICAL VIEW

I have rejected holographic theory as helpful for understanding NDEs and would now like to discuss its relevance more generally to mystical experience. I have been using this term as though it were self-evident what a mystical experience is. In fact it is not easy to define and one of the problems comes from the fact that it is difficult for people who have these experiences even to describe them. The experiences are often ineffable. Nevertheless, there are some common themes. Oneness is the most obvious. People often describe a sense of certainty that the universe is one, including themselves and all the objects in it now and for ever. Space and time seem largely irrelevant, even though an order of events may still be apparent. Love seems to spring naturally out of everything, as though from oneness comes universal love. From this vision, priorities can be changed for ever and a person's attitudes towards death, self and others altered.

Such experiences can come about entirely unexpectedly in the midst of ordinary life; through prayer, fasting, meditation or, as we have already seen, through taking such drugs as nitrous oxide, LSD or mescaline. Whatever their origin, they carry with them a conviction of rightness, that this is how it is and this is somehow more real than the rest of ordinary life.

Nearly a century ago one man described it like this:

Next comes the sensation that the body is just as much a part of the environment as anything else, and it is perhaps this sensation which ... drives him to think that at last the solution of the mystery is dawning upon him. My own experiences under ether I shall never forget ... it seemed to me in the nature of things that I could never know reality. Then it dawned upon me that the only logical position was subjective idealism, and, therefore, my experience must be reality. Then by degrees I began to realize that I was the One, and the universe of which I was the principle was balancing itself into completeness.

(54)

I recently had a letter from an ex-minister of religion who had read something of my work on NDEs. He described a mystical experience he had whilst 'in the theological wilderness'. He had taken LSD and reports

> The experience carried utter conviction of my unity with all things that ever were or will be. It changed my life, and gave a backcloth to the whole of living. I realize now that all is a manifestation of Ultimate Reality, to which, as Koestler and Russell suggested, we will return.

Like NDEs, these experiences carry with them the sense of rightness, or being obviously 'real'. One of the appeals of the holographic theory is that it seems to account for the quality of mystical experience by pointing out that we live in a constructed world; that all the objects of our familiar experience are constructed holographically by our brains. The ordinary world of appearances is not solid, given, self-existing fact. It is a world of illusion or, to use the Hindu term, *maya*. Underlying this is another interconnected realm out of which these experiences are constructed. In the case of the holographic theory they are constructed from the interference of frequencies.

There are other theories that try to do a similar thing. A good example is Bohm's theory of the implicate order (26). A physicist at London's Birkbeck College, David Bohm developed his ideas as a way of dealing with the fragmentation and confusion apparent in particle physics. This physics regarded the universe as made up of particles which were not really particles but also waves and which could only be described by equations and not in terms of a satisfactory world view. Bohm argued that we could not dispense with an overall world view. He proposed that underlying the explicate order, or world of manifest appearances, there is an implicate order. All the structures which make up the world of appearances unfold out of the enfolded implicate order. All that ever was or will be is, in some sense, already there in a timeless and spaceless other order. He talks about unbroken wholeness in flowing movement, for in the implicate order the totality of existence is enfolded within each region of space (and time). So whatever part, element, or aspect we may abstract in thought, this still enfolds the whole and is therefore intrinsically related to the totality from which it has been abstracted.

Ring quotes Pribram as follows:

As a way of looking at consciousness, holographic theory is much closer to mystical and Eastern philosophy. It will take a while for people to become comfortable with an order of reality other than the world of appearances. But it seems to me that some of the mystical experiences people have described for millennia begin to make some scientific sense. They bespeak the possibility of tapping into that order of reality that is behind the world of appearances.

(182 p. 237)

In this way both Pribram's holographic theory and Bohm's implicate order propose an underlying order out of which the world of objects manifests itself. In both cases this underlying order is an unbroken flowing whole, or oneness, out of which separate objects or thoughts come into being. From this point they take the same three steps (although it is often others who do this in the most extreme ways).

Firstly, they conclude that mystical experiences are seeing through the illusion that the ordinary world is 'real'. Secondly, they conclude that they are therefore a glimpse or direct vision of an underlying reality and, thirdly, they conclude that if everything is, underneath, connected to everything else, then paranormal events are explained.

These three arguments are often mixed up, as though they are the same, or as though one follows from the other. Claims of miracles worked by mystics and true visions in mystical states seem to confirm the connection between the mystical vision and paranormal events. But there is no real connection here.

I want to consider the three steps of the argument separately to see which are helpful and which are not. The basic principle is very simple – that the world of appearances is a constructed one. Indeed, I believe this is the heart of the mystical insight. However, the two further arguments do not necessarily follow from it. And although the insight can follow from either Bohm's or Pribram's theories, it follows equally well from many other views of the universe. So one does not need to adopt either of them to share it. Moreover, a more conventional approach to brain function can, I believe, do even better in laying the foundation for understanding mystical experience and without adding on any 'underlying reality' or paranormal phenomena. I shall work backwards and try to demolish both these unwarranted steps before coming back to the basic idea of a world of constructed appearances.

PARANORMAL PHENOMENA (NOT) EXPLAINED

Theories of alternate realities and the like appear to explain the paranormal by positing an underlying interconnected reality from which everything else arises. But it is appearance only. They cannot adequately explain telepathy, clairvoyance, seeing at a distance during an OBE or psychokinesis (effects of mind over matter). Let us take Bohm's theory as an example.

Bohm claims that underlying the explicate order is a totally interconnected implicate order. Every part of that implicate order is enfolded in every region of the explicate order. Some people have taken this to imply that from any region of the universe one could contact any other; that is, telepathy or clairvoyance are possible. Or that one could think something here and now and, through the connections in the implicate, affect something at a vast distance in space and time, i.e. psychokinesis.

Psychologist Stanislav Grof (88) suggests that certain states of consciousness could mediate not only direct experience of the implicate order but also intervention in it. Talbot (223) goes furthest by proclaiming that in addition to psychokinetically moving objects around, the mind may also be able to reach down and reprogram the cosmic motion picture projector that created those objects in the first place ... the mind could alter and reshape the material world in ways far more dramatic than even psychokinesis implies.

Like Ring, they are both assuming a kind of dualist theory of mind – that mind is something separate from matter and can jump in and intervene in the world.

None of this follows from the idea of objects unfolding from an implicate order or from a holographic domain. To become manifest the underlying order has to be revealed. It does this through some kind of process: in the case of holograms through the reconstruction of the original forms from the interference patterns; in the case of the explicate order from the unfolding of the implicate in each region of the universe. One cannot see what a hologram represents except by passing light through it. One cannot see events at a distance in the explicate except by unfolding the implicate here and now into its present form. So the other events are still distant, whether or not their implicate form is essentially everywhere at once. That paranormal communication is still not allowed is made abundantly clear in a recent book honouring the work of David Bohm. It explains that the quantum field may be non-locally connected but 'it can be shown that no signal connecting distant events instantaneously is possible . . .' (94 p. 17). In other words telepathy, clairvoyance and psychokinesis are not explained at all.

THROUGH THE ILLUSION

Having rejected the argument for the paranormal, we are now down to two steps: that the world of appearances is a constructed illusion and that once you have seen through the illusion you can see the underlying reality.

Even if the first statement is true, the second is both unnecessary and misleading. It implies dualism. It implies that consciousness is a separate thing that can look into a new reality. It implies that this reality can be seen independently of construction; that although all our normal experience is 'unreal', this mystical glimpse is 'really real'. This seems to me to be having one's cake and eating it; accepting the difficult insight that all of experience is constructed, without letting go of the idea that somewhere something *is* 'real' and we can get hold of it and 'really' know about it. However, we cannot since anything we 'got hold of' would be part of our experience and also constructed. So we should not – and cannot – take this step. We are now down to just one: the idea that the world of appearances is a constructed illusion.

The joke is that psychologists have been saying this for decades but no one seemed to take on this discovery as though they really believed it; perhaps because it is so hard to accept and so much easier to think there is something else that is 'really real'. I do not think there is. So, I shall present an alternative view of how we construct reality. This builds on much of contemporary cognitive psychology and requires no 'other worlds' or 'underlying realities'. It faces up to the mystical insights and accounts for why the NDE seems so real.

As I have just mentioned, psychologists have known for decades that the world we live in is a constructed one. This became clearer with research into perception during the 1960s. In a classic book, *Eye and Brain*, Bristol psychologist Richard Gregory (77) used visual illusions as a way of explaining. Even a very simple figure gives us many clues (see Figure 8). It is obviously just a few black lines and yet if we look at it for a few minutes we cannot help seeing patterns and even movement and colours in it.

They are obviously illusory and yet we go on seeing them. Even a few dots roughly equally spaced can show how much we try to find pattern in everything. They seem to join together into groups or lines of their own accord (see Figure 9). According to Gregory these effects occur because the brain is trying to build hypotheses about the world – in other words, to construct a 'reality' on the basis of the information gained through the senses. And once we have found what seems to be a stable pat-

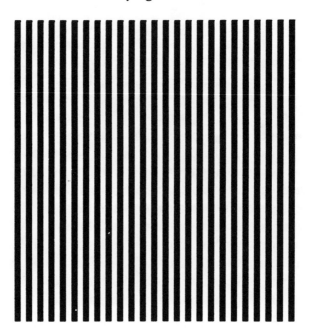

Figure 8.

Figure 9.

tern it is hard to lose it. Can you see any meaning in Figure 10? If you can you will find it hard not to see it ever afterwards.

Some figures have been extensively used by psychologists to explore the way these constructions are made. If the most probable solution is that there is one object blocking out another behind it, that is what we seem to see, even if the illusion is created by a few little pie shapes (Figure 11). The outline of the object in front can even be 'seen' and is said to have 'illusory con-

Figure 10. Is there meaning in this picture?*

tours'. In Figure 12a a set of eight odd-shaped figures are seen. You might try to interpret them as letters but they do not hang together at all. If a few more lines are added, suddenly the figure appears in perspective (12b). There are bars in front and a cube behind. The bars can even be made by taking lines away and leaving illusory contours (12c) and the cube still looks whole.

An even stranger effect can be produced by illusory contours.

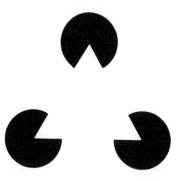

Figure 11.

* Can you read the words 'No Meaning'?

Figure 12.

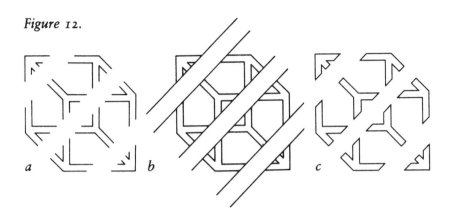

a   b   c

In Figure 13 the cube is transformed into an impossible cube! All these show how strong is our need to interpret what we see as 'real' objects.

Some pictures appear quite different upside down. When they are the right way up we bring to bear all our assumptions about what they represent but upside down we can see them more clearly as patterns and less clearly as objects or people. This is why it can be such fun to copy a drawing upside down. If your drawing skills are, like most people's, far from proficient try copying a photograph upside down. It is a shock to discover how well you can do – presumably because you are not distracted by what you think you ought to draw.

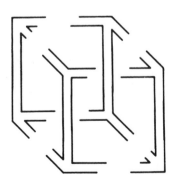

Figure 13.

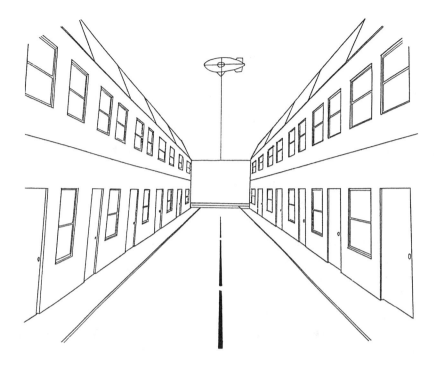

Figure 14.

Simpler still, try to copy the angles of the radiating lines in Figure 14 (leave out the windows and doors). You may well find that you make enormous errors. Turn the picture upside down so that it no longer looks so much like a street and you will probably do better. This led me to wonder whether meditators would do better at this drawing task, on the principle that they have learned to let go of the obvious interpretation and see things more 'as they are'. In a study at Bristol University we found that more experienced meditators made less errors with the upright pictures (23). This might be one rather simple way of discovering how people see through their constructed illusions.

Of course, I have been talking about only two-dimensional figures and yet the world we experience is three-dimensional. In fact, it is the search for three-dimensional structure that gives rise to some illusions. When any part of a figure is interpreted

as nearer than another the automatic constancy mechanisms of
the brain act to reduce the apparent size of the one in front. This
is clearly the best explanation of the famous Ponzo Illusion in
Figure 15, where the upper horizontal line really would be longer
if both were lying on the ground between a pair of railway lines.
Once again, we cannot consciously over-rule our visual systems.
They get on with the job of trying to build a world out of messy,
complicated and incomplete information, whether we want them
to or not.

There are other kinds of illusion too. In just the same way I
think our brain's attempt to make sense of the world produces
'psychic illusions', by which I mean experiences we think are
paranormal when they are not. For example, a chance coinci-
dence may appear 'too good to be true' and so we think there
must be an explanation. If we cannot find one we conclude it
must be paranormal (24).

I may have belaboured the point about illusions somewhat
but they are interesting. By looking at ways in which a system
fails we can learn a great deal about its function. In the case of
vision, the 'failures' of illusions reveal how very efficient the

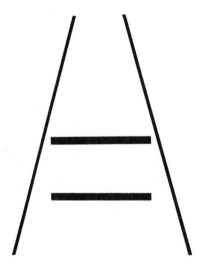

Figure 15.

system is at constructing a three-dimensional world out of a two-dimensional retinal image. They show that the solid world we perceive is constructed. In the case of psychic illusions they show how good the system is at trying to make sense of its world, even when events are purely random.

In the past decade or so, the study of vision has taken great steps forward. The analogy of the brain with a computer has had its problems but has also lead to treating perception in terms of information processing. This lies at the heart of cognitive science, an interdisciplinary approach in which psychologists, computer scientists, mathematicians and logicians try to understand not only how computers can manipulate information so as to interact with the world but how the human brain does so.

This approach, apart from solving innumerable small problems and making artificial vision close to a reality, has solved one of the classic problems in the psychology of vision, a problem recognized right at the start of psychology more than a hundred years ago. If we think of the eye as a camera (which it certainly resembles in many ways) then we are inclined to think that it sends a picture up into the brain. What in the brain looks at this picture? Well, another sort of 'inner eye', I suppose. And how does this inner eye see? Well, it sends a picture . . . and so on. This is known as the homunculus problem because it implies a little person, or homunculus, sitting in the brain looking at the pictures. Either the homunculus has a kind of psychic eye to see with, or there is an infinite regress into a series of homunculi. Either way the problem of understanding perception is not solved.

It *is* solved by the approach of cognitive science. At the moment computers and humans do their tasks in completely different ways but the underlying principle is still the same. Information processing systems can interpret input information so as to interact with the world. It is usually said that they build models or representations of the world. So, the robot walking around a room has to be programmed with or to learn for itself a representation of that room. Only then can it successfully move itself around. Similarly brains build representations of their worlds and of their bodies so that they too can successfully get around.

There is no need for that homunculus. There is no infinite regress. Right from the start of the process of perception, the sensory information is transformed, processed and stored as connection strengths between neurons, in ways that result in successful behaviour. There is a direct throughway from input to output with parallel processing all along the way. There is no ultimate central place, no little woman sitting in the middle and looking out, no little person controlling the actions of the body. There is only a system building models.

MENTAL MODELS

The notions of representation and mental models are central to cognitive science (108). Although some philosophers think the ideas are deeply misleading, recent research is actually making them less and less mysterious. Dramatic developments have been taking place in the field of neural nets. The idea is that nerve cells are connected up into multilayered networks in which the strengths of the connections between the cells change in response to learning. Nets simulated in computers can learn to make discriminations and respond appropriately to new input. They do not need to be told rules for distinguishing things, they can find out ways for themselves from the input they are given. In other words they are building up representations of their world. This approach has revolutionized the study of classic problems in psychology such as how we recognize faces, learn new tasks or see the similarity between a pigeon, an ostrich and Donald Duck (32).

Does our entire world then depend on descriptions of this sort, stored in the connections between brain cells? I think so. I think our brains simply build models of us in the world and that is what makes our 'reality'. Reality is simply a vast set of mental models.

WHO AM I?

If everything experienced is mental models, who or what am I? Presumably 'I' am one of those mental models; a model of a self who appears to be in charge and to 'inhabit' this body. Just as the robot must have a representation of its own 'body' with its wheels and grippers and the position of its television camera, so must I (this brain-based information processing system) have a model of 'myself'. 'I' am no more and no less than a mental model.

This makes it clear that we can use the term 'I' in two senses that are normally confused; I the physical person, the whole system of body–brain, and 'I' the mental model it constructs. To make things clearer I shall refer to these as I and 'I'. In other words, people (systems) construct 'selves' (models). I build 'I'. My brain builds 'me'.

Does this help us understand who or what we are and why we are conscious and seem to live in a real world? Can it explain why some things seem real to me and some not or why I am conscious of some things and not others? Does it provide answers to questions such as – who has NDEs? why do they seem so real? who dies? It does. I have answers to these questions which, unlike all that I have been saying so far, go somewhat beyond what is commonly accepted in cognitive science or psychology, but they are answers that will help us greatly in understanding the NDE.

CONSCIOUSNESS

First we need to ask why some of the models in my system are conscious and some not. My answer is that consciousness is just the subjective aspect of all this modelling. It is how it feels to be a mental model. Of course, 'I' am only one of the models. For all I know all the other models in the system may be equally conscious but they are not conscious of me. Since 'I' am probably the most complex and intricate model being built by my brain

'I' do have some kind of special status but not by being anything essentially different from the others. The only thing that makes any of them conscious to me is being made a part of 'me'. In other words any model that is linked up to or made a part of the self-model automatically becomes conscious to 'me'. All the other mental models being used in the system are unconscious to 'me'.

I am not a special being inside the head directing attention to one thing or another. Rather 'I' am just one of many models built by this system and 'my' awareness is just a product of the way that system builds its model of reality. The model describes 'me' as a separate being, perceiving the world, making decisions and acting independently. Actually that is all illusion too.

This is very difficult to accept but I think it may be true.

WHAT SEEMS REAL?

We may now ask why it is that some models seem real to me and some do not. The system must be building multiple models of all sorts of possible and impossible things and yet only what we take to be the world 'out there' seems real.

My answer is that the brain has to decide which are real and which are imagined and treat them accordingly. Its job is to model an external world with a self in it. It also has to try out possible actions in the imagination and manipulate ideas in dreams and fantasies so as to be able to predict its future actions and those of other creatures around it. To do this successfully it must have a clear idea of which of the models are the experimental ones and which represent 'out there'.

This job is, like the whole of perception, not as easy as it sounds. It might seem that what is real is obvious. After all, it is 'out there' and the information comes in through the eyes and ears and goes to the brain. Surely the brain should know which models have come in that way and which have been invented out of memory and imagination. This is not so. Right from the start of visual processing the information coming in through the eyes is mixed with information from memory. You can only 'see' a cat the way you do because you have seen cats before and have a wealth of knowledge about animals, black objects, chairs and cushions, shadows and textures. The cat perceived, that mental model of your favourite pet lying asleep, is a complicated mixture of input and construction from memory. The brain cannot say 'That came from the eyes so it is real.'

What it can do is check up on any model to see how it behaves. A model that stays there for a long time, that successfully predicts future input from the eyes and ears, that keeps track of plausible movements and so on, is a model that is likely to be based on the world 'out there'. A model that keeps on changing, that can be a black cat one moment and a bird the next, is likely to be an imaginary one. So my proposal is quite simple: that the system takes the most stable of its models and attributes to it the status of 'real'. Our 'reality' at any time is the brain's collection of stable mental models built largely out of sensory input and integrated to form a model of self in the world. It is, if you like, a 'me-now model'. It describes me and my place in an apparently real world.

And is there a real world out there? Well, if we adopt this view we can never know. We assume there is in the way we talk about brains and what they do. But it is only an assumption – a useful working model. It is just another of those ubiquitous mental models. Indeed everything we experience, including ourselves, is a mental model. Every attitude or belief we hold about an outside world or about anything at all, is a description in a mental model. This is all we have. Indeed, it is all we are.

This is where we come back to the notion of alternate realities. From this point of view there can be no alternate realities. Whatever underlies the world of appearances is unknown and unknowable. Any attempt to describe it is creating more mental models, not penetrating into any underlying reality. The best we can say is that it is the formless, the unknowable ground or the void. And even this might be just another mental model.

I said that this theory would be better able to account for mystical experiences and the 'realness' of the NDE. Is it? Both

Bohm's and Pribram's theories, and many others like them, claim that the world of appearances is an illusion and that in mystical experiences one sees through to the underlying reality. My view shares with them the idea that the world is all illusion, or *maya*, but differs from them over the underlying reality. It is not that I propose a totally different underlying reality. Rather that there is not one. Once you see that all 'you' are is a collection of mental models, you see the illusion. Imagine you can see through that illusion to an underlying reality and all you will see is more models of reality – more illusion. Mystical insight is not having a great psychic self that can penetrate through illusion to ultimate reality. Rather it is simply not needing to construct either 'self' *or* 'reality'.

LIVING IN ILLUSION

To do science, to control the world, to predict what will happen, we need to assume there is a world and we need to construct space and time. But all we can ever experience, in mystical states or ordinary having-a-cup-of-coffee states, are mental models. There is nothing beyond this that can be known.

This idea can be just too horrible to accept and we will go to enormous lengths to invent something more substantial to hang on to. 'If I see through this there must be something more!' or 'Now I understand the creation of illusion, I can see the"real" thing.' I believe all these attempts are missing the truly scary truth: that there is nothing substantial to hang on to – not even oneself.

I think this way of seeing things is well expressed in the Buddhist notion of form and emptiness. Behind all forms lies emptiness – not lack of something, but emptiness. Form and emptiness are both aspects of each other. If you try to hang on to form you will find only emptiness. If you try to hang on to emptiness you will keep on finding form. The Buddhist *Heart Sutra* tells of the Bodhisattva Avalokitesvara, a follower of the Buddha, who one day perceived that all sensory experiences are empty. In this way he transcended all suffering. His realization is explained like this: Form is precisely emptiness and emptiness precisely form. So also are sensation, perception, volition and consciousness. Although the language is entirely different and we cannot enter into the assumptions of the people it was written for, I think this is what I have been saying about sensation, perception, volition and consciousness, based on contemporary cognitive psychology.

It was for intellectual reasons that I came to this view but it has strange effects on how you live life. If there is nothing to hang on to, if self is just another model, then experiencing the world is different from the way it is when you live in the illusion that there is a real world out there, or even that there is an underlying reality which can be found. This way there is nothing to find and no self to find it. The only path is just going on being one model after another.

When I was struggling very hard with this I met Baba Ram Dass. Once a successful psychologist, Richard Alpert, he had many experiences with drugs and studied with gurus in the East before becoming a teacher himself. When I met him I was confused. I felt the certainty that so commonly comes with some kinds of insight, and with some NDEs, and yet the implications for living life seemed impossible. I told him about it. He said simply, 'Aha, and you know it's much worse even than that.' Oddly enough this was the most comforting thing he could have said.

And what about NDEs? Who experiences them and who dies?

If there is no underlying reality then the NDE, like every other experience, is a matter of the mental models being constructed by the brain at the time. Therefore to understand the NDE we need to understand the mental models created by the dying brain. To understand why it seems so real we have to see why it is that the brain attributes reality status to those models. To understand who dies we have to ask what model of self was being constructed at the time.

In fact, we have already completed some of this task. We have seen why it is that the brain creates tunnels and bright lights when it is dying or under stress. We can now add that with random firing in the visual cortex and little sensory input, the tunnel form may well be the brain's most stable model of reality at the time. So that is why it seems so real.

This means we can answer the question put at the beginning of the chapter, 'Is the NDE real?'. In the first two senses 'Yes', in the third sense 'No': it happens, it seems real, but the experiences are actually mental constructions.

At the start of this chapter I mentioned the experience of a New Zealander with a congenital heart defect. He had been setting off to go 'tramping' in the bush with friends when he had an accident and was taken to hospital where his heart stopped for about thirty seconds. Yet in his experience he went on with the long walk. He says

> I know that what I thought had happened couldn't have. Yet for many years, it was the most real thing that ever happened to me. Yes, far more real and vivid than any real-life incident. It was so real, detailed and so vivid and consistent (except for the wood smoke); in fact so totally un-dream-like! I actually walked most of those one and a half hours in my mind and conducted lucid conversations. If I had experienced something which could have been even remotely possible, then absolutely nothing would convince me that it was all a dream.
>
> I know how real the experience of 'death' can be. If I were a religious person, then when I felt my heart stopping and having time to prepare myself, I no doubt would have taken an appropriate religious trip. As it was, I'm a tramper, so I went tramping instead!

8

In or Out of the Body?

I did have such an experience in June 1944, whilst at Monty's HQ at Portsmouth, while waiting to land in Normandy with the 'Ultra' network (the outfit which conveyed the secret information to our commanders, derived from the code-breakers at Bletchley Park, StnX.) I was the radio mechanic, serving a group of radio trucks, which would land to receive and transmit 'Ultra' to and from the British and American commanders.

I had the task of checking out regularly the radio equipment and the mobile generators supplying AC to the trucks. On a very wet day – and being diverted by buzz bombs heading our way – I started up a mobile generator supplying high current AC. The mobile generator had an open-ended supply plug, supplying 250V to each truck. I groped in the wet grass for the plug, forgetting it was 'live'! I caught it between the fourth and fifth finger and received a massive electric shock. Whilst still on my feet I had the effects of the voltage – a feeling of being a huge vibrating bear. I managed to let out a cry for help then went on my back in the wet grass – and blacked out.

Here beginneth the surprising experience. Although unable to see, hear or move as the current surged through me to earth I was still able to think. Then suddenly I was floating above my body linked to it by what appeared to be a shimmering cord. I was looking down on myself laying in the grass – with the smoke wreathing up from my fingers as the flesh was burnt away. I looked down on the trucks – and the tent in which my radio operator colleagues were playing cards. I was quite peaceful floating some 15 feet above and could think clearly and observe everything. I clearly remember thinking the following: 'Oh God! here I am dead and I've not even landed! I wonder what Mum will say? I wonder if I'll have a nice funeral and be buried under one of those white stones? I'm not having this!' I willed one of the lads in the tent to quit playing cards and pull the plug out of my hand. Nothing happened and I thought, 'Ah well . . . it's time to go,' and I lifted higher until I was about 25 feet high. Then Corporal Tommy Hitt came out of the tent. I could 'see' his mouth open as he yelled for the others in the tent; I couldn't hear him but saw his mouth open. Then he got hold of the cable and yanked the plug out of my hand. The others spilled out of the tent, got a blanket and rolled me in it. Then Hitt went into the tent and cranked the line telephone to HQ.

I was still blissfully floating above and although there seemed to be a gentle force pulling me away, I was so intrigued that I resisted. A few moments later – it seemed – a 'blood wagon' raced up the sandy road and across the grass. An MO got out and ran over. I noticed the Medical Corps insignia on the battledress, that he had three pips – and as he bent over me I saw he had a bald patch on top. I came down lower to 'see' better: he used a stethoscope, yanking my battle blouse and shirt wide; then he thumped my chest in the approved way, listened again then filled a syringe and plunged it in. Up above I winced then laughed – of course I couldn't feel it! Then he listened again, shook his head and put the blanket over my face. I shouted to him, 'Hey! I'm up here – I'm not dead!' Then the orderly and the lads put me on a stretcher and carried me down the slope towards the ambulance. I didn't want my body to go without me so the 'cord' shortened and I slammed back into my body – and blackness again.

As they carried me I began to hear – far off – the sound of birds singing. It became louder until I could hear everything clearly. Then a spot of light appeared like the end of a tunnel; it widened and grew until I could see – but although I fought to move, not a muscle responded. Then I felt a tingle in my fingertips, which spread up the arms and legs then my body.

I sat up on the stretcher, waved my arms wildly and shouted with joy. The MO, walking in front, turned with a startled look as if he'd seen a ghost, then ran up, pressed me down, wrapped the red blanket around me and said, 'Don't move – we'll have you in hospital in a few minutes!'

In hospital he was examined and his burns were dressed. A week later the consultant told him he could go back to his unit.

'By the way, Corporal,' said the consultant, 'you might be interested to know that the MO pronounced you clinically dead! No heartbeat, no reflexes, not a sign of life. We're all puzzled you recovered; doesn't happen often! You know, one is only supposed to die once!'

He went back to his unit and asked his friends what had happened and they confirmed that it was Tommy Hitt who had dashed out and pulled the plug from his hand and had rung for help. 'How did you know?' Tommy had asked. 'You were out cold.' He asked them if the MO had been a captain with a bald spot on his head but they said they'd been too concerned to notice. Later, however, he carefully questioned others and was told that the MO did have a bald patch and that it could only be seen from above. He asked what the ambulance numberplate had been and nobody could remember, but on a visit to the field hospital to have his fingers dressed he checked the ambulances in the park and, 'There it was – the same serial number I'd written down.'

He went on

I did not tell them of my seeing everything from above; I knew they wouldn't believe me! . . . When I look back over all these years and begin to believe I imagined it all I only have to feel the third and fourth fingers of my left hand, with the healed depressions of the burn wounds!

This story was told to me by a retired engineer who had been a radio and radar technician during his war service from 1940 to 1946. Once again, it did not seem like imagination but 'reality'.

'He' seemed to leave his body and be perfectly conscious outside it.

According to Ring the OBE, or what he calls body separation, is the second stage of the core NDE and involves a sense of detachment from one's physical body. He found it occurring in 37 per cent of his cases (182). Moody also gives many examples. One woman with heart trouble heard the nurses shouting 'Code Pink!' as she felt herself moving out of her body, down between the mattress and the bedrail and then up to a position (typical of OBEs) just below the ceiling. From there, feeling like 'a piece of paper that someone had blown up to the ceiling', she watched the resuscitation. As she saw them beating on her chest and rubbing her arms and legs she thought, 'Why are they going to so much trouble? I'm just fine now' (133 p. 36).

Others react differently, with confusion or fear. Some desperately want to get back to their bodies and do not know how. Some are convinced they must already be dead. Some react with indifference to the sight of their own body, others with surprise at how it looks. Moody gives another example . . .

Boy, I sure didn't realize that I looked like that! You know, I'm only used to seeing myself in pictures or from the front in a mirror, and both of those look flat. But all of a sudden there I – or my body – was and I could see it. I could definitely see it, full view, from about five feet away. It took me a few moments to recognize myself.

(133 p. 39)

What is it that has, apparently, left the physical body? Moody reports that the vast majority of his respondents claimed to have had some other kind of body that left the physical; often a kind of replica or double. It is usually described as something like the traditional ghost: weightless and greyish-silver in colour, more or less transparent and unable to affect anything. Any attempt to turn on a light, for example, results in the duplicate hand passing straight through the light switch. In the same way this out-of-body self is able to pass through any object, walls included.

Although Moody claimed that most NDErs have a duplicate body this has not been found by other researchers. Green (75), in a classic study of OBEs, found that most were 'asomatic' or without a second body. Ring found the same for his NDE cases. Most were not aware of a second body but rather felt as though just their mind or self was out of the body.

There are other strange powers claimed for this new state. Vision and hearing are said to be more powerful and clearer than usual. Some NDErs are baffled that they can see so far and hear so acutely. Some even get the impression that they could see all round at once or hear anything anywhere if they wished to – a sense of limitlessness (154, 133).

All this may sound as though it could only happen near death but in fact, like every other aspect of the NDE, it can occur in many other situations. Many surveys have been carried out to find out how many people have had OBEs. Most researchers have simply given people questionnaires and it is difficult to be sure from a ticked answer to a question just what experience they had. Nevertheless, there is plenty of evidence to suggest that about 15 to 20 per cent of the general population have had an OBE at some time during their life (13, 15, 160).

The people who have OBEs are just as likely to be male or female, educated or uneducated, religious or not religious (though having the OBE may increase the tendency towards non-traditional religion) (67). Some commentators have suggested that OBEs are evidence of psychiatric disorder and have likened the OBE to quite different phenomena such as depersonalization (a state in which oneself seems unreal) or autoscopy (in which one sees a double outside of oneself rather than leaving the physical as a double). It is depressing how often people who have OBEs say they feared to tell anyone about it in case they were thought to be going mad.

Fortunately there is clear evidence that having an OBE does not mean you are going mad – in fact it is rather the reverse. I found that schizophrenics reported the same proportion of OBEs as did a control group of non-psychiatric hospital patients (19). Gabbard and Twemlow (67) in their study of over 300 people who reported OBEs found that they were generally well adjusted with low levels of alcohol and drug abuse and no sign of psychotic thinking.

Some drugs are associated with OBEs; for example, the psychedelics – LSD, psilocybin and mescaline. More specific, however, is the dissociative anaesthetic ketamine which often induces feelings of floating and even dying (87, 195). I have had OBEs myself with this drug, though not as vivid as naturally occurring ones.

OBEs occurring in daily life tend to happen when the person is resting, about to fall asleep, or meditating, but they can also happen in the midst of ordinary activity. Celia Green describes one poor woman who seemed to be sitting on the roof of her car the entire way through her driving test, unable to get back in and 'watching the body part of me making every sort of fool of myself that one could possibly manage in a limited time' (75 p. 64). In another case a priest gave a sermon while feeling as though he were watching the whole proceedings from the far end of the church, and other OBEs have been reported by people acting in a play, riding motorbikes or walking along the road (13). These appear at first sight to be quite unrelated activities with nothing in common but they are all, like coming close to death, conditions that can set off an OBE.

The 'everyday' OBEs are usually very brief, being estimated to last only a few seconds in most cases. The experiencers usually feel as though they can travel anywhere and see anything they wish. In most cases they seem to have another complete body, a sort of double, although in some cases there is just something like a disembodied awareness, or awareness of being at a certain spot but without anything visible being there. The whole experience is usually described as extremely vivid and real – in fact, just like the NDE. Also like the NDE, these experiences are often said to reduce the fear of death and to have a profound effect. In their comprehensive study of OBEs, Gabbard and Twemlow found that many OBErs viewed their OBE as a spiritual experience and were more likely to believe in life after death thereafter (67).

Some people thoroughly enjoy their OBEs and would love to be able to have them more often. Some gain a certain amount of control over where they go and what they see. Some can even induce them at will. There are many books describing the techniques available (194, 93). These range from simple imagery and relaxation methods to complicated regimes involving special diets and sensory isolation. Even so, they all share some common features. To teach yourself to have an OBE you need to be able to relax, withdraw from the sensory impressions coming from the world around you and somehow imagine you are leaving the body. Really all the various methods are variations on this theme.

You might wonder why people would go to such lengths to teach themselves to have OBEs and the answer is that it is a wonderful feeling. At its best it is like flying in a world of incredible beauty and vitality. It can be changed more or less at will and explored by thinking oneself around. However, it is not always like that. Some OBErs find the experience terrifying. Some fear that they are dying or that they will never be able to return to their bodies. From time to time I am called on to help people who have frightening OBEs and want me to teach them how to stop having them. Of course, whether their fears are grounded or not, and how best to deal with them, depends on your view of the OBE. Does something really leave the body – in which case it might actually become separated, stranded, or lost in another dimension? Or is the OBE an experience created by the imagination, in which case one is dealing with the contents of one's own mind and there is no need to fear getting lost because nothing has actually left?

DOES ANYTHING LEAVE THE BODY?

There is no doubt which view is the most popular among NDE researchers. Moody, for example, talks about the double as though it is something that actually leaves the physical body. He calls it the 'spiritual body' and describes its powers as ones to be envied by a spy! For him, the self is something separate from the body and therefore able to leave it. Melvin Morse, in spite of his interest in brain mechanisms, still believes there may be something that survives death. He suggests that there is a part of the brain responsible for NDEs not because the brain alone creates them but because 'such an area represents the seat of the soul, the area of our brain that serves as a trigger point for the release of the soul at death' (139).

Kenneth Ring, as we have already seen, considers the OBE crucial to the core experience. For him, the entire NDE is experienced by the person out of the body. Even the first stage of peace is part of this. He says

> The first two stages actually represent an out-of-body experience, whether or not the individual is aware of it. That is, I believe that what happens when an individual is near the point of apparent death is a *real*, and not just a subjective *separation* of 'something' . . . from the physical body. It is this 'something' that then perceives the immediate physical environment and then goes on to experience events outside of the time-space coordinates of ordinary sensory reality.
>
> (182 p. 221)

Ring is implicitly comparing his theory with one that claims the OBE is just imagination or 'subjective only'. Of course, it is easy to call the OBE imagination but we need to go further than this and construct a valid alternative to theories of souls, spirits or astral bodies. As before, it should be a theory which will account for the specific details of the OBE, avoid invoking any unexplained extra entities or worlds and make testable predictions. Can our theory do this?

MODELS OF REALITY

The essence of my theory so far is that whatever seems real at any time is the most stable model of reality we have. In normal states of consciousness there is a central model of 'me' in the world – a 'me-now' model. It is because this is the best and most stable model at the time that it is usually taken to be 'reality'.

This might prompt us to ask whether there are times when we 'get it wrong', when the normal, sensory-based model of reality breaks down. Perhaps like visual illusions or psychic illusions there are also 'illusions of reality', when the system makes the wrong decision or builds a model of reality that does not work very well. When might this happen? It is by asking this question that we can understand the out-of-body experience.

The normal model of reality is based on sensory information of two main kinds. Firstly, there is all the information coming in to the brain from the outside through the ears, nose, eyes, skin and so on. From this a model of the world is built up that serves very well for us to get around. It appears detailed, accurate and comprehensive but in fact we know that a lot of it is invented; gaps are filled in and plausible bits are created.

The example often given to illustrate this is the 'blind spot'. In the retina at the back of the eye there is one spot where all the fibres from the light-sensitive cells pass out to form the optic nerve. This spot is blind and yet we are not aware that it exists at all. It seems that our brains fill in the missing details. Recent experiments have even shown that this entails an active creation of missing information rather than just ignoring the gap (177).

This process is obviously necessary if we are to perceive a coherent world without wasting too much brain power on processing every detail. The brain can make a lot of assumptions, make the best of limited data and build a complicated world from the bare bones. Only when something surprising happens need it pay more attention and get the details right. In this way we are able to live in what appears to be a real world 'out there' but is actually a construction built up with a lot of guesswork.

The other part of the normal model of reality is the body

image or body schema. This is built up from internal senses which detect the position of our own bodies. It is constantly updated as we move about and keeps track of all our joint and muscle movements. If we did not have this continually changing model of our own bodies we could not accurately move, touch things or respond to anything.

It is also responsible for the sense that 'I' am in my body. This point is interesting and highly relevant to the OBE. If we want to understand how 'I' can apparently get *out* of my body we need to understand why it is that 'I' usually seem to be *in* it. Part of the answer is that building a model from eye-level view is the most efficient way of making use of the information coming in from our predominant sense. Blind people report feeling they are in their fingertips when reading braille. Drivers even wince when something comes close to the bumper and duck when a low branch threatens the roof. It can only be a guess, but I imagine that dogs are more inclined to feel they are inside their noses than we are. So exactly where 'we' are depends on what we are doing.

Another part of the answer concerns what 'we' are able to control. It is the ability to control events that gives rise to a sense of self. This is something most modern children are thoroughly familiar with. Confronted with a new video game the first thing they ask is 'Where am I?' The screen may be full of little green and pink illusory creatures moving about in incredibly complicated ways. But there is only one we are tempted to think of as 'I', the one which moves in response to the keyboard or paddles.

The new technology of virtual realities takes this a step further (179). A virtual reality is a computer-created world in which 'you' can move about as though it were real. A normal computer game can only be controlled with limited means like a keyboard. In a virtual reality what you see changes realistically as you move your head or body. For example, you might be provided with a special helmet which not only displays a computer-created world to your eyes but detects your head movements so that it moves as you do. Add a device that detects your movements back and forth as you walk or turn round and you have a world that changes realistically as you walk about in it. Then add data gloves. These are special gloves that detect your finger movements and relay the information to the computer. It can then change what you see and even give nudges to the skin of your hands so that the 'virtual' hand appears to be your hand. And it seems real. It could be blue, green or pitted with glowing nodules but it will still seem like 'you'. The control that virtual reality gives you creates a 'you' that feels real.

This created 'you' is no more than information being processed in a computer. In the same way the 'you' of our ordinary life is information being processed by our brains. The position where 'I' seem to be depends on the viewpoint of the eyes that take in the information and the parts of the world that can be directly controlled, like fingers, feet and lips. There really is nothing sitting outside the head looking out.

Back now to the normal model of reality. It is a conglomerate of the body image and a model of the outside world. It is a very useful model of reality.

We can now ask that crucial question: when would this model of reality break down?

THE BREAKDOWN

The answer is now quite clear. This model depends on sensory information from inside and outside the body. It will break down when that information is inadequate to construct a plausible model of the world and a coherent body image. So when will this happen?

There are several possibilities. Closing your eyes in a quiet room will not be enough. Vision is lost but there is still the basis for a good body image. Meditation is more effective. Sitting very still for long periods will reduce the body image. All the senses give up responding when the input does not change. Most extreme is vision, which fades altogether if images are kept perfectly still on the retina. Something similar is true of the body sense or somatosensory input. If it does not change we give up feeling it. In this way the body image can become confused.

It can also become confused more actively if wrong information is given. Some techniques to induce OBEs use just this sort of trick. For instance, the 'Christos Technique' entails massaging the head and feet while imagining that you are stretching out and contracting again and again (73). This will confuse the body image and help it break down.

Finally, certain drugs will do the trick. Hallucinogens such as LSD, psilocybin or mescaline can produce sensory distortions that disrupt the stable model of external reality, and distortions of the body image such as limbs growing incredibly long or the whole body expanding or shrinking. Ketamine, on the other hand, is an anaesthetic that at high doses paralyses without abolishing awareness. This reduces the body image or dissociates it from muscular control. I shall never forget my own ketamine experience, the extraordinary sensation of watching the floating parts of a body that seemed to have nothing to do with 'me' coming in and out of vision as 'I' seemed to drift about away from them. These are, of course, the very drugs that cause OBEs.

And near death? Here the body image will also break down but for various different reasons. It may be lack of input, confusion through pain, injury and actual physical distortion; it may be that the brain is no longer capable of building a good body image even if it had the information because it is ceasing to function properly. So already we have the beginning of an answer to what all these conditions have in common – the breakdown of the body image.

There is then the breakdown of the rest of the model of reality – the outside world. Again, cutting off sensory input will be one way and confusing it another. The monotonous input from riding a motorbike or driving on a motorway may confuse the model just as meditating perfectly immobile can. The confused input of a car crash or near-drowning may disrupt it and the dying brain may be unable to sustain a good model. In all these cases we have the answer we need: that the normal model of reality will break down under all these conditions.

What then? What would we expect to happen when the normal model of reality can no longer be sustained? I have already argued that what seems real at any time is the best model we have. Now this model of self in the world is no longer the best model. It is no longer stable and effective. What will take over?

I suppose any other model might take over – anything you are thinking about at the time. But this would mean hallucinating and could be very dangerous for a biological organism that wants to survive.

So what should it do instead? Clearly, if it wants to keep functioning effectively, it must try to keep a hold on reality. It must try to maintain a sense of self in a real world. But this is difficult. What can it do? I suggest that one possibility is to try to get back to normal by using whatever information is available to build a body image and a world. If the sensory input is cut off or confused this information will have to come from memory and imagination. Memory can supply all the information about your body, what it looks like, how it feels and so on. It can also supply a good picture of the world. 'Where was I? Oh yes, I was lying in the road after that car hit me.'

However, there is one crucial thing we know about memory images. They are often built in a bird's-eye view (147). Siegel (214) uses a good example. Recall the last time you were walking along the seashore. Do you see the beach as though from where your eyes would be? Or are you looking from above? Many people recall such scenes in a kind of bird's-eye view. It seems likely, therefore, that in the event of nearly dying, or any other circumstance in which the normal model of reality has broken down, such a bird's-eye memory model may take over as 'real'.

At last we have a simple theory of the OBE. The normal model of reality breaks down and the system tries to get back to normal by building a new model from memory and imagination. If this model is in a bird's-eye view, then an OBE takes place.

ASSESSING THE THEORY

How well does this theory do at accounting for the phenomena? It certainly explains why the OBE seems so real. It is real in the same sense that anything is ever real. That is, the new OB model of reality is the best the system has at the time.

There are many other details that need explaining. There are the sensations of leaving, the fact that the double nearly always seems to be above the physical looking down, its transparency and ability to travel. There is the fact that many OBErs do not have a double at all but simply seem to be looking from a new position in space. There is the appearance of the world in this state, with the added ability to see through things, round corners and long distances. Any theory must also be able to account for when and why the OBE occurs: what is there about relaxing or meditating at home, taking a driving test or riding a motorbike for long hours that is in common with nearly dying? Finally, there are the claims that people when OB see things they could not possibly have known about. Can our theory account for all this?

It easily accounts for the way the world looks and the fact that apparently correct details are often mixed with ones that are obviously false. The system has simply put together the best information it has, some accurate and some not, in the same way as it normally fills in gaps and makes plausible guesses to make a coherent world.

It also accounts for the transparency and glowing appearance of the other world. Memory images are not solid things but are much more fleeting and variable than the sensory world. They are also transparent. Try to imagine your own house and see whether you can move around in it. You will find that in your imagination you can move from room to room, passing through walls like a ghost. Objects seem more stylized than in real life and colours, if you bother to include them at all, less subtle. Of course, it does not seem real, unlike the OBE, because at the moment you have a good body image while you try this. However, the imagined house is much like the OB world in other respects.

In the OBE you actually feel that 'you' are at the imagined point. This makes sense because it is this imagined world that you control. You can no longer control the actual body because you no longer have a good body image. Instead you have either a new body image, outside the physical, created by memory, or you are just a moving position, moving as imagination takes you. In either case, 'you' will seem to be at that location because that is what can be controlled by what you (the system) are thinking about. Think about your own physical body lying in a hospital bed and that is what you will 'see', think about your best friends or your loved ones and you may set off on a trip through your own mind to find them.

The means of travelling is also the same. In your imagination you can move through your house slowly, from point to point, you can whizz through it quickly, streaming through the corridors and walls, or you can simply hop from one point to the next in a kind of magic jump. These three possibilities correspond exactly to the 'three moving speeds' that classic 'astral projection' authors Sylvan Muldoon and Hereward Carrington described (140). They argued that once the astral body has left the physical it can move about in these different ways in the astral world simply by the power of thought. As they put it, 'thought creates in the astral ... In fact, the whole astral world is governed by thought' (140 p. 46). I suggest that thought governs the astral because the entire astral world is a creation of the imagination; a mental model.

Why should people be surprised at seeing themselves as others see them? This is often given as evidence that the OBE cannot be imagination. However, this does not follow. You may have gathered lots of information about yourself, about that bald patch from combing your hair every morning, for example, or that straight long back from stretching it every day, but you may never have put it all together as though looking from above before. When this happens it is unfamiliar and you think 'Wow, is that how I appear to others?' Finally, what all these different conditions have in common is that they destabilize the normal body image and allow another to take over.

This theory of the OBE therefore accounts well for the phenomena described and it does so without inventing any new

worlds, alternate realities, souls, spirits, other bodies or independent selves. Does it make any predictions that allow it to be
tested?

It does and some have been tested. Harvey Irwin, an Australian researcher who has proposed a related theory of the OBE
(101), has done many experiments to try to understand the
experience. When psychological theories of the OBE were first
proposed by parapsychologist John Palmer (159), by Irwin (101)
and myself (16), it was suggested that people with vivid imagery
would be more likely to have OBEs. This was found not to be
the case, suggesting that OBEs are not imagination. However,
since then it has been found that OBErs have superior spatial
abilities; for example, they are better at detecting the viewpoint
from which a three-dimensional object is seen (37) and are better
able to switch viewpoints in their imagination (19).

This relationship with imagery is complicated by the difference
between deliberate and spontaneous OBEs. According to this
theory, to induce an OBE at will takes skills of dissociation from
the normal model and the construction and control of a new
one. On the other hand, if the OBE is induced by external events,
such as being near death, then these skills are not required. So
we should expect correlations with imagery ability for people
having OBEs intentionally or in meditation and so on, but not
in NDEs. In my own experiments I found that dream control
skills were higher in people having deliberate OBEs (17) and
Gabbard and Twemlow found that 'absorption' is higher in
NDErs than other OBErs.

Another prediction concerns the habitual use of bird's-eye
viewpoints. This theory predicts that people who habitually
imagine things or dream in a bird's-eye view should be more
likely to have OBEs (whether deliberate or spontaneous). Both
Irwin and I have found this correlation for dreaming but not for
waking imagery. That is, people who dream in bird's-eye view
or see themselves in their dreams are more likely to have OBEs
(102, 21). However, this has only been tested for OBEs in general. It still needs testing for NDErs. The theory predicts that
NDErs who have OBEs as part of their experience should be

those who use bird's-eye views more in imagination and dreaming.

These are just some of the many predictions that arise from this theory of the OBE. So far the theory has done fairly well in correctly predicting such findings but there is much more research to be done.

What of the major alternatives? I do not think that any of them does very well at accounting for the phenomena, except by the entirely *ad hoc* argument that that is how things are in the astral world or the holographic domain or wherever the other body goes. Why should Moody's 'spiritual body' be transparent, greyish and able to see long distances? Presumably it is just that the person is freed from the constraints of the physical body but this still does not explain the details. Most difficult is to account for why some people have another body and some do not. Is this because some people while in their 'spiritual body' are unable to see it clearly? If so why? and who?

Similar problems face the holographic theory. It does not explain why there should be another body at all, what the self who has left is, or why it has these powers and not others. In general all theories that posit some other self that leaves the body have great difficulty accounting for specific details. It sounds all very well to say that OBEs are just what they seem to be – something leaving the body – but such a theory cannot answer obvious questions such as what that thing is, why it behaves the way it does, and why the world looks the way it does.

And predictions? Most 'something leaves' theories imply that whatever leaves should be detectable. Since the early psychic research of the 1880s and right up to the present there have been innumerable experiments trying to detect the astral body, the soul or the spirit. These have uniformly failed. Although there were some apparent successes at detecting a small weight loss at the moment of death (123) the experiments proved to have been inadequately controlled. Better designed modern experiments have lead to the conclusion that nothing can be reliably detected leaving the body during OBEs (135, 13).

Of course, the spirit or soul might be essentially undetectable but this further weakens the theory and makes it difficult to know what value it has. If whatever leaves is undetectable it follows that it cannot interact with the world. If it cannot interact with the world it could not be seeing it because taking information from the world entails interacting with it. So the theory then has to say that whatever has left is not actually in the same locality at all but in some spiritual or psychic realm, bringing it straight back to all the problems of alternate realities.

If this argument sounds a bit abstruse I think the gist of it was captured by my 7-year-old son's opinion of God's powers. 'It's silly,' he declared. 'If God's transparent then he can't see and feel things. So how can he lift up trees and stuff to put them there?'

This all relates to one crucial prediction that all the 'something leaves' theories share and that distinguishes them from all the psychological theories. They predict that people during OBEs or NDEs should be able to see things correctly at a distance. I predict that they should not. They would say that our engineer 'really' did see the MO with his bald patch and three pips; Tommy Hitt pulling the plug away and the ambulance with its correct numberplate. I would say it was a visual image created from guesswork and residual hearing and sight. They would say the events seemed real because they were real. I would say they seemed real because they were the most stable model available at the time.

And the evidence? There is plenty of evidence for the unreal seeming real and I have explained why it happens. On the other hand we have seen how hard it is to find evidence for the paranormal in NDEs. This case is no exception. The events happened too long ago to be verified now. As the evidence stands it suggests that nothing leaves the body in an OBE. OBEs, like the rest of the NDE, are constructions of the living – or dying – brain.

9

My Whole Life Flashed Before Me

Though the senses were ... deadened, not so the mind; its activity seemed to be invigorated, in a ratio which defies all description, for thought rose above thought with a rapidity of succession that is not only indescribable, but probably inconceivable by any one who has not himself been in a similar situation. The course of those thoughts I can even now in a great measure retrace ... a thousand other circumstances minutely associated with home, were the first series of reflections that occurred. They took then a wider range – our last cruise – a former voyage, and shipwreck – my school – the progress I had made there, and the time I had misspent – and even all my boyish pursuits and adventures. Thus, travelling backwards, every past incident of my life seemed to glance across my recollection in retrograde succession; not, however, in mere outline, as here stated, but the picture filled up with every minute and collateral feature. In short, the whole period of my existence seemed to be placed before me in a kind of panoramic review, and each act of it seemed to be accompanied by a consciousness of right or wrong, or by some reflection on its cause or its consequences.

(152 p. 182)

This very famous case is that of Sir Francis Beaufort who narrowly escaped drowning in Portsmouth Harbour in 1795. Have you ever heard the saying that when you drown 'your whole life flashes before you'? As a child on holiday at the age of eight or nine I can remember being fascinated by this idea and almost wanting to try it out by seeing if I could half drown in the sea.

But I knew I could not deliberately 'half-drown' and anyway I was terrified of the seaweed lurking deep down under the clear water.

It is true, however. And there are very many other cases of a 'life review'. Many NDErs report that, at some point during their experience, they watched, re-experienced or were shown a series of events in their life. Usually it is as though the dying person is a spectator, watching it all happen as if to someone else, but sometimes they seem to be reliving it from the inside. Almost always it is extraordinarily vivid and realistic. Usually it is also in bright colour, although not in every case. For example, Janis had a serious car accident and was in a coma. Later she told Kenneth Ring all about her life review which passed by in a flash, like a 35-millimetre film going 'click, click' in a split second; her whole life passing by precisely in order but in black and white (183 p. 61).

In her case the events went forwards, as they occurred – the opposite of Sir Francis's backwards review. For yet others the recollections do not flow in order at all but seem to be presented, somehow, all at once. There can be a strange sense of timelessness in which everything happens very fast although time is not passing, or a sense that there is not even any order to time any more. In another of Moody's cases the survivor describes how all his childhood thoughts were there 'at the end of this tunnel, just flashing in front of me'. He described it not as pictures but more like thoughts, all there at once. He thought about his mother and father and about things he had done wrong, especially mean little things done as a child: 'I wished that I hadn't done these things, and I wished I could go back and undo them' (133 p. 69). Although the person often seems to be watching the events at a distance they are not neutral or unemotional. Quite the reverse. Moody gives this as his 'representative account' of the life review.

When the light appeared, the first thing he said to me was 'What do you have to show me that you've done with your life?', or something to this effect. And that's when these flashbacks started. I thought, '. . . what is going on?', because, all of a sudden, I was back early in my childhood. And from then on, it was like I was walking from the time of my very early life, on through each year of my life, right up to the present.

(133 p. 66)

This woman went on to describe how she had been back in kindergarten and the Girl Scouts going camping; events in her school life and college. Everything came back in three dimensions and in colour but not from the viewpoint as she had experienced it at the time. Rather, she now saw it as though she were someone else watching the little girl grow up. 'Yet, it was me. I saw myself doing these things, as a child, and they were the exact same things I had done, because I remember them.'

For her, as for many others, the life review was an emotional and educational experience. The events did not seem to be chosen at random or neutrally. It was as though the 'Being of Light' had picked them out to teach her something. There were instances when she had been selfish to her sister and others when she had really shown love to her and shared with her. It was as though the light was showing her the value of learning from experience and the importance of helping others, but all without judgement or accusation.

Others report a similar life review but without the 'Being of Light'. In such cases it seems as if there is a self-judgement; not a judgement in the sense of adding up the rights and wrongs or meting out punishment, but in the sense of accepting what has happened and seeing more clearly its consequences for oneself and everyone else.

Whether this learning is given by some kind of 'being' or experienced alone, it takes place in love and light, and seems to transform the person's attitude towards their own life. One man who had a heart attack while raking leaves in front of his house felt that his life was laid bare to the presence of God. They communicated without words, by 'straight mental instantaneous communication'. He was asked what he had done to benefit or advance the human race. Experiencing his life passing before him, he began to understand what counted. As he puts it, 'What I had counted in life as unimportant was my salvation and what I thought was important was nil.'

In trying to understand the life review we must do justice to the insights it seems to bring. It is not just a matter of 'seeing your life flash before you'. It is seeing your life in a context; almost invariably a context of love and forgiveness. Seeing it this way changes a person's perspective and makes a real difference to their life afterwards.

It is tempting to see the life review as just another stage in the prototypical NDE, comparable to the tunnel or the out-of-body experience and requiring a separate theory. But a good theory must account not only for its occurrence but for its relationship to all these other features and its place in the person's life as a whole. So what would be a good theory? Perhaps the life review could be just a few memories occurring in the midst of other hallucinations, or perhaps a series of images wrongly felt to be familiar and therefore experienced as though they really happened. There are many possible interpretations of the life review, and many theories of its origin, from religious theories to biochemical ones. But before getting embroiled in them we need to find out more about the experience itself. How common is it, to whom does it happen and under what circumstances? For Moody it was a crucial and distinct part of the NDE but nearly twenty years on does it still look that way?

THE INCIDENCE OF THE LIFE REVIEW

First of all, the life review is not very common. In all the cases I have collected over the years I have never come across a classic life review. This is odd because most researchers seem to find them in about a quarter to a third of NDEs.

For example, in their analysis of 205 cases of people who had met with life-threatening danger, Noyes and Kletti (151) found sixty descriptions of panoramic memory (i.e. nearly 30 per cent). Only a slightly smaller proportion (about a quarter) were reported in Ring's sample (182). Greyson (81) found 22 per cent and Greyson and Stevenson (86) in their review of seventy-eight NDEs, found 27 per cent.

In Moody's classic scheme the life review comes after the tunnel, the out-of-body experience, the meeting with other beings and the 'Being of Light' but before the decision to return. Indeed, it is often bound up with the 'Being of Light' who seems to initiate the experience. For Ring, it is also bound up with meeting others and with the choice to go on or go back.

In those schemes that divide up the NDE into factors or subcomponents it is usually included with changes in thought or imagery. Greyson (81) placed it in his 'cognitive component' along with thoughts speeding up, time speeding up and a sudden feeling of understanding. In Noyes and Slymen's factor analysis (154) it came in the first of their three factors, the mystical factor, along with feelings of great understanding, revelation, joy and harmony, sharp and vivid images, colours and visions.

Other research has tried to find out which conditions are most likely to induce the experience. Given the old saying about drowning, it is interesting to learn that life reviews are most common in those who nearly drown. For example, Noyes and Slymen found that of all their subjects who came close to death, nearly half (47 per cent) of those who nearly drowned had 'revival of memories' while only 16 per cent of victims of falls did. The figures were in between for accidents and illness.

I have argued that some features of the NDE are specific to being medically close to death or taking certain drugs while others occur much more widely. Where does the life review fit into this scheme? Do you need to be near death to have a life review?

Moody gives several cases of life reviews in people who were not clinically dead or even close to it. One case, for example, involved a student doing a summer job driving a truck who fell asleep at the wheel. The next thing he knew was fear. The truck was going to hit a bridge. During the brief seconds the truck was skidding he thought of all the things he had done: little details of his school life, of breaking a new red wagon he was given for Christmas when he was five, of his job in a grocery store; things that he later decided would take him at least fifteen minutes to remember and picture to himself, but at the time all of them happened 'in less than a second'. Then it was over and he was standing looking at the truck. It was a total wreck but he did not receive a scratch (133 pp. 71–3).

Moody remarks that the life review can be with or without the 'Being of Light' but is usually more overwhelming when a 'Being' directs it. Nevertheless, it is usually very vivid and rapid regardless of whether the person is medically close to death or not.

Another way of approaching the same question is to look at research comparing NDEs with other OBEs that occur when not near death. In their study of hundreds of OBEs Gabbard, Twemlow and Jones (68) found no difference in the proportion that included peace and serenity or a life review, again implying that one does not need to be medically close to death.

A more directly relevant comparison to make is between NDErs who were genuinely close to dying and those who were not in serious danger. Again there is no difference in the proportion reporting life reviews (157). So we can safely conclude that the life review is part of that general package of experiences that can occur under many circumstances.

Thinking you are about to die is one of those circumstances and of course you do not need to be close to death in any immediate sense to start thinking about it. This might seem to imply a psychological function for having a life review, whether or not you are about to die.

A PSYCHOLOGICAL FUNCTION OF THE LIFE REVIEW?

It is often said that no one can bear to think about their own death. Of course, this is not entirely true. Many people do think about their own death and learning to do so with equanimity forms part of many spiritual practices. Nevertheless, it is certainly true that contemplating my own death is difficult and reveals a lot of resistance and clinging to what is familiar.

This is perhaps why one popular interpretation of the life review is that it is a kind of denial in response to the threat of death, a hallucinatory attempt to escape the reality of death or to go back to pleasant childhood memories instead (80, 100).

The best known exponents of this view have been the psychiatrists Russell Noyes and Roy Kletti. They treat the whole NDE as a kind of depersonalization (150, 152). This is actually a psychiatric condition in which the world appears strange, unreal, distant or dream-like. Things do not feel right and imagery is pale and lifeless. Emotions are flat and even the self becomes lifeless and unreal. This must surely be quite the opposite to the thoroughly 'life-full' experiences of NDErs. Many authors, and even Noyes and Kletti themselves, have remarked on the differences. Beyond this, however, they treat the life review as a form of denial of death.

'Just as the bereaved person clings to symbolic representations of departed loved ones, so the dying individual develops an attachment to memories, symbols of his own existence.' The dying person retreats into timelessness and memories to defend himself against death. As they put it

> In response to the threat of death, the endangered personality appeared to seek the safety of the timeless moment. There death ceased to exist as the person immersed himself in his experience. For that purpose, past experiences of a relatively timeless quality were restored to consciousness, especially blissful ones. Such moments were drawn largely from early childhood, when life was experienced with greatest intensity.
>
> (152 p. 192)

As always, we can ask whether this analysis leads to any testable predictions. It does, and they don't hold up. For example, we would expect the life review to contain mainly childhood images but we have already seen that some contain images from all phases of life. Perhaps more important is that for escapism or denial to be the function the experiences would have to be pleasant and this is certainly not always the case. It is as though they are meaningful and contain lessons to be learned rather than necessarily pleasant. A perhaps rather extreme example comes from the life review of a prisoner described in David Lorimer's *Whole in One*.

This prisoner was in acute pain after repeatedly eating soap to try to get himself transferred to the prison's hospital wing. The success of this attempt brought about something he had not bargained for. He went into a state of emotional and mental terror and a scroll or motion picture began to run before his vision. The only pictures on it were of all the people he had injured. He relived the minute history of his long criminal career. 'Apparently nothing was omitted in this nightmare of injuries, but the most terrifying thing about it was that every pang of suffering I had caused others was now felt by me as the scroll unwound itself' (121 p. 23).

For this man the panoramic life review was only the beginning of many weeks of further agonies, until eventually he came to terms with himself and his life and was able to imagine and remember both the hurt he had caused others and the hurt they had caused him with love and forgiveness.

Few life reviews are as demanding or as dramatic as this one but it serves to show that there can be much more to the experience than just escapism. Few people would choose to escape into a review of all their acts of cruelty or even petty thoughtlessness and unkindness. If the life review does serve a psychological function then I think it is a much more constructive one than mere denial or escape.

Anyone who seriously contemplates the idea of their own death is likely to start asking themselves some difficult questions. 'Who am I? What has my life been all about? Has it served any purpose at all?' One of the most obvious is to wonder 'What will remain of me when I am physically gone?' The prospect of a body in a coffin is not very pleasant to think about – or very relevant. And from the perspective of someone about to die, things like having mowed the lawn or washed the car, or even having written a book or built up a business from scratch seem oddly unimportant. From here it is a small step to wanting to reassess what you have done, to asking other, deeper questions about oneself. 'What have I meant to others – to my family, children, friends? What have I ever done for anyone else?'

As we get older it is natural to start asking these questions, whether death is pressing or not. This may be part of the reason why older people do so much reminiscing, to the irritation of the young who tend to think it is all irrelevant. After all – it's all in the past. It is easy to dismiss the obsession of the aged with the past as a negative trait, as regression, escapism, or as losing touch with life, just as Noyes and Kletti dismissed the life review of the NDE. However, both may serve the same, much more positive, function.

Psychiatrist Robert Butler has argued that reviewing one's life is a naturally occurring, universal mental process. It is not only natural but helps the older person to face up to all their unresolved conflicts and reintegrate them (28). As he points out, life reviews are also reported by the terminally ill and by prisoners condemned to death. So perhaps we should see all life reviews as a positive response to the threat of death.

Here again we can look for predictions. And there is some interesting evidence. First of all, if reviewing one's life is a response to the threat of death it ought to be more common in those who actually think they are going to die. Noyes and Kletti (151) found just this: that life reviews were more common in those who thought they were about to die, whether they were or not.

Next, if the life review serves a positive function then presumably it only has to be gone through until that function is fulfilled. If it were just denial one might go on denying death for ever – or until it finally happens. But if it is a constructive process, then once you have faced up to and dealt with all the problems from your past you no longer have that need. This implies that people who have long expected their death, such as those suffering from long illnesses, would already have had the chance to have reviewed their life and thought about death. So life reviews should be less common for them and more common in cases of unexpected near-death, such as accidents. This is indeed the case, as Ring found in his research (182). His findings suggest that it is the suddenness or unexpectedness of the near-death crisis that prompts the rapid life review.

The most extreme opposite of this must be the suicide case. There are some impulsive suicides, undertaken without much prior thought, but usually people who try to kill themselves have done a lot of thinking about the meaning of their life and the prospect of death as an alternative. Perhaps they should not need the life review (47, 182). Of Rosen's seven survivors of jumps from the San Francisco Bay bridges not one reported a life review. However, this point is not resolved because Ring and Franklin (189) found that nearly a quarter of thirty-six suicide attempters had a life review, not far short of the usual proportion in NDErs. So we cannot draw any very firm conclusions about this yet.

Another interesting comparison is with children. Presumably they do not have so many unresolved conflicts in their lives, so many deeds to cause pride or guilt, so many loves and losses, or so many unfulfilled ambitions and half-forgotten thoughts. For this reason we might expect them to have fewer life reviews. Precisely this difference between adult and childhood NDEs has been remarked on by Melvin Morse (137), by Gabbard and Twemlow (67) in their review of OBEs and by Nancy Bush, who reported seventeen cases of childhood NDEs (27).

All this evidence seems to suggest that the process of reviewing one's life is something that naturally occurs in anyone seriously facing up to the prospect of death; that it is a positive process and serves an important psychological function.

However, this does not provide a complete and adequate explanation. The life review that occurs in the NDE is different from other life reviews in some very important ways. It is not a gradual, well thought-out process, occurring over days or weeks. It is a rapid, realistic and fantastically vivid presentation of life in a moment. It is this aspect of the life review that demands special attention. It might be part of the explanation to say that the person with only seconds to live has to review their life pretty fast. The student with a second or two before his truck hit the bridge thought he only had that long to remember it all. But although this might provide the motivation it cannot, alone, explain how it is possible for an entire life to be apparently reviewed in a very short time or even 'all at once'.

Also, it happens in a very special context. It is sometimes orchestrated by a 'Being of Light'; it can lead on to other realms; and sometimes it ends with a kind of barrier and, finally, the choice of whether to go on or return.

THE POINT OF NO RETURN

I 'died' from a cardiac arrest, and, as I did, I suddenly found myself in a rolling field. It was beautiful, and everything was an intense green – a color unlike anything on earth. There was light – beautiful, uplifting light – all around me. I looked ahead of me, across the field, and I saw a fence. I started moving towards the fence and I saw a man on the other side of it, moving towards it as if to meet me. I wanted to reach him, but I felt myself being drawn back, irresistibly. As I did, I saw him, too, turn around and go back in the other direction, away from the fence.

(133 pp. 73–4)

Some NDErs encounter a visible barrier like this one. Moody gives another example in which the barrier was a large body of water and the woman, a nurse giving birth to her first child, found herself sailing across it towards the farther shore where all her dead relatives were waiting for her. They seemed to be beckoning to her to come on over to their side but she was saying 'No, No, I'm not ready to join you. I don't want to die. I'm not ready to go' (133 p. 74). In yet others the barrier has been a distinct line pointed out by a white light, a grey mist or a door with light shining round the edges of it (133). These are somewhat reminiscent of the medieval bridges across dangerous chasms.

Others find no tangible barrier but instead are told that they have to go back.

> My life started to flash before me. I felt embarrassed every time a stupid thing I had done came up. I sensed that the 'presence' was saying, 'Yes, you did these things, but you were learning at the same time.' It was then communicated to me that I should now go back. I didn't want to, but I understood that there was still a lot of work for me to do.
>
> (79 p. 82)

Yet others seem to confront a choice between going on into the light or coming back to life. This choice is a very strange kind of choice. We are used to making decisions in life. We tend to assume (rightly or wrongly) that we are some kind of autonomous being who has the free will to make choices. Sometimes we make them easily; often we struggle with them. Even more often we do things or say things without ever considering that a choice was being made. We simply get on with life. We rarely ask ourselves just who is making all these decisions. This final choice, however, challenges this assumption. When we try to understand it we shall confront a very difficult question. The decision seems to be a vital one – to live or to die. But who makes it? Any theory that claims to explain these last stages of the NDE will have to deal with perplexing questions like this.

THEORIES OF THE PANORAMIC LIFE REVIEW

How, then, is the rapidity and vividness of the life review and its relationship to other worlds, other beings and the decision to return, to be explained? As we have done before, we need to consider what makes a good theory. Firstly, a good theory is specific. In this case it needs to explain why memories are invoked during the NDE, why they occur in people who expect to die, are less common in long illnesses and why they take the form of a panoramic review. It must explain how the review can happen so fast or even 'all at once', why it takes the specific form it does and how it affects people afterwards.

Secondly, a good theory does not invent extra realms, 'other worlds' or new forces or energies without very good reason and without providing independent evidence that they exist. A theory that builds on well-understood principles is to be preferred to one that invents new ones *ad hoc*.

Finally, to be of any use, a theory must provide testable predictions so that it can be compared with any alternative theories by doing further research. It is on these general criteria that I shall judge the theories dealing with the last stages of the NDE.

There are, in fact, few theories that specifically deal with the life review, apart from the psychological ideas discussed above. Those that do fall mostly into two types: those we might call 'global memory' theories and those that look to processes in the dying brain.

LIGHT IN THE HOLOGRAM

One of the few theories that deals directly with the life review is Ring's holographic theory. In dealing with the last stages of the experience he considers first the light and the 'Being of Light' who often initiates the life review. The light, he claims, has two distinct aspects to it. The first aspect is the 'astral light'; a range of frequencies to which we are sensitive in a fourth dimension or holographic reality. This is closely related to his contention that the worlds explored in the NDE have their own reality, a primary reality in the 'frequency domain'. I have already explained some of the many problems this theory faces and they are as serious when it comes to talking about the light and the life review as they were when considering the OBE.

The other aspect to the light is rather different and concerns the 'Being of Light'. Ring points out that this presence is often identified as God and has the extraordinary powers of being all-knowing and able to communicate directly. Ring's suggestion is that this 'Being' is actually oneself. It is not the ordinary small self but one's higher self or total self. In ordinary life the self operates as though it were a separate entity but in fact it is invisibly tied to the larger self-structure of which it is a part.

Why is this an explanation of the light? Because this higher self is so awesome, loving and accepting, unlike one's normal self, that most people do not grasp that it is themselves at all. Nevertheless, that is why this being seems all-knowing and can initiate a review of one's life. As Ring puts it

> It manifests itself as a brilliant golden light, but it is actually oneself, in a higher form, that one is seeing . . . The golden light is actually a reflection of one's own inherent divine nature and symbolizes the higher self. The light one sees, then, is one's own.

> (182 pp. 240–1)

He goes on to explain that our higher self can initiate a life review and even a life preview. 'At this level, information is stored holographically and is experienced holographically – simultaneously or nearly so. In fact, the life review is a holographic phenomenon *par excellence*' (182 p. 241).

Let us consider the advantages and disadvantages of such a theory. It has some appealing aspects to it. It is nice to think of oneself as being essentially magnificent, golden, awesome, loving and unconditionally accepting (all Ring's words). It also makes a lot of sense to think of the 'Being' that has access to all one's memories as actually being oneself.

So far so good, but the problem is that with Ring's theory we have to take on board much more than this. Taken literally it implies that there is, in some other domain, an autonomous being called the higher self. It has some kind of separate existence and operates in a different plane. It has access to information which the small self cannot access; not just information that is beyond conscious reach, but information that would require paranormal powers to access. He even suggests that it can provide an accurate preview of the person's life ahead.

These are strong claims and I have already dealt with many of them and demonstrated that they make little sense.

We can also easily assess the theory against the general criteria. It does not do very well at the 'specific' test. For example, it cannot explain why the light is 'golden' rather than any other colour, nor even why it is a light at all. I think I could equally well argue that if my higher self is magnificent, awesome, loving and unconditionally accepting, it could manifest itself as a silver bird flying in a cloudless blue sky, the red and white of Father Christmas, an all-encompassing sense of warmth and comfort, a beautiful child with smiling eyes or many things other than a golden light.

Where the life review is concerned the comparison with the hologram looks superficially valid but, again, it does not do very well when it comes to specific details. For example, it cannot account for why the life review is more common in drowning than with other ways of nearly dying. It cannot explain why it is just as common in people who think they are dying even when they are not. Presumably it must be as easy to get propelled into the holographic reality by fear of death as by actual medical proximity to death but, if so, this theory does not specify why. Nor does it explain why the review sometimes goes forwards and sometimes backwards, sometimes is in colour and sometimes in black and white. In fact, it does extremely poorly when it comes to explaining specific details.

Its main success is, of course, in explaining how all the memories are there and present all at once. They are there in the holographic reality. However, any ordinary theory of memory storage implies that all memories are there, all at once, in the brain. It is converting them to a series of experiences that is hard to understand. This brings us to the second criterion. Ring's theory has to invoke another plane or 'holographic reality' in which the astral light shines, the higher self lives (and breathes?) and into which the 'separated consciousness' goes to experience its memories. But there is no independent evidence that such a domain exists. If memories were actually stored holographically it would help but, as we have seen, it is more likely that they are stored by the alteration of synapse strengths in neural networks and retrieved by the activation of those networks. So the holographic theory will have great difficulty in building on or relating to our understanding of brain function.

Finally, it makes no specific predictions that would allow it to be tested and compared with other theories.

The same can be said, for example, of author Gordon Greene's attempt to explain the NDE by recourse to a 'hyperspatial' journey into another dimension (76). It does not help just to invent other worlds and push all the problems into them.

What, though, of another – more serious – attempt to explain the NDE, this time by author David Lorimer, Chair of the UK International Association for Near-Death Studies?

RESONANCE, WHOLENESS AND INTERCONNECTEDNESS

Lorimer tries to break away from the narrow view that memory is just stored in individual brains and so to see the life review as an expansion of the individual into a realm in which all are one. This view of memory and consciousness has a long history. For example, early this century the French philosopher Henri Bergson (11) developed the idea that the brain is more of a filter or limiter than a creator of consciousness. Rather than the brain storing its own memories and producing consciousness, it recalls memories selectively from a much wider realm. According to this theory, telepathy becomes possible if there is a widening of the filter, and survival after death (at least of a non-personal kind) makes sense because once the filter is gone there is total memory or unified consciousness. Rather than perishing at death with the brain that created it, consciousness should expand at death beyond the brain that limited it.

Another more up-to-date version of a similar idea is Rupert Sheldrake's theory of 'morphic resonance'. In a book entitled *A New Science of Life* (213) he tries to explain everything, from the way trees develop similar forms to why scientific discoveries are often made by several people at the same time. 'Like influences like', according to his 'new science'. This is because of 'morphogenetic fields' which carry the influence of one form to any similar form. He uses this to try to explain some puzzles in the way organisms develop their structure, much to the dismay of many biologists. Moreover, the theory seems to make possible telepathy and clairvoyance as well as giving an entirely different meaning to memory. Memories need not be stored in individual brains but could be accessed by similarity to past events through morphic resonance.

The book received what some might consider the ultimate accolade by being called a 'book fit for burning' in the prestigious journal *Nature* (142). Nevertheless, the idea has, now as ever, a certain appeal. It seems to give a scientific basis to the idea that we are all connected; that each of us is not alone but part of a greater whole. Presumably this is why Lorimer calls his book *Whole in One*.

The idea is not workable. The main reason is that it is impossible to define similarity in a way that could make sense of the 'resonance'. What would have to be similar about two forms for them to set up the resonance? Their shape? Their size? If so, what about it? How small a deviation in angle, bumpiness, curvature or number of spots would disqualify a new form from resonating and would the strength of resonance depend more on shape than size, on straight lines rather than curves? Such questions cannot be answered by these theories.

This problem is reminiscent of a similar problem in understanding memory. As we have seen, psychologists have long struggled with the fact that human memory seems to work on similarity and association of ideas yet all the early chemical or digital computer models of memory could not easily deal with notions of similarity. This failure of psychology left the door open for theories such as Bergson's, Sheldrake's and many others (55, 175, 198). Indeed, I myself once found it so appealing that I developed my own theory of ESP and memory based on very similar arguments (12). I was unimpressed by contemporary theories of memory storage and thought that memory might be stored in some global way outside the individual and accessed by anyone under the right circumstances, so allowing for paranormal phenomena.

This idea is also unworkable and for the same reason: that similarity is fundamental to the theory yet remains undefined. Indeed, it was this, as well as my failure to find any paranormal phenomena, that caused me eventually to abandon it (18). Interestingly, the need for it is now also gone. With our increasing understanding of neural networks it is clear that a biological system can create its own notions of similarity on the basis of very simple principles. When a neural network learns to associate two patterns of firing with each other it is found that similar patterns will evoke similar responses in terms of the patterns of firing. Associative memory is at last beginning to make sense. A mystery might be solved. But the similarity is only internal to one system. There is no sense in which *my* idea of a house could be compared for similarity with *your* idea of a house. Our patterns of neural firing might be quite different and idiosyncratic to ourselves; only within one brain is the similarity meaningful. It seems more and more certain that memory is stored in individual brains and less and less likely that we need to argue for global memory in any form.

What, then, of Lorimer's theory? Just like Ring's, it is unspecific, it cannot account for the life review taking the precise form it does. It also needs to invoke other realms and dimensions for which is there is little, if any, independent corroboration. And predictions? It does not make any specific ones which would allow it to be tested against other theories.

For these reasons I reject all these approaches to the life review.

Of course, I can still appreciate that this kind of theory has a strong appeal. How can it be entirely wrong, then? Perhaps, you might argue, my criteria are wrong. Maybe we cannot apply the demands of specificity, parsimony, coherence or prediction to spiritual matters and the life review just *is* the expansion of the self into a holographic domain. Memory *is* connected beyond the individual. We *are* all one. Perhaps it is just that science does not yet understand and cannot deal with mystical truths.

I do not take such a defeatist view of science. Science is not a rigid set of dogmas and theories but a method of enquiry; at its best a completely open and flexible approach to trying to understand the world. I see no reason why it should not eventually explore spiritual matters as well as it has explored neurotransmitters, the chemistry of common salt or the life-cycle of the earth worm. However, if it is going to do so it needs to start by being clear about what has to be explained and what criteria are appropriate to judge its success. I reject Ring's and Lorimer's theories according to the criteria I have given, but that does not mean I must reject all their ideas. Perhaps the 'Being of Light' is myself. In fact, in any materialist view of the NDE it simply must be, because there is no other outside force or entity that it could be. Maybe at some level I am or could be magnificent, golden, awesome, loving and unconditionally accepting. Undoubtedly at some level we *are* all one, even if only in the sense that the universe is all one and the separations we make are part of the illusion we create for ourselves. The life review can be a spiritual experience but to agree to that does not mean also agreeing that it takes place in another 'spiritual realm'. What I need is a theory that can do justice to these ideas without invoking the unnecessary and unlikely realms of global memory and holographic reality.

Such a theory is possible. It can build on the understanding we have so far of the origin of NDEs. It starts with the role of the endorphins and takes us on to question the very nature of time and ourselves.

10

All At Once and Timeless

Specific memories: a trip to Yosemite or to Reading; a scene in her home; lying on a couch watching football; a particular telephone conversation; a chocolate coke she drank once in a small town . . . her brother's graduation from college and her son's first day in school.

(91 p. 92)

Everything's changing really fast, like pictures in a film, or television, just right in front of me. I am watching it happen right there.

(218 p. 116)

No – these are not more descriptions of NDEs. The first is a series of memories evoked by directly stimulating the exposed temporal lobe of one woman's brain. The second is a description of the way images flow fast and film-like when taking hallucinogenic drugs. It is clear that experiences resembling the NDE can be induced in other ways but is this enough to give us a real understanding of how the final stages of the NDE come about?

Our starting point is that the life review, like the experience of bliss and joy, is common to many situations. It is therefore unlikely to be induced specifically by anoxia and more likely to be induced by general factors, including the endorphins which are released in response to pain, fear and stress. So why should the endorphins lead to something as specific and meaningful as a life review?

ENDORPHINS AND THE TEMPORAL LOBE

Perhaps we need to recap a little on the endorphins. These are the morphine-like chemicals produced in the brain itself in times of pain and stress. They act on receptor cells in various brain areas and serve to modulate the brain's activity. Among their effects are pain reduction and feelings of euphoria and bliss. In chapter 5 I explained how these internally generated chemicals could induce the typical emotions of the NDE but why should they produce a life review?

The answer lies in another effect these substances have. They can set off seizures. This happens in two important areas of the brain, the limbic system and the temporal lobe of the cortex, which are the areas where the endorphins and their receptors are most commonly found. They are also, as previous researchers have pointed out, areas implicated in other experiences that are comparable to NDEs (139, 151, 202).

The limbic system includes structures in the midbrain, the hypothalamus, hippocampus, septum, amygdala and reticular formation. The functions of these areas are quite well known and are mostly concerned with such essential matters as regulating the sleep-wakefulness cycle; maintaining homoeostasis such as a constant temperature, or intake of food and drink; and in the control of emotion and motivation. These areas, or analogues of them, occur in many animals apart from humans and concern basic survival needs. In humans they have developed further and can be seen as contributing to the sense of self in its relationship to space and time.

In addition, the hippocampus is involved in memory. It is still not clearly understood exactly what its function is. Yet damage to the hippocampus, for example in Korsakoff's syndrome produced by chronic alcohol abuse, seems to prevent new memories being laid down even though it does not interfere with the retrieval of older memories. It may be that its role is in indexing or organizing memories. The hippocampus is also the most sensitive part of the brain to anoxia.

All these areas are rich in endorphins and enkephalins and in the receptor cells these chemicals act upon. Presumably it is here that they produce their emotional effects. But they also have another important effect, which is to reduce the seizure threshold.

It has long been known that morphine has this effect and more recently it has been confirmed that the endogenous opioids do too (229). The seizure threshold is the level of activity at which a group or area of cells will go into uncontrolled firing. The best known example of this kind of seizure is in epilepsy when a focus of damage can set off uncontrolled activity leading to epileptic fits. The form the epilepsy takes depends on the area of the brain that is affected. As far as the endorphins and enkephalins are concerned this means that when their levels are high there is an increased chance of seizures in the limbic system and associated temporal lobe.

The way this seizure activity is brought about is probably by disinhibition. It is known that enkephalins suppress neural activity in many brain areas but in the hippocampus they inhibit the action of cells that are themselves inhibitory. The result is disinhibition and an increase of activity leading to seizures.

It is interesting to compare this with the mechanism I suggested for the origin of the tunnel, namely disinhibition in the visual cortex brought about by the effects of anoxia. Here we have a similar disinhibition brought about by the effects of the stress-related endorphins and enkephalins. There may of course be other mechanisms having similar effects elsewhere. The difference is that the endorphins only affect certain brain areas. They are not found in large quantities in the visual cortex and so would not be expected to produce tunnel experiences directly.

We now have to find out what effects these seizures have in the affected areas. The answers come from three kinds of evidence: Firstly, there is epilepsy, secondly, studies of unstable temporal lobe activity and, thirdly, direct electrical stimulation of the brain.

THE SACRED DISEASE

In early Greek and Roman times epilepsy was thought to be sacred, possibly because of the mystical states and apparent insights that its sufferers sometimes report. It is an illness characterized by epileptic fits that can involve major convulsions and unconsciousness or brief periods of abnormal awareness, strange perceptions or feelings. They can range from frequent and highly damaging attacks, effectively ruining a person's life, to mild, barely noticeable or very infrequent episodes. Sometimes there is an epileptic 'aura' a sensation or series of sensations which precede the full-blown seizure and by which the patient can recognize that one is coming.

More than 2,000 years ago Hippocrates recognized that epilepsy was due to a physical abnormality of the brain and he even noted that convulsions on one side of the body can be set off by damage to the opposite side of the brain. It was only in the nineteenth century that brain functions were more effectively mapped and it was understood that different areas control different functions; in many cases those of the opposite side of the body. It is now recognized that there are many kinds of epilepsy, set off by different brain abnormalities. Some involve generalized abnormal activity while others start with abnormal firing in one specific location which then spreads to other parts of the brain. In one common form the epileptic focus is in the temporal lobe of the cortex or in closely associated limbic structures such as the amygdala and hippocampus. This is then known as temporal lobe epilepsy.

It is perhaps temporal lobe epilepsy that gives us the clearest insight into what may be happening in NDEs, since it is the limbic system and temporal lobe that are especially sensitive to the effects of endorphins.

Temporal lobe epilepsy takes many forms. For example, some people get strange feelings in their body such as pains, cramps, odd tastes, nausea or tickling sensations. Others suddenly begin automatic behaviours such as smacking their lips together or twitching repeatedly, or undergo disturbances of vision, distortions of colour, size or time and even illusions and fully formed hallucinations. Some epileptics experience sudden emotions such as anxiety, inexplicable fear, sadness, peace, or overwhelming happiness.

Perhaps most interesting from the point of view of NDEs is that some epileptics have sudden flashbacks of memories from their past. Many get feelings of *déjà vu* as though everything seems entirely familiar even though it is not (144). Some have out-of-body experiences and some even see apparitions of dead friends and relatives (128). Indeed, the Chilean neuroscientists Juan Saavedra-Aguilar and Juan Gomez-Jeria have developed a 'neurobiological model' of the NDE, suggesting that all the phenomena of the NDE occur because of abnormal functioning of similar parts of the brain to those involved in temporal lobe epilepsy (202).

Déjà vu is a most fascinating experience. Most people know what it feels like and have experienced it more than once in their lives (160). Suddenly everything is terribly familiar even though you may objectively know that you are in a place for the first time, or doing something very ordinary for which this extreme feeling of familiarity is inappropriate. It is difficult, when you have such a feeling, to understand it. It seems natural to look for an explanation. Some people think they must have dreamed of that very event before, which would entail precognition in dreams. Others wonder whether they have lived before and seen the place in a past life – though this never seems very convincing because most places would have changed dramatically in the interim, acquiring cars and televisions, sky-scrapers and digital watches. Others conclude they must have visited the place in an OBE and that is why it is familiar. In these and many other ways people try to make sense of their odd experiences and often assume that they must be paranormal (144).

It is difficult to find out whether such paranormal explanations are ever valid. However, it is certain that they are not usually necessary. The real explanation may be disappointingly prosaic. The feeling of familiarity, like many other feelings, appears to be controlled by neural activity in the limbic system. It is likely that when events really are familiar the hippocampus is activated and signals this fact. However, the same mechanism can be set off in abnormal activity and give rise to the sensation of familiarity without any actual recognition having taken place (91, 144). That abnormal activity is what occurs in epilepsy, direct brain stimulation and in NDEs.

But, you might object, I am not epileptic and have often experienced *déjà vu*. This is because many people have occasional spurious activity in these parts of the brain and research is only just beginning to reveal its implications.

TEMPORAL LOBE SIGNS

It may be that temporal lobe epileptics are not in a totally separate category from everyone else but rather that there is a continuum of temporal lobe instability. There may be many people who have unstable activity in their temporal lobes which never reaches the strength of epilepsy or causes obvious seizures but none the less affects their behaviour and experiences. These people are said to have varying degrees of temporal lobe signs.

Vernon Neppe, a South African psychologist, has made a special study of temporal lobe phenomena. He developed a questionnaire to assess what he calls 'possible temporal lobe symptoms'. These include not only having fits, blackouts, dizziness and severe headaches or migraines but things like 'losing control of yourself', having fluctuating moods, getting very tired even when you have had enough sleep, having difficulty concentrating, and attacks of inexplicable fear. Also included were *déjà vu*, feelings of unfamiliarity, odd feelings in the stomach, tastes, smells or other bodily sensations when there is no apparent cause, sometimes feeling that you are not quite yourself or you are watching yourself. Most people have some of these experiences from time to time and only the more severe of them are likely to be anything to worry about. The relevant point here is that people who have many of these experiences may have particularly unstable temporal lobe activity and this may help us understand the NDE.

Neppe hypothesized that many psychic experiences are actually set off by temporal lobe instability. He referred to prior research in which a group of twelve trance mediums were studied with the electroencephalogram and ten were found to have temporal lobe instability, even though none had epilepsy (143). Rather than getting embroiled in the difficult issue of whether any psychic experiences were genuinely paranormal, he then studied 'subjective paranormal experiences', in other words, any experiences perceived by the experiencer as being paranormal. These, he suggested, should be more commonly reported in people with more temporal lobe signs and this is exactly what he found (145). A similar relationship has been found by London neuropsychologist Peter Fenwick (59). Neppe also points out that some temporal lobe epileptics report having psychic experiences and are considerably upset when their medication puts an end to them! (146).

At the same time, a Canadian neuroscientist, Michael Persinger, developed an entire theory about the role of the temporal lobe in religious experience (168). He pointed out that the temporal lobe and its associated structures, especially the amygdala and hippocampus, are involved in memory, strong emotions and in the sense of self in time and space. It is activity in these areas, he argued, that is associated with the sense of deep meaningfulness, as well as recall of early memories and even out-of-body experiences. The more unstable the activity in a person's temporal lobe, the more liable they are to have such experiences, and everyone can be placed somewhere along a continuum from very stable to very unstable.

Persinger developed questionnaires to assess temporal lobe and epileptic-like signs. In several studies he found higher scores in people who reported more paranormal and mystical experiences (169) and in a group engaged in psychic studies (171). These experiences included telepathy and clairvoyance, a sense of 'presence', out-of-body experiences and precognition, as well as feelings of being close to a 'Universal Consciousness'(172).

To be sure that this really has anything to do with temporal lobe activity it was necessary to measure it directly. This he did by measuring the number of 'spikes' per minute in recording from the temporal lobe using an electroencephalogram, or EEG. A strong correlation was found between this activity and both temporal lobe signs and psychic experiences. No such correlation was found for activity in other brain areas (125).

An even more specific hypothesis is that the psychic and mystical experiences actually occur at the time of brief activity in this area. This is much harder to test, of course, since you cannot easily get someone to have a mystical or psychic experience at will. However, Persinger has gathered some very interesting evidence suggesting this may be true. Ten subjects meditated while their EEG was studied. It is known from much research that meditation is often associated with increased alpha waves in the EEG and sometimes with even slower theta activity (60). In this experiment one subject was a 32-year-old meditation teacher who had been meditating for about ten years. After about nearly twenty minutes of meditation Persinger noted clear delta frequencies, an unexpected spike in the recording and slow waves which lasted for about 15 to 20 seconds. This was seen on the temporal lobe electrodes only with no obvious changes in other areas. Afterwards she said that her experience had been especially meaningful and she had felt very close to 'the cosmic whole'. None of the other nine meditators had specially meaningful experiences nor did they show similar temporal lobe activity.

In another experiment a young woman who claimed she could 'speak in tongues' also had spikes in her temporal lobe during these episodes. Persinger concluded that religious experiences are natural correlates of temporal lobe activity, raising some very difficult questions about the interpretation of mystical and paranormal experiences, questions to which I shall return soon.

It is now clear that temporal lobe signs correlate with many experiences that occur in the NDE. This raises a most interesting possibility. I have already alluded to the puzzle that some people who come close to death have full core experiences while others, in apparently similar circumstances, experience nothing at all.

Perhaps it is those who already have more unstable temporal lobe activity who are more prone to having an NDE.

There is even some possible support for this idea in Greyson and Stevenson's finding (86) that their NDErs had had more mystical experiences prior to their NDE than the average population. Other researchers have also found that NDErs reported more OBEs, psychic experiences and intense spiritual experiences than non-NDErs (111, 225).

It is also interesting to think about Ring and Rosing's (190) 'NDE-prone personality'. This type of person, according to them, has more sensitivity to alternate realities, more childhood experiences with non-ordinary realities, claims more psychic and healing abilities, and scores higher on a measure of psychological dissociation. Perhaps these strangely assorted experiences now begin to fall into place. Persinger and his colleagues have found that scores on an inventory of childhood memories and imaginings correlate with both temporal lobe signs and the number of spikes per minute over the temporal lobes measured with the EEG (126). They also used a Dissociative Experiences Scale and this too correlated with temporal lobe signs (180). All this suggests a physiological basis for Ring and Rosing's NDE-prone personality. The connection is nothing to do with personality itself or people's ability to enter into alternative domains of reality but to do with temporal lobe instability (188).

Clearly this needs pursuing in further research. It would be most interesting to compare the number of temporal lobe signs in NDErs and in people who have come close to death but experienced nothing.

ELECTRICAL BRAIN STIMULATION

The pioneer of direct brain stimulation was Wilder Penfield, an American neurosurgeon. He was born in the 1890s and studied at Princeton and Oxford, where he was much influenced by the famous physiologist Sir Charles Sherrington. He went on to found the world renowned Montreal Neurological Institute and it was there that he pioneered new techniques in neurosurgery. But what really motivated him was a life-long quest to understand the 'mystery of the mind'. Brain research was the way to study it, he decided, 'if only one could deal with the human brain as Sherrington had analyzed the reflexes of the animal brain' (166 p. ix).

Much of experimental brain research seems to have little direct bearing on the study of the mind. We may learn about the interactions of neurotransmitters and the signalling of neurons but it is often frustratingly difficult to relate any of this to the mental events of our experience. Penfield's research, however, is an outstanding example of how probing the brain can directly induce unusual experiences.

In the 1930s Penfield was treating patients for epilepsy. This was well before the invention of the electroencephalogram which allows electrical activity in the brain to be picked up by electrodes on the scalp without ever getting close to the brain itself. Nowadays we have even better techniques which allow precise localization of activity, such as PET scanning and various other kinds of tomography. But before any of these were developed the only way to find out about brain activity directly was to open the brain up for surgery.

Of course, no scientist would carry out surgery just to find out about brain function. However, it could be explored during the course of necessary operations. Sometimes epilepsy is caused by scar tissue in the cortex; if this is removed the seizures can be stopped or reduced, and this is what Penfield tried to do. In the course of his surgery it was often necessary to stimulate different points on the brain's surface to find the appropriate place for the excision. The patient was only given a local anaesthetic on the scalp which is all that is needed since the brain itself is insensitive to pain. She or he could then be perfectly conscious during the operation and report on what was experienced. In this way Penfield was able to find out that stimulating some areas of the brain (the sensory cortex) produced sights, sounds, smells or other sensations, while stimulating other areas (the motor cortex) produced twitches and muscle movements.

When such twitches were evoked the patients were often surprised and said that *they* did not do it, 'You did.'

In the course of this stimulation Penfield explored the effects on the temporal lobe. What he found surprised him, and his patients, greatly. One suddenly exclaimed, 'Oh God! I am leaving my body' (165 p. 458). More often they suddenly seemed to go back in time to a specific memory. They had memory 'flashbacks'. Penfield describes his surprise.

> On the first occasion, when one of these 'flashbacks' was reported to me by a conscious patient (1933), I was incredulous. On each subsequent occasion, I marvelled. For example, when a mother told me she was suddenly aware, as my electrode touched the cortex, of being in her kitchen listening to the voice of her little boy who was playing outside in the yard. She was aware of the neighborhood noises, such as passing motor cars, that might mean danger to him.
>
> A young man stated he was sitting at a baseball game in a small town and watching a little boy crawl under the fence to join the audience. Another was in a concert hall listening to music.
>
> (166 pp. 21–2)

Another woman was able to hear music and, when Penfield stimulated the same point thirty times, she heard the melody again each time, beginning at the same place. She could even hum in accompaniment.

There are a good many problems in trying to understand what is going on here. For a start, it is not entirely clear that these 'flashbacks' were actual memories. Penfield himself describes them as the 'reactivation of consciousness' but of course no one could ever find out whether this exact event ever did happen; for example, was the mother ever in that exact position listening to those exact words spoken by her little boy? An alternative is that it was a reconstruction of a typical kind of moment condensed from general recollections. We now know that the feeling of familiarity can also be evoked by temporal lobe activity. So it is possible that any imagined scene might be felt to be terribly familiar whether it was a genuine memory or not.

With fifty years of further research into memory it now seems that the second type of explanation is more likely. Memories are distributed in the brain and constantly overlaid and reordered by subsequent learning. It is not possible to 'reactivate' an event that happened long ago because every precise detail of that event was never stored. Outlines of events are retained in memory and when we recall an event we probably fill in (or invent) a lot of the detail to make the recollection more realistic. Add a strong sense of familiarity (also evoked by temporal lobe stimulation) and it will make it seem even more convincing as a replay of the past.

Precisely the same argument applies to the memory flashbacks occurring near death. They might arguably be exact recollections of actual events reawakened from their holographic or brain-based store. Alternatively they might be convincing recreations of plausible past events. In the case of the life review we can no more go back and check on the memories than we can in the case of Penfield's research. We can only accept the person's word that these felt like memories and were convincingly realistic and vivid. However, in a sense it does not really matter which they were. Either way we have learned that direct electrical stimulation of groups of cells in the temporal lobe can induce convincing 'flashbacks'. They feel like memories and are vivid and realistic, just like in NDEs – and stimulation of temporal lobe cells is just what we expect when endorphins are released in response to stress.

These flashbacks are not the only NDE features to be evoked by electrical stimulation. Penfield only used electrodes near to the surface of the cortex but more recent research has probed deep inside the temporal lobe. The effects produced include floating and rising sensations, out-of-body experiences, mystical and religious experiences and dream-like sequences (221). Given what we now know it seems certain that unusual activity in the temporal lobe occurs during the NDE.

We now have a clear theory of how the NDE flashbacks occur.

Endorphins are released during stress and one of their effects is to lower the threshold for seizures in the limbic system and temporal lobe. The resulting abnormal activity in the temporal lobe causes the flashbacks and associated feelings of familiarity and meaningfulness. The hippocampus which is concerned with memory is also especially sensitive to anoxia and so can become disinhibited, leading to similar effects on memory.

OBJECTIONS TO THE THEORY

Karl Jansen (106), of the University of Auckland, New Zealand, has argued that the endorphins are not potent hallucinogens and do not produce the kind of dissociated state or out-of-body experiences so common in NDEs. He suggests that a different chemical produced by the brain may be more relevant.

The brain contains another kind of receptor called the NMDA receptor. Cells with these receptors can be killed by excessive excitation in cases of low blood pressure, anoxia and epileptic brain damage but this can be prevented by blocking the receptors with ketamine, the dissociative anaesthetic that we know induces OBEs. Perhaps, Jansen suggests, the brain produces its own blockers to protect the cells in the event of cardiac arrest or near death. As a side-effect they would produce a brief dissociative state and the hallucinations and OBEs characteristic of ketamine. One possible candidate has been discovered called alpha endo-psychosin.

In a further twist he points out that the NMDA receptor is also involved in memory formation. Memories are normally suppressed by a kind of 'gate' which is open to sensory information from outside. Blocking the receptor with ketamine or endopsychosin may be the equivalent of closing the gate to the outside and so allowing for the emergence of old memories. So this could provide another clue to the origin of the life review and Jansen suggests that this provides a better explanation than the endorphins.

This should remind us that our understanding of the brain

and its myriad chemicals is only just beginning. It could be that this is an additional mechanism and that there are many more yet to be discovered. As this exciting progress continues we shall add to our understanding of what happens in the dying brain and soon our present attempts will look very sketchy indeed. Even so, from all the evidence presented here, it still seems clear that the temporal lobe and limbic system play an important part in the life review.

Some researchers remain unconvinced, however, even though the relevance of temporal lobe symptoms to NDEs has often been pointed out. One such is Michael Sabom who, while acknowledging that NDEs cannot strictly count as evidence for survival, still prefers to interpret them as mind separating from body and even as evidence for a soul (204). He rejects the idea of temporal lobe involvement and his arguments will do well as examples of some frequently voiced objections.

Sabom compares the features of direct temporal lobe stimulation and epileptic seizures with the NDE and claims they are quite different, concluding that temporal lobe stimulation cannot account for the NDE. I think he is right that there are differences but wrong in his conclusion. The differences result from the varying way in which the temporal lobe is stimulated in these different conditions.

In direct electrical stimulation the electrode is inserted in one place without knowing what the cells in that place are doing and regardless of what is going on in the rest of the brain at the time. In other words it is essentially meaningless. Similarly an epileptic seizure starts at the focus point and spreads from there, again with no relationship to other experiences going on at the time. In the case of the NDE, however, the stimulation is widespread. It depends on the whole state of the person undergoing the NDE and may amplify activity already going on in the brain.

Some examples of Sabom's arguments will make the importance of this difference clear.

Sabom points out that the characteristic emotion during a seizure is fear, sadness and loneliness, whereas calm, peace and joy pervade the NDE. This difference can easily be explained by the fact that in the NDE, but not in brain stimulation or epilepsy, the limbic system and temporal lobe are flooded with endorphins. It is these that bring about the calm and peace as well as the temporal lobe activity. So naturally the overwhelming emotional tone will be positive.

Next he points out that there is forced thinking in the seizure but not in the NDE. Again the same argument applies. When an electrode stimulates a group of brain cells, or a damaged area sets off an epileptic seizure, the thoughts evoked will depend on that area and may have little relevance to what the person was thinking about a moment before. In the NDE, by contrast, the increasing activity comes in the context of ongoing activity and so is more likely to feel natural and unforced.

This is closely related to his most powerful argument, that in a seizure 'The reliving of past life events involves a random, single event of no particular significance but in the NDE it consists of multiple significant events experienced in rapid succession' (204 p. 238). There are two points here: one is the connected flow of the NDE flashback and the other its personal significance.

It is obvious that directly stimulating one area and then another will produce disconnected experiences. But this is not what we suppose happens in an NDE. Rather there is generalized amplification of activity and so lots of memories can be invoked all at once or in sequence. You might then object that such generalized activity could only produce random memories and not the connected and meaningful experiences of the near-death life review. However, more recent research on direct brain stimulation in epileptics has shown that the mental phenomena evoked depend on the personality and life experiences of the patient. For instance, one group reports that patients who were more fearful in their ordinary life were more likely to report fear while those who had schizophrenic tendencies were more likely to report hallucinations (91). Other experiments, by Ernst Rodin, who himself had an NDE, showed that the mental content was tied to the patient's fears, hopes and neurotic preoccupations. Rodin used this evidence to argue that the devout Christian may well meet Jesus when lack of oxygen affects his brain, whereas the Buddhist might accept his last experiences as *maya* and face them with equanimity (192).

As far as the feeling of 'personal significance' is concerned, we have already seen that this feeling can be evoked by activity in the deep structures of the limbic system.

This opens the way to understanding how it is that the life review is so personal and so relevant. It is the concerns of each individual and their own personal interpretations that will be evoked when their temporal lobes are affected near death.

From this I conclude that there are genuine differences between directly stimulating the brain and the NDE life review but this is what we would expect. Direct brain stimulation is not the same as the NDE but we can understand just why not and why studying temporal lobe phenomena still gives us great insights into how the NDE comes about.

THE LIFE REVIEW EXPLAINED?

How good is our theory? We can assess it, by comparison with the previous theories, against the usual criteria.

It handles specific details quite well. It makes sense of the fact that life reviews occur in those who expect to die even if they are not close to death, as well as in those who are actually dying. It explains why the experience depends on the individual and is meaningful in terms of their own lives and why the images feel so very familiar. It requires no other realms or worlds and builds on our current understanding of memory.

Does it lead to any testable predictions? Its main prediction is that anyone having a panoramic life review should have seizures or intense activity in the temporal lobe and limbic system. This would be hard to test directly since patients who are close to death are rarely studied with an EEG or related techniques. However, if this activity is promoted by endorphins these might be measurable. Also drugs, such as naloxone, that inhibit the action of endorphin should prevent a life review or terminate it if it has begun.

Another prediction already discussed is that people with more temporal lobe signs should be more likely to have an NDE. This could be investigated by comparing NDErs with those who have come close to death but had no experience. This suggestion has also been made by Persinger (170) and Neppe (146) in discussing the Chileans' neurobiological theory of NDEs, and Ring (188).

We can now make this prediction even more specific by thinking about the difference between NDEs close to death and other NDEs. When people are really close to death there may be both anoxia and endorphins to precipitate the experience. It is the NDEs occurring when death is not imminent that have no immediately obvious cause. It is in these cases that unstable temporal lobe activity may be crucial. So I would predict that the highest level of temporal lobe signs would be found in those who have NDEs when not medically near death, next highest in those who have NDEs near death and lowest in those who come close to death but have no NDE.

A question remains over why drowning most often produces life reviews. According to this theory we might suggest that drowning is more likely to lead to endorphin release than accidents or cardiac arrest. This is certainly plausible since the anoxia sets in slowly and there is time enough for other mechanisms to come into play. Alternatively, the slow anoxia might produce disinhibition in the hippocampus leading to experience of memories. This area is known to be especially sensitive to anoxia and prone to disinhibition (202). However, further research is clearly needed on this point.

On all these criteria I believe this theory does far better than the others we have considered.

You may think I have left out some important aspects – pinned down only the bones of the last stages of the NDE and not done justice to its more mystical qualities. And indeed I have. There is more to mystical experiences than their parallels in temporal lobe function. To start with there is what might seem a relatively straightforward example: that strange sense of 'timelessness'.

DISSOLVING TIME

Time seemed to have no existence.

(Cannabis experience, 54 p. 68)

It was like I lost time.

(NDE, 182 p. 97)

There was no time, no space, no 'I', no 'You', only – the Becoming of Being.

(LSD experience, 127 p. 308)

'I found myself in a space, in a period of time, I would say, where all space and time was negated.

(NDE, 182 p. 98)

A complete loss of time can happen in the last stages of the NDE but it is also characteristic of other kinds of experience. These include naturally occurring mystical experiences and also those induced by drugs, especially the hallucinogens such as LSD, mescaline, psilocybin and, perhaps to a lesser extent, cannabis. It is a more peculiar feeling than the simple distortions of time that can happen with many drugs; that is, when events seem to pass either very quickly or very slowly and half an hour can seem like a lifetime. The speeding up or slowing down of time is easier to remember and conceptualize than is the sense of complete timelessness. It is as though time itself no longer had any meaning. In some cases there still seems to be an order to events but no sense that time can be measured. In others, even this disappears and everything that ever happened seems to be happening all at once, outside of time, through all of space.

This sense is often considered part of the mystical experience. For example, 'Being non-spatial and non-temporal' is considered to be one characteristic of mystical states of mind. Another description includes 'transcendence of space and time' (127, 59). This state seems to have a kind of peculiar certainty or truthfulness to it, as though this is how it is and always has been.

Something similar is described in NDEs. Ring found that 95 per cent of his core experiencers claimed that time was either expanded or absent and 65 per cent said there was no sense of time. Greyson and Stevenson found distortions of the sense of time in 79 per cent of their NDErs, though about half reported a slowing of time, and they do not say for how many time actually disappeared. They do, however, note that of the 27 per cent of people who had a life review nearly 40 per cent claimed that the memories appeared all at once rather than in some particular sequence (86).

Noyes and Kletti (150) found a difference between those who thought they were about to die and those who did not. Eighty per cent of those who believed death was imminent reported an altered passage of time but only 65 per cent of those who did not think they were about to die had this experience. Since endorphins are more likely to be released in those who think they are dying this is at least compatible with temporal lobe involvement in the altered time sense. Further confirmation comes from the finding of Greyson and Stevenson (86) that time distortion was significantly correlated with positive emotions during the experience.

But what is happening? Do we have to start inventing other worlds outside of time to understand this mystical experience? Do we need to relate it to precognition and other paranormal effects? Some researchers clearly think so. Ring, for example, says that 'From the standpoint of recent formulations of brain functioning, the near-death experience seems to represent a "frequency domain" where time and space collapse and everything merely "coexists"' (182 p. 98).

I think recent formulations of brain functions actually have something much more interesting to teach us about the relationship between time and consciousness; something that ought to make us overthrow some of our most persistent illusions. To understand this we need to think a bit more about our normal sense of time and order – indeed about what time means anyway.

TIME AND REALITY

In chapter 7 I explained how I think things come to seem real. The brain constructs multiple models of the world all the time. Among the most important of these is the model of self. This is relatively persistent and is the basis for our talking and thinking as though there is 'someone' in there. It is closely linked to other models based on the senses and others from memory. The most stable and persistent of these models are taken as 'reality'. But, of course, reality is no more than this collection of changing mental models. And 'I' am no more than the evolving model of self.

What then of time? Well, time and order of events are crucial in the whole model building process. We have to remember the purpose of all this modelling. It is to enable the organism, the human being, to get around in the world, to interact with others, to find food, carry out jobs and generally survive. To do this our behaviour has to be ordered. But what about our thoughts and experiences? Is there an underlying time for them? Do they occur in order?

To understand the problem we need to be able to look at what is happening in the brain from two different perspectives: firstly, from the objective point of view in which many things are happening in the brain at once; secondly, from the point of view of 'me', the self-model created by the brain. We can do this for any series of events or actions we like, even, to take an example, walking down to the shops.

Let us take the first perspective. In walking down to the shops the brain is doing countless jobs all at once. Visual input is being processed through multiple stages so that the body can respond appropriately. The eyes are swept back and forth across the ground a little way ahead. Bumps, bits of rubbish, a running dog, are all dealt with. The step is shortened a little, now lengthened a little. The edge of the pavement is kept at a steady distance. Passing faces are observed. The automatic head-turning system responds to an insect coming into view from the side. The hand comes up to brush it away. Simultaneously sounds are processed, recognized, no action taken. The smell of a bonfire processed, no action taken. Suddenly the face recognition system comes up with something. The whole body responds. The head turns. The speech construction systems start operating. Out come the words, 'Sam, I haven't seen you for ages. How are you?' The pace of walking is adjusted, bumps and obstacles still dealt with, sounds processed. As far as the whole system is concerned a massive number of jobs are all being done at once – far more than I can begin to mention here.

We could ask questions like 'Which happened first, seeing the fly or smelling the bonfire?' The problem is that we could not realistically answer such a question. It is a meaningless question. Many processes went into coordinating the hand response to swipe away the fly. None exactly corresponds to 'seeing the fly'. Indeed, it is not appropriate to talk about a moment of seeing at all as far as the whole brain system is concerned. Similarly for the bonfire. If bonfires had been specially relevant that day no doubt the person would have responded to it. They were not. There was no exact moment at which the bonfire was smelt. All these processes were going on and overlapping. The idea of a precise order is nonsensical.

Now let us look at it from the point of view of the 'self'. It might be described like this: 'This morning I was walking down to the shops when I met Sam. I hadn't seen him for ages. We walked down together and had a chat.' None of the rest of the multiple parallel processing comes into this story. It is a serial, sequential, ordered story about what 'you' did. You could reasonably ask which happened first. You might say, 'Yes, I remember that I had already seen that fly when I met Sam.' Of course, 'you' may never really have 'seen' the fly at all; or rather, you may only have been able to say you saw it long after you had already brushed it away. The response to moving objects at the edge of vision is very fast. The hand probably came up to swipe it long before 'you' could have consciously noticed anything. However, you then concluded that you had seen the fly and so could describe it that way. In this story there is an order. There is the order of actions, the order of a remembered sequence in memory and the order of speech. As far as 'you' are concerned, things happened all in order and one at a time.

Why am I making this distinction between the whole system and 'you' (the model of self)? Because it shows how the normal sequence of events that we all take for granted is, like the self-model it depends on, a mental construction. It is a fiction created to make sense of the world. It is, once more, an illusion. Underlying it are the multiple processes and multiple mental models for which we cannot ask in precisely what order they happened.

You might now want to ask how the sense of order and sequence comes about. The American philosopher Daniel Dennett explains in a slightly different, but related view (46). Dennett, like me, thinks that we are prone to a very special kind of illusion. This he calls the 'Cartesian Theatre'. Most people, he argues, are able to reject the old Cartesian idea of a separate mind or soul but they still hang on to something else just as erroneous – the idea that somewhere inside us there is a place where it all happens; a kind of theatre in which the show goes on and in which we, the audience, watch the world go by. This is the place where our mental images are 'seen' by us; where events come in one by one and go out again in order; the place where we observe. This, he explains, is a very difficult illusion to dispel.

Why is the illusion created and why is it so difficult to dispel? Dennett's answer is that the brain is building 'Multiple Drafts' of the world all the time and in parallel. What creates the sense of order is the 'probes' that are used. For example, speech is constructed. Speech is, by its very nature, serial, and so events are ordered in speech and seem as though they were always ordered that way. Or events are laid down in memory by constructing a model of a series of events which represents them as happening in order. It is not that seeing the fly and meeting Sam came into the Cartesian Theatre one after the other. Rather, a model of events was constructed that represented one as happening before the other. In this way the probes of speech and memory construct an ordered world.

Of course, brain events do follow one another and if a longer time interval is looked at, walking to the shops came after setting out from the house and before going to bed that night. What both Dennett's view and my own deny is that there is a place inside the head where 'I' am and where events are experienced one at a time.

I would add that the illusion that events come into our consciousness one by one is all part of the illusion that there is a 'me' who experiences them. In fact, there are just multiple mental models coming and going, overlapping, growing and fading away. Only when there is a big, central, persistent model of self does it seem as though events happen in order to me.

We can now go back to the NDE and see how this helps us understand the sense of timelessness.

Parts of the limbic system and temporal lobe are involved in constructing the sense of self in time and place. During an NDE these areas are flooded with endorphins which lower the seizure threshold and make unstable activity more likely. Other things have also been happening in the brain to break down the self-model. The body image has become unstable because of lack of input. Decisions about what is real are being made and come up with real tunnels because of stable tunnel forms in the visual cortex, or real lights or sounds because of cortical disinhibition. The self may seem to be travelling down a tunnel or leaving the body. Now the self-model begins to break down completely. There is no longer any central self to hold it all together or to give rise to the illusion of order in time. Time starts to dissolve. There is no more self in time.

This is, I think, how the sense of timelessness comes about. Experience goes on but it is not experience of self. This is why it is timeless and this is also why it is so hard to describe.

This timelessness does not imply any other world that any version of oneself has gone to. It does not imply that suddenly paranormal things are possible. It does not imply precognition, reincarnation or any of the other fanciful notions sometimes linked with it. It involves only the simple insight that time and self are all part of the same mental construction.

It is a genuine insight. Whether this state is arrived at by taking drugs, by having a temporal lobe seizure, by meditating for years, by fasting or prayer, or by coming close to death, it is an insight into the essential non-existence of self. To this extent all such mystical experiences are equally valid. They all dissolve the model of self. They all dissolve the illusion.

But that leaves us with a new and difficult question. We know who nearly died. We know that before death threatened there was a strong self-model, with views and opinions, memories and desires and even a name. But who is there now? Who makes the decision to come back? Who returns from the NDE?

11

I Decided to Come Back

'Please, God, don't let my children grow up without a mother.'
I was back and I never went there again.

The traditional account of the NDE includes a dramatic moment
at which the released soul is confronted with a choice: 'Do I go
on into this bliss and peace, or do I return to my responsibilities,
my loved ones and the pain?' Is it really a choice? and if so, who
makes it?

The choice is described in many ways. It is often tied up with
the life review, but who makes it varies. Sometimes it seems to
be made by the 'Being of Light' or the 'Presence'; sometimes by
a dead relative or friend. Sometimes the dying are brought back
by the living and sometimes they seem to make the choice for
themselves.

In the first two instances someone (or something) else is
involved. According to Ring, most people have either a presence
or dead relatives and friends, but not both. And their roles seem
to be different. The 'presence' most often gives the dying person
a choice of whether to stay or return; the spirits almost always
urge them to go back (182).

Occasionally the decision seems to be made offstage, as it
were, by someone unseen. Sometimes it is the Lord who 'permits
them to live', or 'sends them back'. One person who surrendered
to death got an unexpected surprise: 'I looked up and said,
"Lord, here I am. If you want me, take me" . . . He shot me
back so fast it felt like I almost lost my breath' (133 p. 77).

It is tempting to think of these beings as real 'entities'
inhabiting some other realm which is now opening to the dying

person. This is certainly the implication of Ring's holographic theory and of the views of writers like David Lorimer and Margot Grey who believe that telepathy can occur in NDEs and beyond death and that there are surviving spirits with whom we communicate. Aside from the logical problems in making sense of such theories, some examples just do not seem to fit this prescription.

I interviewed one man who had had more than one cardiac arrest. He went into the ' perfect peace' several times in one day. Then, as he was being wheeled into the operating theatre, he saw a group of tall people, like Lowry figures, surrounded by light. 'They looked like angels,' he said. 'I've never seen an angel. I'm not good enough to see angels.' They were welcoming him with open arms. Yet he was quite sure that they were the doctors and nurses waiting for him in the theatre. I asked him to try to draw them for me (see Figure 16).

It was obvious to me that this experience touched him deeply. The sense of welcome was profound even though he insisted that the angels were a transformed version of the doctors and nurses. He was, if you like, simultaneously being welcomed to another imagined realm and back to life.

In another case a woman nearly suffocated after an operation.

> I have a distinct recollection of struggling along a dark tunnel in which someone was trying to hold me back. The figures in the bright light at the end of the tunnel proved to be the ward sister and her staff trying to resuscitate me. I never stopped to inquire who was trying to hold me back, but whoever it was, they were very anxious for me to stay.
>
> (98)

Neither of these cases make much sense if you think the beings seen in NDEs are 'real entities' inhabiting another realm. They make perfect sense if you think of them as part of the mind's own creations as it tries to make sense of the physical struggle going on between life and death.

If the tunnel is held to be a passageway to another realm the

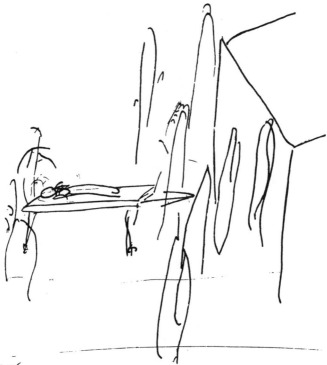

Figure 16.

figures in the light should surely have been spirits of the departed or some religious figure, not the living medical team whose intent was to bring her back. So such a theory cannot account for this example. On the other hand, it makes perfect sense according to the theory I have been developing here. The tunnel form is produced by effects in the visual cortex and the abnormal activity in the temporal lobe transforms the limited sensory information about the real doctors and nurses into figures in the bright light. The real physical struggle the body is going through is then experienced as a pull between the different imagined figures. The experience is real enough but its origin lies in the brain and the whole situation then and there – not in some other realm of the beyond.

A man from India, in intensive care after a bypass operation, was just coming round when he felt someone calling him away, saying 'Now you have to go.' But, of course, he did not have to go. Another saw himself in his coffin with his mother weeping over him but soon recovered and realized the 'vision' had to have been false. Again, these make far more sense if you see the experience as a mental creation rather than a glimpse into another world.

In other cases it is clearly the living who bring the experience to an end. A mother of six children became unconscious after a stillbirth. She told me

I found myself sitting on a high wall looking down at this mother whose baby had just died. I felt so sorry for her, and looked at the child who lay naked on a table in the corner of the room . . . The next thing that happened was I was walking into a garden There were no sounds of any kind, and I had the impression that it was sunlit, but not excessively so.

The flowers were in all colours, but not colours I knew. It was as though they were lit up from the inside, they glowed and resembled nothing on earth at all. There was a very strong perfume, sweet and delightful, but indescribable. Unique.

The further I walked into the garden, the more beautiful it became and the sweeter the scent of the flowers, but I became aware of a voice calling my name, and telling me to turn round and come back. I was very reluctant to do so, but the voice persisted, and eventually I succumbed and returned. My husband had been told to remain at my side and to keep calling my name. He did this for five hours without ceasing and, of course, it worked.

Finally, there are some cases in which it seems as though the dying person makes the final choice themselves. One woman who had just got married was involved in a car accident and in a coma for four days. She found herself contemplating whether to live or die. She went back over her unhappy childhood, recalling the pain and wondering whether she would have to go through it all again in her marriage. It became a question of whether she could trust her new husband or not. As she reviewed her past she began to experience happy events as well as all the pain and she saw her husband and their future together with two children. She saw him looking worried, seeming to pat her hand and encourage her to come back. Finally she made her choice. There was no religion, no one else involved. It was her decision to make and she decided to come back (182 p. 74)

Another woman suffered a cardiac arrest during a tonsillectomy and was told afterwards that she had been clinically dead for nearly three minutes. She encountered a presence who seemed to be telling her to go down and she was torn between wanting to go down and wanting to stay. There was no pain and no fear, only peace. She reported 'I was being drawn back. It was a choice, evidently, that I made.'

The interviewer then asked her, 'Do you feel that you made the choice?' and she replied, 'Yes, I think so. I wasn't afraid to go that way. And yet I'm sure it was my choice to come back.' She explained that it was for the sake of her two little children who needed her and this outweighed her own desire to stay in that peace and joy (182 pp. 70–1).

As in this case, the reasons for coming back are usually said to be either the pull of loved ones still living or the sense of there being 'unfinished business' to be completed before succumbing to death. The pull of death and the blissful scenes that seem to await the dying person can be very powerful. Sabom recounts the experience of a physician who was helped in his work by having an NDE himself. He says, 'I didn't want to come back because the tranquillity and peacefulness is so great,' but he was successfully resuscitated. Another patient had an extended cardiac arrest and reported later that he wanted to go on but didn't want to go. He didn't want to leave his wife and kids and believed that if it hadn't been for them he would have fought to carry on. It seemed as though he had to make a decision (204 pp. 204–5).

One thing that impresses me in all of these accounts is the hesitancy expressed about who made the decision. The NDErs seem to be saying both 'I made the choice' and 'It wasn't really a choice.' Many writers discuss the choice as though it is just that, the disembodied being rationally and consciously making a decision. And yet the NDErs themselves clearly have trouble in describing this choice/non-choice.

Margot Grey gives just four accounts of a decision to return. One woman had the decision made for her by robed Indians with silvery turbans on their heads. Another patient's father communicated that it was time to go back. The other two are more ambivalent. One actually says 'I was given a choice, although it wasn't really a choice, to go on or go back', and goes on to describe the agony of making the decision (79 p. 83). The other describes how he understood that he had the choice of continuing or going back and how he considered that he could follow and surrender to the light, fight the unbearable pain or find a middle way and accept the pain in order to come back. All this sounds very much like making a deliberate and conscious choice and yet even he states 'It was very much a choice. I felt I could have gone the way of the light, but at the same time I had a feeling – this is very hard to put into words – that I was not ready to go' (79 p. 84). In other words, he did not really have a choice.

I can understand this feeling very well. I remember it from an experience of my own (13). It had begun as a classic out-of-body experience in which I seemed able to fly around the room, the town, and eventually large parts of the globe. Later it became much harder to describe and I went through a series of experiences which are difficult even to think about in ordinary language. In the attempt to turn them into words I was left with such phrases as 'However far you go there is always somewhere further.' Soon after this I began to get the sense that I had to return. I can remember contemplating the timeless light ahead, the rapture and wonderful rightness of where I was and comparing it with the realities of the normal routine of life if I returned. In one sense there seemed to be a choice; in another, I knew there was not. I knew I would return, whether you call it 'choose' to return or not.

The paradox took another turn too. Coming back was a terrible struggle. I had to fight to make sense of the world again. I had to persuade myself that 'I must try to get back inside the head and look out through the eyes.' I had to try to make sense of time and the order of events again. I worked very hard at it but it was as though I could not do otherwise – rather like the labour of childbirth. 'You' work terribly hard but also 'you' have no choice about it.

This leaves the whole question very confused and such perplexity in itself tells us something about the nature of the experience as it comes towards its end.

So who does make the choice to return to life? Is it the 'Being of Light' or spirits from another world? Or even God? Is it the relatives of the dying? Or the dying themselves? Is it sometimes one and sometimes another? There does not seem to be a clear answer. It could be that there are genuine choices available to some NDErs and not others; that some can really make a choice and others have it made for them. To me this seems unlikely. It seems more likely that they are all trying, and with difficulty, to describe something that is not either their own choice, nor someone else's choice. It seems paradoxical. And whenever that happens it is time to ask whether the question makes sense – for nonsensical questions lead to nonsensical answers.

I think that is what we have here and the question 'Who makes the decision to return?' is not a valid one. On the surface it looks perfectly reasonable: if there is a choice someone must have made it. However, that means making two very interesting assumptions. The first is that by this stage in the NDE there is still someone there to make a choice. The second, in some ways more fundamental, is that in our everyday lives 'we', some conscious person inside ourselves, actually makes all those choices. I shall try to explain why I think both these assumptions are false.

DECISIONS WITHOUT A SELF

First, let us think about the self in the NDE. I have argued that the self is no more and no less than a mental model; a construction of the brain. And, as I explained in the last chapter, some strange things have been happening to the self-model during the NDE. The lack of sensory input, the stable tunnel patterns and unstable activity in the temporal lobe have all begun to destroy that persistent model of self which is such a strong feature of ordinary life. And along with the destruction of the model of self has gone the normal model of sequential and ordered time. There is continuing activity and continuing experience but it is not centred around a self.

This alone might be enough to explain the difficulty people have in saying whether they, or some other being, made the final choice to return. But I think this apparent choice gives us the chance to think about something much more fundamental. That is, what happens in ordinary life. Do 'I' make all the choices I think I make? Do I really make them consciously and deliberately? Could I not make them?

It all depends on whom you mean by 'me'.

Obviously people make choices. They live in one house rather than another. They watch one television channel rather than the others. They eat seaweed stew or beefburgers and baked beans for dinner. Choices are made by people. But are they made by selves?

I have suggested that the self is a mental construction. If so, then it is not the kind of thing that can make choices. So this implies that most of us live our lives under a huge illusion; that there is someone inside us who is doing all our actions and making all these choices.

Am I really saying this is an illusion?

If so, I shall have to explain how it is that we all come to share the same illusion. At least part of the answer lies in the way we are brought up and the way we learn to use language. Guy Claxton, a psychologist, long-time meditator and student of Buddhism, describes this very well in *The Light's On But There's Nobody Home*. The young learner of language discovers that he is allowed to say 'I am drinking my milk' but not 'I am gurgling my tummy'. And has to learn to understand what people mean by 'I didn't mean to do that' or 'You shouldn't have done that'. Systematically we are taught to use the words

'I', 'me' and 'myself' as though they refer to an autonomous and persistent thing. We learn to separate this self from its body, as though they were two different things and we learn to attribute actions and choices to this thing.

In the process we acknowledge that there are lots of actions that just seem to happen. We wake up, scratch, yawn, even clean our teeth, without any sense that 'we' really decided to do it. We accept that many actions do not require a deliberate or conscious choice and allow them to go on automatically. Others are more problematic but even so we fail to notice the paradox when we say we'll do one thing and another happens. We have all sorts of ways out of the dilemma which manage to preserve the sense of self.

As Claxton puts it, 'I meant to keep my cool but I just couldn't. I'm supposed not to eat pork but I forgot. I'd decided on an early night but somehow here we are in Piccadilly Circus at four a.m. with silly hats and a bottle of wine.'

How can we sustain the idea that 'I' am in control? Easy, says Claxton. If someone presses us we can retort with 'Really, Richard, you can be such a bore sometimes' or try to divert their attention some other way.

> If all else fails – and this is a truly audacious sleight of hand – we can reinterpret our failure of control as an actual success! 'I changed my mind', we say, temporarily withdrawing our identification from the 'mind' that has been 'made up', and aligning ourselves instead with some higher decision-maker and controller who can 'choose' to override this mind. Somehow or other 'I' manages to emerge from this potentially embarrassing situation, like an astute politician, with its reputation not only intact but enhanced.
>
> (34 pp. 59–60)

So we get out of the failures and sustain the illusion of self. But what about the successes? Aren't there cases when we rationally and deliberately and consciously choose to do something and we do? Of course there are, but even this does not require a separate self to do it. The whole system learns to weigh up alternatives very effectively. Some of this processing results in conscious experience and some does not; some can be verbalized and some cannot. 'We' may have the impression that 'we' did the weighing up but an alternative view is that the whole system did it and came up with a verbal description of a self who did. If the describable processes appear rational we congratulate ourselves on our decision-making. If not we may say 'I just had a hunch' or 'I let my "intuition" decide.'

You might still argue, on behalf of the real self, that there are times when we spontaneously, without reference to anything else, decide to do something and do it. In those cases isn't there really a self, an indispensable ghost in the machine, who does the deciding? It certainly feels that way but is this, too, just illusion? This might seem to be more of a philosophical than an experimental question. Nevertheless, one pioneering researcher has found a way to try to investigate something very close to it and his experiments have raised a storm of protest and argument.

SPONTANEOUS AND DELIBERATE?

Californian neuroscientist, Benjamin Libet has long been fascinated by the problem of voluntary action (119). If someone decides to move their fingers we know that certain brain events are involved. Research using the EEG has shown that for any simple action there is a 'readiness potential', or ramp-like change in potential, which begins in the brain's cortex a few hundred milliseconds before the action begins. The action itself is coordinated by the cerebellum, a part of the brain specialized for controlling skilled action. Signals are sent along the motor neurons to the appropriate muscles and the action takes place. So where does the conscious decision to move come in? This was Libet's question.

In particular he wanted to know about the order of events. It certainly feels as though 'I' decide to act first and then the action follows. From this perspective it looks as though the first event in the sequence must be my conscious decision to act, otherwise I could not be said to be making a real decision at all. The brain events would then follow and finally the action.

Libet set up a simple task with which to investigate this. His subjects were given plenty of time and told that whenever they wanted to, completely spontaneously, they were to flex their wrists. They were fitted with electrodes on the scalp to measure the EEG and, by averaging the patterns obtained on many trials, to detect the start of the readiness potential. So the action itself and the start of the brain events could be timed. The difficult part was timing the moment of the conscious decision to act. Libet did this by asking the subjects to watch a revolving spot on a clock face and to tell him where the spot was at the precise time they made their decision to act. With control tests he showed that this was something they could easily and accurately do. It was then a simple matter of timing the three events. Would the conscious decision to act start the process?

The answer was straightforward. It did not. The readiness potential began about four hundred milliseconds before the conscious decision to act. In other words the events that would eventually lead up to the movement had begun well before the person had actually decided to move. It seemed that the conscious decision to act was not what it seemed to be at all.

Libet published his findings and dozens of other scientists and philosophers responded with criticisms and numerous different interpretations (119). Libet himself argued that though the results appeared to go against the idea of free will, there was still room for a conscious veto on any action or – as Richard Gregory put it – there might not be any free will but there is still 'free won't' (78).

Although the reaction to these experiments was heated and argumentative the basic point is simple. They show that the conscious decision to act does not happen before any brain events connected with the action begin.

To the dualist this might seem all wrong. The dualist believes that there is a separate self or mind or soul and that conscious decisions come from that separate thing. For this view to hold, the mind's decision must be the first stage in the process. So the results seem to be another nail in the coffin for dualism.

As we have seen there are many dualists among NDE researchers, but in the rest of neuroscience, psychology and philosophy there are very few. Most of these people believe that all experience depends on brain events and, in a sense, Libet's results are obvious if you accept that premise. If experience and brain events are inseparable then at the very earliest the awareness of wanting to act would have to start at the same time as the brain events which gave rise to that awareness. More likely some build-up in those events would be required to produce conscious experience and that is, of course, what Libet found.

So if this is obvious why were the arguments so heated and protracted? I think because many scientists, while professing to have rejected dualism, still live in the illusion of Dennett's Cartesian Theatre. It feels as though there is some central place where it all happens; a place where 'I' am; a place to which all the incoming signals come and a place from which 'I' send out my instructions to 'my' body and to the world.

But there is no such place. The brain is a complicated system, doing lots of things in parallel, and making lots of decisions at once. There is no one person in there doing it all. There is no one time or place at which decisions are made. Decisions are the consequences of lots and lots of parallel processes coming together to produce an action, a word or a remembered sequence.

Am I saying, then, that every time I think I have made a decision, it was actually an illusion? 'I' didn't really make it? Yes – if by 'I' you mean something separate from the rest of the system, then that is precisely what I am saying.

It is hard to think this way but one trick that is helpful is to try to look at the same events from two perspectives, as I did in the last chapter, one from the point of view of the fictitious self, 'I', and the other from the perspective of the whole system. Let's go walking down to the shops again. I might say 'I walked down to the shops and when I met Sam I decided to postpone the shopping and walk along with him.' It sounds like a simple enough choice made by a self and can be easily described in language. From the perspective of the whole system it looks quite different. Multiple processes were going on, objectives being worked out, timing coordinated, walking coordinated. This whole complicated system, weighing up all the pressures and constraints, did end up talking to Sam. It then put on a mental construction afterwards that 'I' decided to do so.

I think all our lives are like this. And perhaps the trick of looking at it in these two ways helps to free us a little from the illusion. It is all right to let go of the self. The world won't fall apart if you (the whole system) lets go of 'you' (the self-model). The problem is that it is very difficult and it goes against the habits of a lifetime. The fascinating thing about the NDE is that it forces this 'letting go' upon the dying person. The brain can no longer sustain that usual illusion of self. It has begun to break down. For perhaps the first time in its life this system is experiencing events without a central self. No wonder it is hard to explain afterwards. No wonder there is doubt and ambiguity about who made the decision to come back.

GIVING UP THE GHOST

The NDE may force the dissolution of the self but there are other ways to do it. Meditation is one. Practising mindfulness is another. Some kinds of contemplation and prayer can do it, too. These are all centuries old techniques, often allied with particular religions but, in their essential practice, quite separable from them.

Mindfulness is a difficult technique, perhaps best described as 'being in the moment'. Whether it is performed in everyday life or as a form of sitting meditation, the basic practice is to pay attention to everything and anything without choosing, categorizing or in any way discriminating anything from anything else and without projecting ideas or thoughts into the past or future. It might sound easy but it goes against everything we normally do. Usually paying attention means selective attention –

attending to the thing we want to attend to and not to other things. In mindfulness the attitude required is not discrimination but attending impartially to everything.

The initial effect is one of confusion because there is so much happening all at once, but after a time this clears. The odd thing is how such a seemingly simple practice can wreak havoc with the self. As the person (the whole system, not the self-model) goes on practising, events keep on happening. Choices are made. The body goes on walking, digging the garden, even cooking the dinner – and (with a lot of practice, for this is much more difficult) conversing. These things seem to happen without intention. Without self. With such practice the superfluity of the self becomes obvious. It isn't needed. And after all, it was only an illusion.

The connection to mindfulness appears in accounts of the aftereffects of NDEs. Some NDErs report that their experience forced on them something like a mindfulness of the present. As one of Sabom's patients explained

> It [the NDE] just changed my whole life like a flipflop . . . I used to worry about life and living it and trying to get ahead, trying to make life easier by working harder to make more money to make life easier. I don't do that no more . . . I just live from day to day. I used to live for what was ahead or behind me. You can't live a day in advance or a day behind. You can only live for the day you're living.
>
> (204 p. 181)

In Moody's original collection of cases one person says 'Before that heart attack I was too busy planning for my children's future, and worrying about yesterday, that I was losing the joys of the present. I have a much different attitude now' (133 p. 91). It is as though being forced into the present moment creates an increased capacity to enjoy the present thereafter.

The same kind of effects can come about through meditation on the nature of self. There are many questions that can be contemplated in meditation; not asked in an intellectual way but simply asked, so that endless answers keep arising in a mind calmed by quiet sitting. They might be 'Who am I?' or 'Where do thoughts come from?' or 'Who was there before I was born?' When the answers run out there arises a sense of watching the thoughts, the events, the struggles. Thoughts just seem to happen rather than being caused by 'me'. It is always tempting to lapse back into thinking there is someone in charge inside but the alternative is to think of it as a system building models. In meditation and mindfulness that system builds different models – it may just build up a world without any model of self (20).

The question that naturally springs to mind next is an ethical one. If 'I' am not there, who is responsible? Won't that body do all sorts of terrible things? Why should it bother to do anything? Isn't letting go of the self a prescription for disaster? Wouldn't it mean more thoughtless and selfish behaviour? It seems not. Indeed selfishness is just what it would not mean – for selfishness, in its mean and thoughtless sense, is precisely what is created along with the creation of the self. Letting go of the self can also mean the end of selfishness.

Guy Claxton explains what happens as the inquiry through meditation progresses. We start by thinking that the control is real and so we think we can and must control ourselves. From this perspective the thought of giving up control seems really dangerous. In fact, of course, it was based on a false premise and the consequences of giving it up are quite the reverse to what was expected. As he puts it

> I do not take up wholesale rape and pillage and knocking down old ladies just for fun.
> The thing that does happen is the reverse . . . Guilt, shame, embarrassment, self-doubt, self-consciousness, fear of failure and much anxiety ebb away, and as they do so I seem to become, contrary to expectations, a better neighbour. As I can look inwards with more acceptance and compassion, so I can look outwards at others. My needs to dominate and censure, to be wary and manipulative, they melt too. It is truly

startling to discover how much of the mischief and misery in the world is attributable to this simple ontological mistake.

(34 p. 69)

There seems to be a contradiction here. If the self is let go, who is left? Who is going to be the 'better neighbour'?

At first it seems there is a watcher, an observer, or witness. This is a position encouraged in some kinds of mystical training and mentioned by many NDErs. It is certainly a first step away from identification with the false self but what is this observer? It is all too easy to think of it as the 'real self', the 'higher self' or some such phrase. This sense of leaving behind one self and finding another may be the origin of many ideas of this kind. But this just recreates all the same problems on a new level.

The alternative is to see that this new self is also only a creation. There is nothing inside that corresponds to it. It is another construction; another point of view. Dennett's view is that an observer comes about whenever a portion of the world composes a skein of narratives. So, if the brain is still capable of stringing together a story about an observer then it will feel like there is something being that observer. If the brain ceases constructing such a narrative, then there won't be.

So this 'higher self' can also be let go of. And what happens then? The body and everything else carries on but without this 'narrative centre'; this artificial construction. There are still actions but no actor. It still makes sense to talk of the person and the actions but not of one 'doing' the other. At this point it could be said that the individual is lost in the whole.

We can again make the useful distinction between the whole system and the self-model. Now the self-model has ceased but there is still a system of body and brain. It is still acting, making decisions and choices. It is the person who has a name. It is the person who becomes a better neighbour. But there is no one in there who does anything.

How, then, can such a person be responsible?

This is another of those funny things that happens through meditation and mindfulness. As the self dissipates and actions just seem to happen, rather than losing a sense of responsibility it is as though the perspective changes from the self to the whole system. Instead of 'me' feeling deadly responsible for all those things I thought I could control, the whole system becomes responsible for everything it ever did, and soon the realization occurs that there is no real boundary between this body and brain and the rest of the circumstances in which it finds itself, indeed the rest of the world. An extraordinary sense of responsibility for the whole of creation can arise – another route to the experience of one-ness.

I am reminded here of the many NDErs whose life review throws them into a sense of responsibility for everything they ever did, whether it was intentional or not, whether they had previously remembered it or not. Phyllis Atwater (2) nearly died three times. In her experience she seemed to relive every thought she had ever thought, every word ever spoken and every deed ever done; plus the effect of each of those on everyone and anyone who had ever come within her environment or sphere of influence whether she knew them or not; plus their effect on weather, plants, animals, soil, trees, water and air. She suddenly realized that we are responsible and accountable for every single thing we do and she found it overwhelming.

This is a description of broadening the sense of responsibility from the smaller self to something larger but there is still a boundary between self and other. I get the impression that many NDErs take a step in the direction of oneness but end up simply grasping on to a new 'higher' self. This may help them become more generous and more responsible but there is a further step to take, to the truly scary thought that there is no real boundary between self and other.

SO YOU DECIDED TO COME BACK?

I asked the question 'Who decides to come back?' And I can now answer it. The decision to come back is like all other decisions in life. It happens because it happens. The experience we have of 'making' the decision is all part of the verbal construction put on to the events. This is as much true of getting up in the morning as it is of coming back from heaven. The particular body either pulls through and goes on living or it does not. If it does, it rebuilds a model of self and tells the story of the NDE, including the fact that 'I' decided to come back.

For some NDErs the boundaries of self really have disintegrated. They have gone far enough down the road of dying for the self-model to have fallen apart completely. For these few, more extreme, cases the normal parameters of life have temporarily disappeared. There is no time, no sequence of events, no self and no other. There is just how it is. However, it is only a temporary state, forced on them by coming close to death. Unlike the meditator, yogin or mystic who learns to fall in and out of this state, the NDEr comes back. Their body recovers and the brain resumes its normal functioning. Inevitably it starts at once to build again that model of self.

We must remember that all we have from NDErs is their descriptions given after they have recovered from their brush with death. By then, if I am right about the dissolution of the self-model, the recovering brain will have reconstituted the 'self' afresh and, in the usual language of selves and decisions and actions, will try to describe something that just does not fit that language. What comes out is the story of someone who has had an NDE.

But . . . and this is an important 'but' . . . the self may never be quite the same again. That brain has existed for a while in a state without a central self-model. Its limbic system and temporal lobe have been in abnormal states and its cortex has constructed new models of the world. Perhaps it may be easier for it in future to do the same again. This, I want to argue, is why NDErs are changed by their experience: because they have, however briefly, had experience without an experiencer, action without an actor and being without a self.

But I am getting too far away from the evidence. It is time to draw together what is known about NDE transformations and try to work out just how and why people are changed by their experiences.

12

Who Returns?

There is no doubt that the NDE seems to transform people's lives. Again and again NDErs describe how different are their priorities, hopes and fears, after their experience.

Not surprisingly there has been much research on the extent and nature of these transformations. Even before Moody first wrote about NDEs, doctors had studied the effects of surviving a cardiac arrest and reported a reduced fear of death (49, 53). Since then all the major reports, from the earlier ones of Moody, Ring and Sabom to the more recent work of Grey, Lorimer and Rogo, have commented on such important life changes as an increase in reverence for life and a transformation of priorities away from material gains and achievements towards other people and the spiritual values of love, compassion and acceptance.

It is perhaps this last that is most often reported. For example Flynn (62) carried out a questionnaire survey of twenty-one NDErs and found that an increase in concern for others was the most consistent effect. Ring summarizes the changes that take place like this:

Someone who survives a core experience usually reports that the experience was so striking and so singular that the passage of time does nothing to dim its vividness . . . such experiences . . . tend to exert a powerful effect on a person's motivations, values, and conduct . . . however one chooses to interpret near-death phenomena, they are unquestionably real in their effects.

(182 p. 138)

He adds that even those people who recall nothing from being close to death had their lives altered in significant ways.

This raises the question of whether it is just coming close to death that brings about these changes or whether an NDE itself is essential.

CHANGES WITHOUT AN NDE

You certainly do not need to be very close to death to undergo a change.

As one woman told me,

> Two years ago my husband came extremely close to dying when his artery burst. If he had a NDE, he did not remember it when he regained consciousness. Certainly I did not have a NDE – the most life threatening thing I did was to drink hospital coffee. Yet both of us found that the experience had a profound and lasting effect, very similar to those you attribute to NDEs ... simply coming very close to dying also shakes the very foundation of your existence – with or without NDE.

There are many other experiences that can and do bring about comparable transformations in people. Among them are the drug experiences we have already considered, naturally occurring mystical experiences, out-of-body experiences and even UFO encounters, which some researchers have compared to NDEs (186). UFO encounters might seem totally different from NDEs but they too can include experiences of light and leaving the body. One study showed that they also produced aftereffects such as an increased appreciation of life and concern for others, though to a lesser extent and with less consistency than do NDEs (45). Several investigators have concluded that there is a commonality between these experiences and some have compared them to the changes of identity found in initiation rites (186) or status passage (110).

I have already mentioned the effect that being close to someone else's death can have. Even stranger is that just imagining
someone else's death can also have profound effects, at least it
did in one case where the experiencer was the man who fired
the gun. A kind of 'NDE by proxy' was reported by an Australian
researcher, Cherie Sutherland, in her study of the sociological
implications of NDEs (222). Robert was interviewed at a
maximum security prison in New South Wales where he was
serving a sentence for murder. One night he was sitting in his
cell reading and rereading a letter which asked him why he had
shot his victim. He began to feel guilt and then describes how
he sensed that he would learn something if he could 'go with'
the feelings he was experiencing.

Next he found himself changing places with the man he had
shot; putting himself through the anguish and terror that he had
previously put the other man through. He saw himself being
shot and the body writhing in pain. Then he left, met with other
beings and travelled towards a tiny speck like a foetus in a
spotlight. He came back to a sense of oneness, love, purpose
and direction. As he put it,

> I died in a sense in that experience. I died to the past because
> when I had that experience, when I came out of it, my percep-
> tion was so different to what I had before. Basically my atti-
> tudes towards many things, my understandings of many things
> was changed. It happened instantly. It was a total transforma-
> tion . . . and it wasn't till I came out of the experience that I
> realized that I was a different person.
>
> (222 pp. 244–5)

Subsequently Robert's life changed considerably. He lost
his fear of death, became a vegetarian, gave up smoking and
drinking, learned to meditate and taught meditation in the
prison.

This story is comparable to the changes in people who actually
did come close to death. There are many cases of NDErs changing their careers to become nurses, take up other helping pro-

fessions or do volunteer work (63, 183, 222). One woman had a series of cardiac arrests and three experiences; two pleasant and one frightening and devastating. During the third experience she felt she was 'turned completely around', 'made over', 'made different'. There was a feeling of tremendous love for all humanity and she made a promise to care for children. During the next seventeen years she opened her home to nearly a hundred homeless and unwanted children (167).

Such cases suggest that physically coming close to death is not needed for the transformations, and nor is having a core experience. Lots of different things can set off important life changes. Contemplating death can of itself bring some of them about. However, to find out more precisely what produces the transformation we need to look at research that has made the relevant comparisons.

WHAT CAUSES THE CHANGE?

There are numerous problems involved in tackling the question of transformations. The most difficult is that usually one can only interview the person after the experience has happened. They may then claim, and sincerely believe, that their fear of death has been reduced but unless they had been asked about it beforehand you cannot be sure that this was so. They might report such a change because they feel better about life in general, because they think that this is what is expected of them, because they can remember extreme fear of death immediately before the experience or for any of a number of other reasons. So interviewing someone and just asking 'Is your fear of death changed in any way?' is not a reliable method.

The same problem arises using questionnaires. For example, one study used the Life Attitude Profile and showed positive changes in every one of twenty-eight NDErs (5). However, the NDErs had to complete the form for their attitudes now and as they recalled them from the past. This could not reliably measure their attitudes before the experience because it could not take account of how their recollections had changed in the intervening time.

To be sure whether it really was the NDE that brought about the change we would have to interview people or give them psychological tests both before and afterwards. No one has done this. You cannot predict who is going to have an NDE in advance and although it might be possible to give death anxiety scales to all patients with cardiac disease, even this would present ethical problems.

In spite of these difficulties there are two kinds of research that can address the question. These have been discussed before and make two comparisons: one is between people who have OBEs or other NDE-like experiences and are or are not close to death; the other is between people who have come physically close to death and do or do not have an NDE.

The first approach has been taken by psychiatrists Gabbard, Twemlow and Jones (68) who studied over three hundred OBErs. Only about 10 per cent of the experiences occurred near death and there were statistically significant differences between these and the non-death OBEs. For example, the people whose experiences occurred near death were more likely to feel that there was a purpose connected to the experience, that it was of lasting benefit, that it was a religious or spiritual experience and that their life was changed by it. This all seems to show that it is not just the experience itself (in this case an OBE) that brings about the change. Being close to death in itself makes a difference to the changes.

The exception was in belief in life after death. Two-thirds of all the subjects became more convinced of survival, regardless of whether they had been near death. The authors concluded that it was their perception of consciousness being separate from the body which brought about this change in belief.

A different approach has been taken by Kenneth Ring who compared two groups of people who had all come close to death; some had had core NDEs and others had not. This comparison should show which changes are brought about by the experience itself and which by physical proximity to death. (There were, of course, no non-experiencers in Gabbard, Twemlow and Jones's study.) His results were most interesting. Some changes happened to those in both groups, regardless of whether they had had an experience or not. These included changes in values and personality, a sense of increased appreciation for life, increased sense of purpose and a changed attitude towards other people. One said:

> My priorities have definitely changed ... it suddenly made me realize that nothing is important unless you have people around you that you love ... Now I feel that I feel more for people. Just a greater concern for living and how to make people appreciate their surroundings, or something like that. I just feel that I have a greater appreciation of being here.
>
> (182 p. 142)

Compare this with a second claim:

> I love people now ... I've never had the ability to love before. I have a great capacity for listening to people. I think I accept people – most of all – as they are ... And it's made me richer.
>
> (182 p. 157)

The first of these comes from a woman who was nearly killed by a car explosion but had no recall whatsoever for any experience at the time. The second, by comparison, comes from a woman who was apparently clinically dead for about three minutes and did have a core experience. So these changes seem attributable to the proximity to death, rather than to having any particular experience.

Other changes depend upon having a core experience, including an increase in religiousness, increased belief in God and in life after death and a decrease in the fear of death. This latter confirms what Gabbard and his colleagues found, that belief in life after death is brought about by the experience itself, not by being close to death.

So we can now answer the question about whether you need

an NDE to be changed by coming close to death. The answer seems to be no, but the changes are different depending on the circumstances and experience.

NO EXPERIENCE

The effects of having an NDE are often talked about. The direct effects of *not* having an NDE are not. I get the impression that this may have something to do with the recent popularity of positive interpretations of the NDE. It is certainly interesting that two of the studies which predate Moody report serious difficulties people had in adjusting to having had a cardiac arrest and also the effects on those who had no NDE. One survivor of a cardiac arrest considered his atheistic beliefs confirmed because 'there is nothing there' (49). Another stated that now he knew there was no afterlife because during the time he had died all he could remember was 'nothingness' (53).

Of course, this is unlikely to cause problems if the person is already an atheist but it can have a more serious effect on a believer. I interviewed one survivor of cardiac arrest who told me how his beliefs were changed by his close brush with death. He was a keen church-goer, editing its newsletter and working in other ways for his local church. When he had a cardiac arrest he experienced nothing. As he put it, 'I know now that you don't see the pearly gates or anything. I know you just pass out. At least that's the way it was with me. I just stopped living.' He explained that this weakened his faith rather than strengthened it and this was mainly because he realized it was the skill of the doctors and nurses that saved him, not people's prayers.

This not only affected his life but his wife's too. Her faith was tested at a time when she needed it to help her support him through his recovery.

An even more unusual experience was told to me by one of my students. While suffering from dangerously low blood pressure after an operation she passed out, seemed to leave her body and travelled down a tunnel that gradually filled with light. She felt exhilarated by a sense of power and speed until she was brought back to earth by the sound of someone at the door. For many years after this experience she felt that she was living in a state of grace as if she were on a spiritual path. But that state was abruptly brought to an end by her second brush with death during a miscarriage. This time she seemed to be in a deep hole and unable to move or signal to anyone. Not only was this an unpleasant experience but it was the end of her 'state of grace' and the end of her path.

This, however, is rare. Far more common is an enthusiastic 'Now I know there is heaven because I've been there. Now I know there is nothing to fear in death because I've died. Now I know there is life after death because I've seen it for myself.' This raises a very interesting question – are they right? There seems no doubt that people do change. The question is, do the changes take place because people have genuinely seen the truth of the afterlife? Or could it be that they happen in spite of the fact that they've jumped to the wrong conclusion?

NOW I KNOW THE TRUTH

For many researchers the truth is obvious. People are transformed because their consciousness has been freed from its physical constraints. They become more spiritual because they have had a glimpse of the spirit world and of life after death. They are better people because they have seen a mystical realm and been touched by its qualities. The person who returns is not the same person but someone more in touch with a higher aspect of themselves.

Such a view takes many forms. Ring contrasts the physical self with the 'essential self' or the 'overself'. 'We are ensouled selves,' he argues, 'and our true being does not merely survive death but is immortal' (184 p. 19). Margot Grey concludes that we access spiritual reality when our consciousness is freed from dependence on the physical body (79). Pennachio (167) says that the ego is transcended and the psyche moves beyond the confines of the skin, the material world and the limitations of time and space. For them, and many others, the transformation comes about because there is a *bigger* self, not because there is no self.

If additional proof is needed it can be gleaned, they say, from the paranormal effects. Grey notes that one aftereffect of NDEs is an increase in claimed psychic experiences and healing powers. She gives many examples of people who seemed to acquire the gift of healing others after going through their NDE. Ring reports flash-forwards, as well as flashbacks, in which people claimed to see psychically into the future during their NDEs. For him such effects are only to be expected because people have contacted the holographic domain in which time and space are transcended and the changes they undergo reflect their contact with this domain.

He has gone even further than this and in a recent study investigated what he calls 'Kundalini Activation'; that is, signs of a special kind of energy said to develop from the base of the spine during training in yoga. Comparing NDErs with a control group he found more signs of 'Kundalini Activation' in the NDErs. He sees all these changes as heading towards a higher kind of consciousness, a goal for us all that he calls Omega (183, 188, 190). The NDEr is a kind of 'Omega prototype', a harbinger of a better future for mankind.

Kundalini may seem to be a spiritual matter, far removed from brain mechanism theories of the NDE, but oddly enough it may not be. Michael Persinger (170) notes that people who survive cardiopulmonary resuscitation often develop a special form of limbic epilepsy. He suggests that after such a trauma the temporal lobe and limbic system are more unstable and therefore more likely to produce the religious feelings, mystical and psychic experiences associated with temporal lobe signs. Indeed, these experiences are just what you would expect from a nervous system damaged by trauma, anoxia or extreme stress.

If these views seem poles apart, a fascinating point of contact is that many of Ring's 'Kundalini Activation' items sound very much like temporal lobe signs. His scale includes such statements as 'I would occasionally experience sensations of tickling, itching, or tingling on or underneath my skin', 'I would sometimes feel a deep ecstatic sensation, something like an orgasm, for no reason' and even 'I experienced severe or migraine-type headaches more often than before.' Both types of people are creative, intuitive and have a rich fantasy world. This suggests that Persinger's temporal lobe changes and Ring's 'Kundalini Activation' may be the same thing.

As always, a useful theory leads to specific predictions. This theory suggests that 'Kundalini Activation' will only occur after an NDE that involves the temporal lobe. An increase in subsequent psychic and mystical experiences should correlate with an increase in temporal lobe signs after the NDE and both should be more common if the NDE includes those features that depend on temporal lobe activation; that is the life review, visions and mystical components. Since we have so little evidence about these details of NDE transformation an answer will have to wait for further research.

It might seem a crude analysis to say that Kundalini *is* temporal lobe instability. Nevertheless, if you accept the dependence of experience on brain events then there has to be some correlate of these experiences in the brain and this may well be it. Of course, the dependence of experience on brain events is precisely what many NDE researchers deny. Indeed, their theories are mostly based very clearly on that denial. They acknowledge that the NDE cannot be *proof* that something can separate from the brain and survive without it, but that is certainly their preferred interpretation.

What, though, if it is not true? What if we are nothing more than biological creatures living out our lives which will one day come to an end? What if there is no higher realm? What if there is no consciousness beyond the experience that depends on the activity of brains and nervous systems. If all that is so, as I believe it is, then why are people transformed?

I have already explored the grounds for my answer. It is because the NDE breaks down, if only for a brief moment, the self-model which was the root of all our greed, confusion and suffering. There never was any real persistent self; a self that makes conscious choices, a self that observes the objective world at a distance, a self that takes responsibility or is the centre of experience. There never was a separate self who lived through all those experiences, who had all those memories or who made all those decisions. There never was any permanent self and there is no permanent self to survive when the body is gone. There was only a mental model that said there was one.

We can do without such a model. It is possible for living organisms to live as they truly are: ever-changing, owning nothing, a part of the universe as a whole and inseparable from it. This is the truly mystical vision – that it is all just like it is and nothing ever stays the same.

Am I denying all those spiritual transformations by saying this? No, I honestly do not think I am. For what I am saying is that NDEs can give a genuine insight, an insight rightly called 'mystical'; but it is not the insight some people think it is. It is an insight into what the self is *not* rather than what it *is*.

DAZZLING DARKNESS

So am I always at odds with what other NDErs themselves are saying? Do they all adhere to the theory of a self that survives and a world beyond? No, not all.

John Wren-Lewis was a mathematical physicist who gave up an industrial career to pursue a humanistic faith as an independent scholar. In 1983, while travelling in Malaysia, he was poisoned, probably with morphine, and had an experience that changed his life (237, 238). It was not a classic NDE but he came into a state of paradoxically 'shining darkness', a most wonderful deep and dazzling darkness in which he felt utterly secure and at home. The extraordinary thing was that it never really left him. Long after he had recovered he described the experience as being 'all still here, both the shining dark void and the experience of myself coming into being out of, yet somehow in response to, that radiant darkness'. He goes on

My whole consciousness of myself and everything else has changed. I feel as if the back of my head has been sawn off so that it is no longer the 60-year-old John who looks out at the world, but the shining dark infinite void that in some extraordinary way is also 'I'.

(238 p. 116)

He suggests that by comparison ordinary consciousness is 'an illusion of separate selfhood'(238 p. 106).

The changes wreaked in him were profound. Pain became something he could not only accept but even enjoy, though he still kept some aspirin just in case! More importantly, his whole experience of life was transformed; every moment lived for what it is. Through this change his views on mysticism turned full circle, not because he took on the idea of a permanent surviving self, but because he saw through the myth of that self and was able to let go. Like so many NDErs he lost his fear of death; not because he knew that 'he', John Wren-Lewis, would survive, but because he understood 'why the mystics of all religions have said that the pearl of great price is not immortality but eternal life, which is lived in every moment' (238 p. 118).

This seems to be another of those paradoxes that appear when we try to explain mystical insights from the point of view of ordinary language. Nevertheless, it seems to be valid. Letting go of oneself leads to living more fully and more directly.

LETTING GO

Steven Levine is an American poet and teacher of meditation who has worked for many years with people who are dying. In his work he encourages the dying not to put their faith in some hoped for future after death but in an attitude of 'don't know'. There is only the present to work with and the work is all about letting go. He explains how much of our suffering is caused by hanging on to how things might have been or should have been and to the idea of a separate self that has to be defended at all

costs. The real task is to let go of all that and open to what
is rather than what the constructed self wants it to be. The
extraordinary thing is that this task is the same in living as it is
in dying – 'Whatever prepares you for death enhances life' (117
p. 28).

This preparation can be done in many ways and at any time.
We can cut through our resistance by investigating what is real
and who is hanging on to a false sense of security.

> We see that our pain arises in pulling back from the unknown
> and the imagined. It is by playing this edge that we expand
> beyond the fear of death, beyond the idea of 'someone' dying,
> and come into the wholeness of being, the deathless.
>
> (117 p. 34)

The problems and suffering of life are all created by hanging on
to a false sense of self. Some people seem able to let go of it
completely. So what is there when there isn't this kind of self?
There is just a person, a body, an individual with a name, acting
in the circumstances that exist at the time. It is the resistance
and clinging that is gone. It is the end of preferring one thing to
another and of 'minding' about what happens. What happens
happens. With that transformation seems to come a completely
new vigour for life: energy, openness, simplicity, joyousness and
even compassion.

It may seem odd that compassion arises but with the end of
a separate self other people's suffering becomes more immediate
and there is nothing to block the appropriate response. It may
seem perverse, but the death of self can be the beginning of
living, not the end.

Why, then, is it so hard? Why does it take a lifetime of practice
in prayer, meditation or mindfulness, or an extraordinary near-
death experience even to begin to open up to this? The answer
may be simply biological. Survival of our genes is helped by a
body that protects itself and creates the idea that it is separate
and that it matters. This is a good enough reason why the
thought of annihilation should be so scary.

But the scary thought has to be faced. Maybe this 'me' is not what I thought it was. And it is not a spirit either, nor a soul, nor an immortal being of any kind. Not a higher self, not an overself, nor a bundle of Kundalini energy. In fact, it isn't any thing at all. And it never was.

This view has a long history and so does resistance to it. It was certainly resisted in the time of the Buddha and he was well aware of the problem. A monk once asked him whether one can be tormented when something permanent within oneself is not found. The Buddha explained that a person may think he will exist for eternity, after death, permanent, abiding and unchanging. Then he hears the doctrine aiming at the destruction of all craving and attachment, 'Then that man thinks: "I will be annihilated, I will be destroyed, I will be no more." So he mourns, worries himself, laments, weeps, beating his breast, and becomes bewildered' (176 p. 56). He is only able to think in terms of either existing or ceasing to exist, so naturally he is afraid.

The Buddha's view on life after death is simple. In one of his teachings he said,

O bhikkhus [monks], when neither self nor anything pertaining to self can truly and really be found, this speculative view: 'The universe is that *Atman* [soul]; I shall be that after death, permanent, abiding, ever-lasting, unchanging, and I shall exist as such for eternity' – is it not wholly and completely foolish?

(176 p. 59)

I agree it is foolish but the resistance is natural. When we are so used to thinking of ourselves as having that eternal central 'something' we can only think of non-self in terms of annihilation. The resistance takes a lot of letting go.

Of course, this is just one religious outlook and one that many people would not share. However, it is my contention that present day psychology, physics, biology and philosophy are all beginning to converge on something like this same view. It is talked about in different ways and in different contexts but there is an essential similarity. Here are just a few examples:

There is no observer inside the brain.

philosopher (46 p. 106)

There is no stage, no screen, no ground, no experiencer, no knower, no self.

psychologist (34 p. 52)

It will be ultimately misleading . . . to suppose . . . that each human being is an independent actuality.

physicist (26 p. 210)

Ordinary consciousness is . . . an illusion of separate selfhood.

NDEr (238)

You, the person, are not a separately existing entity.

philosopher (161 p. 23)

There is in reality no one to die.

counsellor of the dying (117 p. 251)

Enlightenment is a permanent freeing of the individual from the illusion that he is 'doing'.

psychiatrist (60 p. 117)

Actions do exist, and also their consequences, but the person that acts does not.

The Buddha (161 p. 21)

Appreciating that we are just bodies that will die and not selves who will go on for ever is the way to understand NDEs and to live our own lives and deaths more fully.

BUT I KNOW

I have to face a real problem here. I have encountered it often enough already and I expect to meet it many more times. Many NDErs come back from their experiences convinced that they have seen the spirit world, convinced that they have grasped their 'overself', 'higher self' or 'ultimate being'; convinced that 'they' have met their dead loved ones and that they will live after they die. I am denying that they are right. I am not denying their experiences but I am disagreeing with the conclusions they have come to. They may, with some justification, think I am insulting them by saying 'You have not seen what you thought you saw.' I am not surprised when people come back at me with 'But I know it because I have been there.' To this I can only say – I have experienced it too and I have come to a different conclusion from you.

I also have another problem: many people find the idea of an eternal soul and an afterlife a great comfort. Adopting this view may even help them to live their lives more fully and more lovingly. They find this view a comfort when facing their own death, the death of others they love and even in the midst of life. It may actually be easier to live life in the false hope that you will live for ever than in the scary openness of nothing but the present. So by saying what I believe to be true I may be denying people that comfort. I can only hope that people who prefer that view will simply disagree with me and say – I have come to a different conclusion from you.

My conclusion is that the NDE brings about a breakdown of the model of self along with the breakdown of the brain's normal processes. In this way it can cut right through the illusion that we are separate selves. It becomes obvious that 'I' never did exist and so there is no one to die. The funny thing is that when a whole system drops the idea of there being anyone in there to die, it seems to become a nicer person to have around. To the extent that this happens, the person is changed. Here is the real loss of the fear of death. Here lies the true transformation of the NDE.

13

And After Death?

It is time now to return to the major question. Which hypothesis best accounts for the evidence: the 'Afterlife Hypothesis' or the 'Dying Brain Hypothesis'? Are NDEs a glimpse of life after death or the visions of a dying brain?

The arguments are now strong enough to take on the challenge offered by many NDE investigators. Melvin Morse claims that 'There is no scientific explanation for the Light' (136), Michael Talbot refers to 'the inability of our current scientific understanding of reality even to begin to explain NDEs' (223 p. 244), and philosopher and parapsychologist Michael Grosso has said that 'Explaining NDEs is obviously a large undertaking. The most that can be said now is that they cannot be adequately accounted for by any of the reductionist theories' (89 p. 23).

But the most direct challenge is, not surprisingly, offered by Kenneth Ring in his book *Life at Death*.

I would like to advise any neurologically minded researcher interested in investigating this issue of one important constraint: Any adequate neurological explanation would have to be capable of showing how the entire complex of phenomena associated with the core experience (that is, the out-of-body state, paranormal knowledge, the tunnel, the golden light, the voice or presence, the appearance of deceased relatives, beautiful vistas, and so forth) would be expected to occur in subjectively authentic fashion as a consequence of specific neurological events triggered by the approach of death . . . I am tempted to argue that the burden of proof has now shifted to those who wish to explain near-death experiences in this way.
(182 p. 216)

I am happy to take on this burden.

In the very first chapter I listed four arguments commonly used as evidence for the Afterlife Hypothesis. I can now reassess them all.

1. The first was the 'consistency argument'. This is that NDEs are similar around the world and throughout history. The only possible explanation for this, so the argument runs, is that NDEs are just what they appear to be – a journey through a real tunnel to another world which awaits us after death. Consistency, it is argued, amounts to evidence for an afterlife.

The consistency is certainly there. We have explored many different kinds of NDEs and seen that, although no two are the same, there are consistent patterns: the joy and peace; the tunnel; the light; the out-of-body experience; the life review and the dissolution into timelessness; the return to life and the changes it brings. The consistency is there but this does not mean there is an afterlife.

The joy and peace are consistent because of the natural opiates released under stress. The tunnel, light and noises are consistent because they depend on the structure of the brain's cortex and what happens to it when it is deprived of oxygen or is affected by disinhibition and random activity. The OBE is consistent because it is the brain's way of dealing with a breakdown in the body image and model of reality. The life review is consistent because the endorphins cause random activation and seizures in the temporal lobe and limbic system where memories are organized. The same effect leads to the breakdown of time and its relationship to self. And it is this dissolution of self that accounts for the mystical experiences and aftereffects.

No afterlife hypothesis is required to account for the consistency of NDE across times, peoples and cultures. Indeed, the dying brain hypothesis accounts for it better.

2. The second argument I called the 'reality argument'. It is that NDEs feel so real that they must be what they appear to be, a real journey to the next world.

By exploring the reasons why things seem real I have provided an alternative interpretation. It is useful for us, as biological organisms, to separate what is real from what is not. However, the distinction is largely artificial. All we have is model-building and we call some models 'real' and some 'imaginary'. The most stable and persistent ones, like those based on the senses, we call real. The ones that affect the limbic system in certain ways we feel as 'familiar' or 'meaningful'. Mostly this works well but during the NDE it leads us astray. Stable tunnel forms in the cortex seem real. An out-of-body perspective taken on in imagination seems real. So the felt 'realness' of NDEs is no evidence that there is anyone to travel out of the body or any next world to go to. The dying brain hypothesis thus accounts better for why the experience seems so real and can also account for why obviously 'unreal' things are seen in NDEs as well.

3. Third comes the 'paranormal argument'. That is that NDEs involve paranormal events which cannot be explained by science. Since they cannot be explained in any normal way they must be evidence that the NDE involves another dimension, another world, or the existence of a non-material spirit or soul.

This is not a good argument for the afterlife hypothesis for two reasons. Firstly, I have cast considerable doubt on the evidence itself. Many cases are simply very weak to start with, others become weaker the deeper you look into them and some have even been invented altogether. Secondly, even if the evidence were compelling, it could not be explained just by claiming 'There is an afterlife'. If the evidence changes in the future and truly convincing paranormal events are documented then certainly the theory I have proposed will have to be overthrown – along with a lot more of psychology, physics and biology – but the afterlife theories we have encountered here will not do instead.

By contrast, the dying brain hypothesis explains why people seek paranormal evidence to bolster their impression of realness and how the stories are passed on and elaborated. By understanding the role of the limbic system and temporal lobe it accounts for the experiences of familiarity, insight and *déjà vu* and for the increase in psychic experiences after the NDE. I shall keep looking for the evidence that might prove it wrong but for now the dying brain hypothesis accounts better for what we know.

4. Finally, there is the 'transformation argument'. This is that people are changed by their NDEs, sometimes dramatically for the better, becoming more spiritual and less materialistic.

The afterlife hypothesis attributes this to NDErs having a spiritual experience in another world. In fact this does not really explain it at all. There is no obvious reason why an afterlife should be a better one nor why contact with it should make people who return nicer. This is simply assumed.

By contrast, the dying brain hypothesis is compatible with two reasons for transformation. One is simply that being made to think about death can affect a person's priorities deeply, whether it is their death or another's and whether they have an NDE or not. This alone can make them less selfish and more concerned for others. The other is that coming close to death can provoke the insight that the self was only a mental construction; that all the struggles, attachment and suffering of life depend on that artificial construction and that it can be let go. There never was any solid self and there is no one to die. With this insight fear is left behind and life can be lived more directly and fully. The dying brain hypothesis accounts better for the mystical insight of the NDE and the changes it can bring about.

All things considered, I can see no reason to adopt the afterlife hypothesis. I am sure I shall remain in the minority for a long time to come, especially amongst NDErs, but for me the evidence and the arguments are overwhelming. The dying brain hypothesis, for all its shortcomings, does a better job of accounting for the experiences themselves. And it reveals not a false hope of the self surviving for ever but a genuine insight beyond the self.

We are biological organisms, evolved in fascinating ways for no purpose at all and with no end in any mind. We are simply here and this is how it is. I have no self and 'I' own nothing. There is no one to die. There is just this moment, and now this and now this.

References

1 Appleby, L., 1989. 'Near-death experience: Analogous to other stress-induced psychological phenomena', *British Medical Journal* 298 976–7.

2 Atwater, P., 1988. *Coming Back to Life*, New York, Dodd Mead.

3 Ayer, A.J., 1988. *That Undiscovered Country*, unpublished paper.

4 Baker, D.M., n.d. *The Techniques of Astral Projection*, London and New York, Regency Press.

5 Bauer, M., 1985.'Near-death experiences and attitude change', *Anabiosis: The Journal of Near-Death Studies* 5 39–47.

6 Becker, C.B., 1982. 'The failure of Saganomics: Why birth models cannot explain near-death phenomena', *Anabiosis: The Journal of Near-Death Studies* 2 102–109.

7 Becker, C.B., 1985.' Views from Tibet: NDEs and the Book of the Dead', *Anabiosis: The Journal of Near-Death Studies* 5 3–19.

8 Becker, C.B., 1990. 'Extrasensory perception, near-death experiences, and the limits of scientific knowledge', *Journal of Near-Death Studies* 9 11–20.

9 Becker, E., 1973. *The Denial of Death*, New York, The Free Press.

10 Beloff, J., 1962. *The Existence of Mind*, London, MacGibbon & Kee.

11 Bergson, H., 1911. *Matter and Memory*, trans. N.M. Paul and W.S. Palmer, London, Swan Sonnenschein.

12 Blackmore, S.J., 1980. *ESP as a Cognitive Process*, unpublished PhD thesis, University of Surrey.

13 Blackmore, S.J., 1982. *Beyond the Body*, London, Heinemann.

14 Blackmore, S.J., 1983. 'Birth and the OBE: An unhelpful analogy', *Journal of the American Society for Psychical Research* 77 229–38.

15 Blackmore, S.J., 1984. 'A postal survey of OBEs and other experiences', *Journal of the Society for Psychical Research* 52 225–44.

16 Blackmore, S.J., 1984.'A psychological theory of the out-of-body experience', *Journal of Parapsychology* **48** 201–218.

17 Blackmore, S.J., 1986. 'Spontaneous and deliberate OBEs: A questionnaire survey', *Journal of the Society for Psychical Research* **53** 218–24.

18 Blackmore, S.J., 1986. *The Adventures of a Parapsychologist*, Buffalo, New York, Prometheus.

19 Blackmore, S.J., 1986.'Out-of-body experiences in schizophrenia: A questionnaire survey', *Journal of Nervous and Mental Disease* **174** 615–19.

20 Blackmore, S.J., 1986. 'Who am I?: Changing models of reality in meditation', in *Beyond Therapy: The Impact of Eastern Religions on Psychological Theory and Practice*, ed. G. Claxton, London, Wisdom, 71–85.

21 Blackmore, S.J., 1987. 'Where am I?: Perspectives in imagery, and the out-of-body experience', *Journal of Mental Imagery* **11** 53–66.

22 Blackmore, S.J., 1988. 'Out of the body?' in *Not Necessarily the New Age: Critical Essays*, Buffalo, New York, Prometheus, 165–84.

23 Blackmore, S.J., 1991. 'Is meditation good for you?' *New Scientist* 6 July.

24 Blackmore, S.J., 1992. 'Psychic Experiences: Psychic Illusions', *Skeptical Inquirer* **16** 367–76.

25 Blackmore, S.J. and Troscianko, T., 1988. 'The Physiology of the Tunnel', *Journal of Near-Death Studies* **8** 15–28.

26 Bohm, D., 1980. *Wholeness and the Implicate Order*, London, Routledge & Kegan Paul.

27 Bush, N., 1984. 'The near-death experience in children: Shades of the prison-house reopening', *Anabiosis: The Journal of Near-Death Studies* **3** 177–93.

28 Butler, R.N., 1963. 'The life review: An interpretation of reminiscence in the aged', *Psychiatry* **26** 65–76.

29 Carr, D., 1981. 'Endorphins at the approach of death', *The Lancet* 14 February, 390.

30 Carr, D.B., 1982. 'Pathophysiology of stress-induced limbic lobe dysfunction: A hypothesis relevant to near-death experiences', *Anabiosis: The Journal of Near-Death Studies* **2** 75–89. Also reprinted in B. Greyson and C.P. Flynn, 1984, 125–39.

31 Castaneda, C., 1968. *The Teachings of Don Juan: A Yaqui Way*

of Knowledge, University of California Press and 1970, London, Penguin.

32 Churchland, P.S. and Sejnowski, T.J., 1992. *The Computational Brain*, Cambridge, Mass., MIT Press.

33 Clark, K., 1984. 'Clinical interventions with near-death experiencers', in *The Near-Death Experience: Problems, Prospects, Perspectives*, ed. B. Greyson and C.P. Flynn, Springfield, Ill., Charles C. Thomas, 242–55.

34 Claxton, G., 1986. 'The light's on but there's nobody home: The psychology of no-self ', in *Beyond Therapy: The Impact of Eastern Religions on Psychological Theory and Practice*, ed. G. Claxton, London, Wisdom, 49–70.

35 Comer, N.L., Madow, L. and Dixon, J.J., 1967. 'Observations of sensory deprivation in a life-threatening situation', *American Journal of Psychiatry* 124 164–9.

36 Comper, F.M.M., 1917. *The Book of the Craft of Dying*, London, Longmans, Green and Company.

37 Cook, A.M. and Irwin, H.J., 1983. 'Visuospatial skills and the out-of-body experience', *Journal of Parapsychology* 47 23–35.

38 Cowan, J.D., 1982. 'Spontaneous symmetry breaking in large-scale nervous activity', *International Journal of Quantum Chemistry* 22 1059–82.

39 Crookall, R., 1961. *The Supreme Adventure: Analyses of Psychic Communication*, Cambridge, James Clarke.

40 Crookall, R., 1961. *The Study and Practice of Astral Projection*, London, Aquarian Press.

41 Crookall, R., 1964. *More Astral Projections*, London, Aquarian Press.

42 Cytowic, R.E., 1989. *Synesthesia: A Union of the Senses*, New York, Springer-Verlag.

43 Daniel, P.M. and Whitteridge, D., 1961. 'The representation of the visual field on the cerebral cortex in monkeys', *Journal of Physiology*, 159 203–21.

44 Darwin, C., 1859. *The Origin of Species*, reprinted, London, Penguin, 1982.

45 Davis, L., 1988. 'A comparison of UFO and near-death experiences as vehicles for the evolution of human consciousness', *Journal of Near-Death Studies* 6 240–57.

46 Dennett, D.C., 1991. *Consciousness Explained*, Boston, Little, Brown & Co.

47 Dlin, B.M., 1980. 'The experience of surviving almost certain death', *Advances in Psychosomatic Medicine* 10 111–18.

48 Dlin, B.M., Stern, M.D. and Poliakoff, S.J., 1974. 'Survivors of cardiac arrest: The first few days', *Psychosomatics* 15 61–7.

49 Dobson, M., Tattersfield, A.E., Adler, M.W. and McNicol, M.W., 1971. 'Attitudes and long-term adjustment of patients surviving cardiac arrest', *British Medical Journal* 3 207–12.

50 Dossey, L., 1989. *Recovering the Soul: A Scientific and Spiritual Search*, New York, Bantam.

51 Dossey, L., 1991. Personal communication.

52 Drab, K., 1981. 'The tunnel experience: Reality or hallucination?' *Anabiosis: The Journal of Near-Death Studies* 1 126–52.

53 Druss, R.G. and Kornfeld, D.S., 1967. 'The survivors of cardiac arrest: A psychiatric study', *Journal of the American Medical Association* 201 291–6.

54 Dunbar, E., 1905. 'The light thrown on psychological processes by the action of drugs', *Proceedings of the Society for Psychical Research* 19 62–77.

55 Dunne, J.W., 1927. *An Experiment with Time*, London, Faber and Faber.

56 Evans, J.M., 1987. 'Patients' experiences of awareness during general anaesthesia', in *Consciousness, Awareness and Pain in General Anaesthesia*, ed. M. Rosen and J.N. Lunn, London, Butterworths, 184–92.

57 Evans-Wentz, W.Y. (ed.), 1957. *Tibetan Book of the Dead*, trans. Kazi Dawa-Samdup, London, Oxford University Press.

58 Fenske, E.W., 1991. 'From the President', *Vital Signs* 10(2) 1–2.

59 Fenwick, P., 1983. 'Some aspects of the physiology of the mystical experience', in *Psychology Survey No. 4*, ed. J. Nicholson and B. Foss, Leicester, British Psychological Society, 203–23.

60 Fenwick, P., 1987. 'Meditation and the EEG', in *The Psychology of Meditation*, ed. M.A. West, Oxford, Clarendon Press 104–17.

61 Fenwick, P., 1991. 'Progress in IANDS research', *IANDS News Bulletin (UK)*, Autumn 1991.

62 Flynn, C.P., 1982. 'Meanings and implications of NDEr transformations: Some preliminary findings and implications', *Anabiosis: The Journal of Near-Death Studies* 2 3–13. Also reprinted in B. Greyson and C.P. Flynn, 1984, 278–89.

63 Flynn, C.P., 1986. *After the Beyond: Human Transformation and*

the Near-Death Experience, Englewood Cliffs, New Jersey, Prentice-Hall.

64 Forster, E.M. and Whinnery, J.E., 1988. 'Recovery from Gz-induced loss of consciousness: Psychophysiologic considerations', *Aviation, Space, and Environmental Medicine* **59** 517–22.

65 Frenk, H., McCarty, B.C. and Liebeskind, J.C., 1978. 'Different brain areas mediate the analgesic and epileptic properties of enkephalin', *Science* **200** 335–7.

66 Fujiwara, N., Higashi, H., Shimoki, K. and Yoshimura, M., 1987. 'Effects of hypoxia on rat hippocampal neurons in vitro', *Journal of Physiology* **384** 131–51.

67 Gabbard, G.O. and Twemlow, S.W., 1984. *With the Eyes of the Mind*, New York, Praeger.

68 Gabbard, G.O., Twemlow, S.W. and Jones, F.C., 1981. 'Do "near-death experiences" occur only near death?' *Journal of Nervous and Mental Disease* **169** 374–7.

69 Gallup, G., 1982. *Adventures in Immortality*, New York, McGraw Hill, and London, Souvenir Press, 1983.

70 Gallup, G.H. and Newport, F., 1991. 'Belief in paranormal phenomena among adult Americans', *Skeptical Inquirer* **15** 137–46.

71 Georgeson, M.A. and Harris, M.G., 1978. 'Apparent foveofugal drift of counterphase gratings', *Perception* **7** 527–36.

72 Gibbs, J.C., 1987. 'Moody's versus Siegel's interpretation of the near-death experience: An evaluation based on recent research', *Anabiosis: The Journal of Near-Death Studies* **5** 67–82.

73 Glaskin, G.M., 1974. *Windows of the Mind: The Christos Experience*, London, Wildwood House.

74 Gliksman, M.P.H. and Kellehear, A., 1990. 'Near-death experiences and the measurement of blood gases', *Journal of Near-Death Studies* **9** 41–3.

75 Green, C.E., 1968. *Out-of-the-Body Experiences*, London, Hamish Hamilton.

76 Greene, F.G., 1979. 'A glimpse behind the life review: A summary', *Anabiosis: The Journal of Near-Death Studies* **1** 3–5.

77 Gregory, R.L., 1966. *Eye and Brain*, London, Weidenfeld and Nicolson.

78 Gregory, R.L., 1991. Personal communication.

79 Grey, M., 1985. *Return from Death*, London, Arkana.

80 Greyson, B., 1981. 'Toward a psychological explanation of near-death experiences: A response to Dr Grosso's paper', *Anabiosis: The Journal of Near-Death Studies* 1 88–102.

81 Greyson, B., 1983. 'The near-death experience scale: Construction, reliability and validity', *Journal of Nervous and Mental Disease* 171 369–75. Also reprinted in B. Greyson and C.P. Flynn, 1984, 45–60.

82 Greyson, B., 1985. 'A typology of near-death experiences', *American Journal of Psychiatry* 142 967–9.

83 Greyson, B., 1990. 'Near-death encounters with and without near-death experiences: Comparative NDE scale profiles', *Journal of Near-Death Studies* 8 151–61.

84 Greyson, B. and Bush, N.E., 1992. 'Distressing near-death experiences', *Psychiatry* 55 95–110.

85 Greyson, B. and Flynn, C.P., 1984. *The Near-Death Experience: Problems, Prospects, Perspectives*, Springfield, Illinois, Charles C. Thomas.

86 Greyson, B. and Stevenson, I., 1980. 'The phenomenology of near-death experiences', *American Journal of Psychiatry* 137 1193–6.

87 Grinspoon, L. and Bakalar, J., 1979. *Psychedelic Drugs Reconsidered*, New York, Basic Books.

88 Grof, S., 1985. *Beyond the Brain*, Albany, State University of New York Press.

89 Grosso, M., 1981. 'Toward an explanation of near-death phenomena', *Anabiosis: The Journal of Near-Death Studies* 1 3–26.

90 Groth-Marnat, G. and Schumaker, J.F. 1989. 'The near-death experience: A review and critique', *Journal of Humanistic Psychology* 29 109–33.

91 Halgren, E., Walter, R.D., Cherlow, D.G. and Crandall, P.H., 1978. 'Mental phenomena evoked by electrical stimulation of the human hippocampal formation and amygdala', *Brain* 101 83–117.

92 Haraldsson, E., 1985. 'Representative national surveys of psychic phenomena: Iceland, Great Britain, Sweden, USA and Gallup's multinational survey', *Journal of the Society for Psychical Research* 53 145–58.

93 Harary, K. and Weintraub, P., 1989. *Have an Out-of-Body Experience in 30 Days*, New York, St Martin's Press, and Wellingborough, Northants, Aquarian, 1990.

94 Hiley, B.J. and Peat, F.D., 1987. *Quantum Implications: Essays in Honour of David Bohm*, London and New York, Routledge.

95 Holaday, J.W. and Loh, H.H., 1981. 'Neurobiology of beta-endorphin and related peptides', in *Hormonal Proteins and Peptides. Vol. X. Beta-Endorphin*, ed. C.H. Li, New York and London, Academic Press, 203–91.

96 Holck, F.H., 1978. 'Life revisited', *Omega* 9 1–11.

97 Honneger, B., 1983. 'The OBE as a near-birth experience', in *Research in Parapsychology 1982*, ed. W.G. Roll, J. Beloff and R.A. White, Metuchen, New Jersey, Scarecrow Press, 230–31.

98 Hryniewicz, M., 1968. 'Back from the Brink', letter to *New Scientist* 2 June 1968.

99 Hutchison, M., 1984. *The Book of Floating*, New York, Quill.

100 Hunter, R.C.A., 1967. 'On the experience of nearly dying', *American Journal of Psychiatry* 124 122–6.

101 Irwin, H.J., 1985. *Flight of Mind: A psychological study of the out-of-body experience*, Metuchen, New Jersey, Scarecrow Press.

102 Irwin, H.J., 1986. 'Perceptual perspective of visual imagery in OBEs, dreams and reminiscence', *Journal of the Society for Psychical Research* 53 210–17.

103 Irwin, H.J., 1987. 'Out-of-body experiences in the blind', *Journal of Near-Death Studies* 6 53–60.

104 Irwin, H.J. and Bramwell, B.A., 1988. 'The devil in heaven: A near-death experience with both positive and negative facets', *Journal of Near-Death Studies* 7 38–43.

105 James, P., 1991. *Twilight*, London, Victor Gollancz.

106 Jansen, K., 1989. 'Near-death experience and the NMDA receptor', *British Medical Journal* 298 1708.

107 Johnson, R.C., 1959. *Watcher on the Hills*, London, Hodder and Stoughton.

108 Johnson-Laird, P.N., 1983. *Mental Models*, Cambridge, Cambridge University Press.

109 Judson, I.R. and Wiltshaw, E., 1983. 'A near-death experience', *The Lancet* 3 September 561–2.

110 Kellehear, A., 1990. 'The near-death experience as status passage', *Social Science and Medicine* 31 933–9.

111 Kohr, R.L., 1983. 'Near-death experiences, altered states, and psi sensitivity', *Journal of Near-Death Studies* 3 157–76.

112 Kluver, H., 1926. 'Mescal visions and eidetic vision', *American Journal of Psychology* 37 502–15.

113 Kluver, H., 1967. *Mescal and Mechanisms of Hallucination*, Chicago, University of Chicago Press.

114 Kubler-Ross, E. 'Life, Death and Life After Death', tape-recorded lecture distributed by Friends of Shanti Nilaya, London. Quoted in Wilson 1987.

115 Kulli, J. and Koch, C., 1991. 'Does anesthesia cause loss of consciousness?' *Trends in Neuroscience* 14 6–10.

116 Leao, A.A.P., 1944. 'Spreading depression of activity in the cerebral cortex', *Journal of Neurophysiology* 7 359–90.

117 Levine, S., 1986. *Who Dies? An Investigation of Conscious Living and Conscious Dying*, Bath, Gateway.

118 Li, C.H. (ed.), 1981. *Hormonal Proteins and Peptides. Vol. X. Beta-Endorphin*, New York and London, Academic Press.

119 Libet, B., 1985. 'Unconscious cerebral initiative and the role of conscious will in voluntary action', *Behavioral and Brain Sciences* 8 529–66. Including commentaries following this article.

120 Locke, T.P. and Shontz, F.C., 1983. 'Personality correlates of the near-death experience: A preliminary study', *Journal of the American Society for Psychical Research* 77 311–18.

121 Lorimer, D., 1990. *Whole in One*, London, Arkana.

122 Lovelock, J., 1979. *Gaia: A New Look at Life on Earth*, Oxford, Oxford University Press.

123 MacDougall, D., 1907. 'Hypothesis concerning soul substance together with experimental evidence of the existence of such substance', *Journal of the American Society for Psychical Research* 1 237–44.

124 MacMillan, R.L. and Brown, K.W.G., 1971. 'Cardiac arrest remembered', *Canadian Medical Association Journal* 104 889–90.

125 Makarec, K. and Persinger, M.A., 1985. 'Temporal lobe signs: Electroencephalographic validity and enhanced scores in special populations', *Perceptual and Motor Skills* 60 831–42.

126 Makarec, K. and Persinger, M.A., 1987. 'Electroencephalographic correlates of temporal lobe signs and imaginings', *Perceptual and Motor Skills* 64 1124–6.

127 Masters, R.E.L. and Houston, J., 1966. *The Varieties of Psychedelic Experience*, London, Anthony Blond.

128 McHarg, J.F., 1978. 'Review of *At the Hour of Death* by K. Osis and E. Haraldsson', *Journal of the Society for Psychical Research* 49 885–7.

129 McHarg, J.F., 1989. 'Comments on "A neurobiological model for near-death experiences"', *Journal of Near-Death Studies* 7 229–31.

130 Meduna, L.J., 1950. 'The effect of carbon dioxide upon the functions of the brain', in *Carbon Dioxide Therapy*, Springfield, Illinois, Charles C. Thomas.

131 Menz, R.L., 1984. 'The denial of death and the out-of-the-body experience', *Journal of Religion and Health* 23 317–29.

132 Monod, J., 1971. *Chance and Necessity*, trans. A. Wainhouse, New York, Knopf, and London, Fontana, 1972.

133 Moody, R.A., 1975. *Life after Life*, Atlanta, Georgia, Mockingbird.

134 Moody, R.A., 1977. *Reflections on Life after Life*, Atlanta, Georgia, Mockingbird, and London, Corgi, 1978.

135 Morris, R.L., Harary, S.B., Janis, J., Hartwell, J. and Roll, W.G., 1978. 'Studies of communication during out-of-body experiences', *Journal of the American Society for Psychical Research* 72 1–22.

136 Morse, M., 1990. *Closer to the Light*, London, Souvenir Press.

137 Morse, M., Castillo, P., Venecia, D., Milstein, J. and Tyler, D.C., 1986. 'Childhood near-death experiences', *American Journal of Diseases of Children* 140 1110–14.

138 Morse, M., Conner, D. and Tyler, D., 1985. 'Near-death experiences in a pediatric population: A preliminary report', *American Journal of Diseases of Children* 139 595–600.

139 Morse, M.L., Venecia, D. and Milstein, J., 1989. 'Near-death experiences: A neurophysiological explanatory model', *Journal of Near-Death Studies* 8 45–53.

140 Muldoon, S. and Carrington, H., 1929. *The Projection of the Astral Body*, London, Rider & Co.

141 Mullin, G.H., 1986. *Death and Dying: The Tibetan Tradition*, London, Arkana.

142 *Nature*, 1981. 'A book for burning?' Editorial, *Nature* 293 245–6.

143 Nelson, G.K., 1970. 'Preliminary study of the electroencephalograms of mediums', *Parapsychologica* 4 30–35.

144 Neppe, V.M., 1983a. *The Psychology of* Déjà Vu: *Have I Been Here Before?* Johannesburg, Witwatersrand University Press.

145 Neppe, V.M., 1983b. 'Temporal lobe symptomatology in subjective paranormal experients', *Journal of the American Society for Psychical Research* 77 1–29.

146 Neppe, V.M., 1989. 'Near-death experiences: A new challenge in temporal lobe phenomenology? Comments on "A neurobiological model for near-death experiences"', *Journal of Near-Death Studies* 7 243–8.

147 Nigro, G. and Neisser, U., 1983. 'Point of view in personal memories', *Cognitive Psychology* 15 467–82.

148 Noyes, R., 1972. 'The experience of dying', *Psychiatry* 35 174–84.

149 Noyes, R. and Kletti, R., 1972. 'The experience of dying', *Omega* 3 45–52.

150 Noyes, R. and Kletti, R., 1976. 'Depersonalization in the face of life-threatening danger: A description', *Psychiatry* 39 19–27.

152 Noyes, R. and Kletti, R., 1977a. 'Panoramic memory: A response to the threat of death', *Omega* 8 181–94.

153 Noyes, R. and Kletti, R., 1977b. 'Depersonalization in response to life-threatening danger', *Comprehensive Psychiatry* 18 375–84.

154 Noyes, R. and Slymen, D., 1979. 'The subjective response to life-threatening danger', *Omega* 9 313–21.

155 Osis, K., 1979. 'Insiders' views of the OBE: A questionnaire survey', in *Research in Parapsychology*, 1978, ed. W.G. Roll, Metuchen, New Jersey, Scarecrow Press.

156 Osis, K. and Haraldsson, E., 1977. 'Deathbed observations by physicians and nurses: A cross-cultural survey', *Journal of the American Society for Psychical Research* 71 237–59.

157 Osis, K. and Haraldsson, E., 1977. *At the Hour of Death*, New York, Avon.

158 Owens, J.E., Cook, E.W. and Stevenson, I., 1990. 'Features of "near-death experience" in relation to whether or not patients were near death', *The Lancet* 336 1175–7.

159 Palmer, J., 1978. 'The out-of-body experience: A psychological theory', *Parapsychology Review* 9 19–22.

160 Palmer, J., 1979. 'A community mail survey of psychic experiences', *Journal of the American Society for Psychical Research* 73 221–52.

161 Parfit, D., 1987. 'Divided minds and the nature of persons', in *Mindwaves*, ed. C.Blakemore and S.Greenfield, Oxford, Basil Blackwell.

162 Parkin, A.J., Miller, J. and Vincent, R., 1987. 'Multiple neuropsychological deficits due to anoxic encephalopathy: A case study', *Cortex* 23 655–65.

163 Pasricha, S. and Stevenson, I., 1986. 'Near-death experiences in India: A preliminary report', *Journal of Nervous and Mental Disease* **174** 165–70.

164 Peale, N.V. 'The power of positive thinking', 51, quoted in *Revitalised Signs* **8**(4) 1989, 5.

165 Penfield, W., 1955. 'The role of the temporal cortex in certain psychical phenomena', *The Journal of Mental Science* **101** 451–65.

166 Penfield, W., 1975. *The Mystery of the Mind*, Princeton, New Jersey, Princeton University Press.

167 Pennachio, J., 1988. 'Near-death experiences and self-transformation', *Journal of Near-Death Studies* **6** 162–8.

168 Persinger, M.A., 1983. 'Religious and mystical experiences as artifacts of temporal lobe function: A general hypothesis', *Perceptual and Motor Skills* **57** 1255–62.

169 Persinger, M.A., 1984. 'Propensity to report paranormal experiences is correlated with temporal lobe signs', *Perceptual and Motor Skills* **59** 583–6.

170 Persinger, M.A., 1989. 'Modern neuroscience and near-death experiences: Expectancies and implications. Comments on "A neurobiological model for near-death experiences"', *Journal of Near-Death Studies* **7** 233–9.

171 Persinger, M.A. and Fisher, S.D., 1990. 'Elevated, specific temporal lobe signs in a population engaged in psychic studies', *Perceptual and Motor Skills* **71** 817–18.

172 Persinger, M.A. and Makarec, K., 1987. 'Temporal lobe epileptic signs and correlative behaviors displayed by normal populations', *Journal of General Psychology* **114** 179–95.

173 Popper, K.R. and Eccles, J.C., 1977. *The Self and its Brain: An Argument for Interactionism*, Berlin, Springer.

174 Pribram, K., 1971. *Languages of the Brain*, Englewood Cliffs, New Jersey, Prentice-Hall.

175 Price, H.H., 1939. 'Haunting and the "Psychic Ether" hypothesis', *Proceedings of the Society for Psychical Research* **45** 307–43.

176 Rahula, W., 1959. *What the Buddha Taught*, London, Gordon Fraser.

177 Ramachandran, V.S. and Gregory, R.L., 1991. 'Perceptual filling in of artificially induced scotomas in human vision', *Nature* **350** 699–702.

178 Rawlings, M., 1978. *Beyond Death's Door*, Nashville, Thomas Nelson.

179 Rheingold, H., 1991. *Virtual Reality*, London, Secker and Warburg.

180 Richards, P. and Persinger, M.A., 1991. 'Temporal lobe signs, the Dissociative Experiences Scale and the Hemispheric Quotient', *Perceptual and Motor Skills* 72 1139–42.

181 Ring, K., 1979. 'Further studies of the near-death experience', *Theta* 7(2) 1–3. Also reprinted in B. Greyson and C.P. Flynn 1984.

182 Ring, K., 1980. *Life at Death: A Scientific Investigation of the Near-Death Experience*, New York, Coward, McCann and Geoghegan, and New York, Quill, 1982.

183 Ring, K., 1984. *Heading Toward Omega: In Search of the Meaning of the Near-Death Experience*, New York, Quill.

184 Ring, K., 1984. 'The nature of personal identity in the near-death experience: Paul Brunton and the ancient tradition', *Anabiosis: The Journal of Near-Death Studies* 4 3–20.

185 Ring, K., 1988. 'Paradise is paradise: Reflections on psychedelic drugs, mystical experience and the near-death experience', *Journal of Near-Death Studies* 6 138–48.

186 Ring, K., 1989. 'Near-death and UFO encounters as shamanic initiations: Some conceptual and evolutionary implications', *ReVision* 11 14–22.

187 Ring, K., 1991. Personal Communication.

188 Ring, K., 1992. *The Omega Project*, New York, William Morrow.

189 Ring, K. and Franklin, S., 1981–2. 'Do suicide survivors report near-death experiences?' *Omega* 12 191–208.

190 Ring, K. and Rosing, C.J., 1990. 'The Omega Project: An empirical study of the NDE-prone personality', *Journal of Near-Death Studies* 8 211–39.

191 Roberts, G. and Owen, J., 1988. 'The near-death experience', *British Journal of Psychiatry* 153 607–17.

192 Rodin, E.A., 1980. 'The reality of death experiences: A personal perspective', *Journal of Nervous and Mental Disease* 168 259–63. Also reprinted in B. Greyson and C.P. Flynn 1984.

193 Rogo, D.S., 1982. 'Psychological models of the out-of-body experience', *Journal of Parapsychology* 46 29–45.

194 Rogo, D.S., 1983. *Leaving the Body: A practical guide to astral projection*, Englewood Cliffs, New Jersey, Prentice-Hall.

195 Rogo, D.S., 1984. 'Ketamine and the near-death experience', *Anabiosis: The Journal for Near-Death Studies* 4 87–96.

196 Rogo, D.S., 1989. 'An experimentally induced NDE', unpublished manuscript.

197 Rogo, D.S., 1989. *The Return from Silence: A Study of Near-Death Experiences*, Wellingborough, Northants, Aquarian Press.

198 Roll, W.G., 1966. 'ESP and memory', *International Journal of Neuropsychiatry* 2 505–12.

199 Rosen, D.H., 1975. 'Suicide survivors', *Western Journal of Medicine* 122 289–94.

200 Rosen, M. and Lunn, J.N., 1987. *Consciousness, Awareness and Pain in General Anaesthesia*, London, Butterworths.

201 Royce, D., 1985. 'The near-death experience: A survey of clergy's attitudes and knowledge', *Journal of Pastoral Care* 39 31–42.

202 Saavedra-Aguilar, J.C. and Gomez-Jeria, J.S., 1989. 'A neurobiological model for near-death experiences', *Journal of Near-Death Studies* 7 205–22.

203 Sabom, M., 1979. 'Beyond Death's Door: A book review', *Anabiosis: The Journal of Near-Death Studies* 1(3) 9.

204 Sabom, M.B., 1982. *Recollections of Death*, London, Corgi.

205 Sabom, M.B. and Kreutziger, S., 1982. 'Physicians evaluate the near-death experience', in *A Collection of Near-Death Research Readings*, ed. C.R. Lundahl, Chicago, Nelson Hall, 148–59.

206 Sagan, C., 1979. *Broca's Brain*, New York, Random House.

207 Sagan, C., 1984. 'The Amniotic Universe', in *The Near-Death Experience: Problems, Prospects, Perspectives*, ed. B. Greyson and C.P. Flynn, Springfield, Illinois, Charles C.Thomas, 140–53. Reprinted from Sagan 1979.

208 Schoolcraft, H.R., 1825. *Travels in the Central Portion of the Mississippi Valley*, New York, Collins and Henry, 404–20.

209 Schorer, C.E., 1985–6. 'Two native American near-death experiences', *Omega* 16(2) 111–13.

210 Serdahely, W.J., 1989–90. 'A pediatric near-death experience: Tunnel variants', *Omega* 20 55–62.

211 Serdahely, W.J., 1990. 'Pediatric near-death experiences', *Journal of Near-Death Studies* 9 33–9.

212 Sheils, D., 1978. 'A cross-cultural study of beliefs in out-of-the-body experiences', *Journal of the Society for Psychical Research* 49 697–741.

213 Sheldrake, R.A., 1981. *A New Science of Life*, London, Blond & Briggs.

214 Siegel, R.K., 1977. 'Hallucinations', *Scientific American* 237 132–40.

215 Siegel, R.K., 1980. 'The psychology of life after death', *American Psychologist* 35 911–31.

216 Siegel, R.K., 1981. 'Accounting for "afterlife" experiences', *Psychology Today*, January 65–75.

217 Siegel, R.K. and Hirshman, A.E., 1984. 'Hashish near-death experiences', *Anabiosis: The Journal for Near-Death Studies* 4 69–85.

218 Siegel, R.K. and Jarvik, M.E., 1975. 'Drug-induced hallucinations in animals and man', in *Hallucinations: Behaviour, Experience and Theory*, ed. R.K. Siegel and L.J. West, New York, Wiley.

219 Siegel, R.K. and West, L.J. (eds) 1975. *Hallucinations: Behaviour, Experience and Theory*, New York, Wiley.

220 Slade, P.D. and Bentall, R.P., 1988. *Sensory Deception: A Scientific Analysis of Hallucination*, Baltimore, Johns Hopkins University Press.

221 Stevens, J.R., 1982. 'Sleep is for seizures: A new interpretation of the role of phasic events in sleep and wakefulness', in *Sleep and Epilepsy*, ed. M.B. Sternman, M.N. Shouse and P. Passouant, New York, Academic Press, 249–64.

222 Sutherland, C., 1990. 'Near-death experience by proxy: A case study', *Journal of Near-Death Studies* 8 241–51.

223 Talbot, M., 1991. *The Holographic Universe*, London, Grafton.

224 Thalbourne, M.A., 1989. 'On the psychology of belief in life after death', in *Exploring the Paranormal: Perspectives on Belief and Experience*, ed. G.K. Zollschan, J.F. Schumaker and G.F. Walsh, Bridport, Dorset, Prism, 215–36.

225 Thomas, L.E., Cooper, P.E. and Suscovich, D.J., 1982. 'Incidence of near-death and intense spiritual experiences in an intergenerational sample: An interpretation', *Omega* 13 35–41.

226 Tobacyk, J. and Milford, G., 1983. 'Belief in paranormal phenomena: Assessment instrument development and implications for personality functioning', *Journal of Personality and Social Psychology* 44 1029–37.

227 Twemlow, S.W. and Gabbard, G.O., 1984. 'The influence of demographic/psychological factors and pre-existing conditions on the near-death experience', *Omega* 15 223–35.

228 Twemlow, S.W., Gabbard, G.O. and Coyne, L., 1982. 'A multivariate method for the classification of pre-existing near-death

conditions', *Anabiosis: The Journal of Near-Death Studies* 2 132–39.

229 Urca, G., Frenk, H., Liebeskind, J.C. and Taylor, A.N., 1977. 'Morphine and enkephalin: Analgesic and epileptic properties', *Science* 197 83–6.

230 Vernon, J., 1965. *Inside the Black Room: Studies of Sensory Deprivation*, London, Souvenir Press.

231 Way, E.L. (ed.), 1980. *Endogenous and Exogenous Opiate Agonists and Antagonists*, New York and Oxford, Pergamon Press.

232 Wilson, I., 1987. *The After Death Experience*, London, Sidgwick and Jackson.

233 Whinnery, J.E., 1990. 'Psychophysiologic correlates of unconsciousness and near-death', unpublished paper.

234 Whinnery, J.E., 1990. 'Acceleration-induced loss of consciousness: A review of 500 episodes', *Archives of Neurology* 47 764–76.

235 Whinnery, J.E., 1990. Personal communication.

236 Whinnery, J.E., 1990. Interview in *Code One* 5 2–6.

237 Wren-Lewis, J., 1987. 'The darkness of God: An account of lasting mystical consciousness resulting from an NDE', *Anabiosis: The Journal of Near-Death Studies* 5 53–66.

238 Wren-Lewis, J., 1988. 'The darkness of God: A personal report on consciousness transformation through an encounter with death', *Journal of Humanistic Psychology* 28 105–22.

239 Zaleski, C., 1987. *Otherworld Journeys: Accounts of near-death experience in medieval and modern times*, Oxford, Oxford University Press.

Index

Index